# VISUALLY™

# iPhone® 5s and iPhone® 5c

## Guy Hart-Davis

**V** **isual**
A Wiley Brand

**Teach Yourself VISUALLY™ iPhone® 5s and iPhone® 5c**

Published by
**John Wiley & Sons, Inc.**
10475 Crosspoint Boulevard
Indianapolis, IN 46256

www.wiley.com

Published simultaneously in Canada

Library of Congress Control Number: 2013939153

ISBN: 978-1-118-66103-1

Manufactured in the United States of America

10  9  8  7  6  5  4  3  2  1

### Trademark Acknowledgments

### Contact Us

For general information on our other products and services please contact our Customer Care Department within the U.S. at 877-762-2974, outside the U.S. at 317-572-3993 or fax 317-572-4002.

For technical support please visit www.wiley.com/techsupport.

**Sales** | Contact Wiley at (877) 762-2974 or fax (317) 572-4002.

# Credits

**Acquisitions Editor**
Aaron Black

**Sr. Project Editor**
Sarah Hellert

**Technical Editor**
Dennis Cohen

**Copy Editor**
Scott Tullis

**Editorial Director**
Robyn Siesky

**Business Manager**
Amy Knies

**Sr. Marketing Manager**
Sandy Smith

**Vice President and Executive
Group Publisher**
Richard Swadley

**Vice President and Executive
Publisher**
Barry Pruett

**Project Coordinators**
Patrick Redmond
Kristie Rees

**Graphics and Production Specialists**
Ana Carrillo
Carrie Cesavice
Ronda David-Burroughs
Jennifer Mayberry

**Quality Control Technician**
Lindsay Amones

**Proofreader**
Judith Q. McMullen

**Indexer**
Potomac Indexing, LLC

## About the Author

**Guy Hart-Davis** is the author of *Teach Yourself VISUALLY iPad, 4th Gerneration and iPad mini*; *Teach Yourself VISUALLY iMac,* 3rd Edition; *iMac Portable Genius,* 4th Edition; *iLife '11 Portable Genius*; and *iWork Portable Genius,* 2nd Edition.

## Author's Acknowledgments

My thanks go to the many people who turned my manuscript into the highly graphical book you are holding. In particular, I thank Aaron Black for asking me to write the book; Sarah Hellert for keeping me on track and guiding the editorial process; Scott Tullis for skillfully editing the text; and Dennis Cohen for reviewing the book for technical accuracy and contributing helpful suggestions.

# How to Use This Book

## Who This Book Is For

This book is for the reader who has never used this particular technology or software application. It is also for readers who want to expand their knowledge.

## The Conventions in This Book

### ① Steps

This book uses a step-by-step format to guide you easily through each task. **Numbered steps** are actions you must do; **bulleted steps** clarify a point, step, or optional feature; and **indented steps** give you the result.

### ② Notes

Notes give additional information — special conditions that may occur during an operation, a situation that you want to avoid, or a cross-reference to a related area of the book.

### ③ Icons and Buttons

Icons and buttons show you exactly what you need to click to perform a step.

### ④ Tips

Tips offer additional information, including warnings and shortcuts.

### ⑤ Bold

**Bold** type shows command names or options that you must click or text or numbers you must type.

### ⑥ Italics

*Italic* type introduces and defines a new term.

# Table of Contents

## Chapter 3 Working with Voice and Accessibility

## Chapter 4 Setting Up Communications

# Table of Contents

| Chapter 6 | Networking and Social Networking |

**Chapter 7**   Working with Apps

# Table of Contents

## Chapter 9 | Keeping Your Life Organized

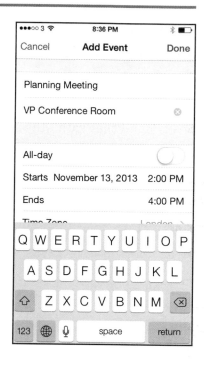

## Chapter 10 | Playing Music and Videos

# Table of Contents

## Chapter 13   Taking Photos and Videos

## Chapter 14   Advanced Features and Troubleshooting

# CHAPTER 1

# Getting Started with Your iPhone

In this chapter, you set up your iPhone to work with your computer or iCloud. You choose items to sync and learn to use the iPhone interface.

# Unbox Your iPhone and Charge It

Once you have gotten your iPhone 5s or iPhone 5c, your first move is to unbox it, identify the components, and set the iPhone to charge. The iPhone 5s and iPhone 5c come with the same components. This task shows the iPhone 5s.

To get the best battery life out of your iPhone, you should first fully charge the battery, even if it came partly charged. So no matter how eager you are to set up your iPhone, sync it with iTunes or iCloud, and start using it, take a few hours to charge it fully first.

## Unbox Your iPhone and Charge It

① Open the iPhone's box and remove its contents.

② Make sure you have the iPhone itself and the following components:

ⓐ The EarPods headset in its storage and travel case.

ⓑ The USB-to-Lightning cable.

ⓒ The power adapter.

③ Peel the protective stickers off the front and back of the iPhone.

**4** Connect the USB end of the USB cable to the power adapter.

**5** Plug the power adapter into a power socket.

**6** Connect the Lightning connector end of the USB cable to the iPhone.

**Note:** The connector is reversible, so you can plug it in either way up.

A Charging readout appears on-screen.

**7** Leave the iPhone to charge until the battery readout shows that the battery is fully charged.

**Can I charge the iPhone from my computer's USB port instead of using the power adapter?**

Yes, you can. Charging from the USB port offers the convenience of charging the iPhone at the same time as syncing data with it. You must make sure that the USB port provides enough power to the iPhone; some USB ports on keyboards, other external devices, and even some computers do not provide enough.

For the first charge, using the power adapter is better than charging from a USB port. This is because the power adapter delivers a more consistent power feed, which charges the iPhone as fast as possible.

# Turn On Your iPhone and Meet Its Hardware Controls

After charging your iPhone, turn it on and meet its hardware controls. For essential actions, such as turning on and controlling volume, the iPhone has a Power/Sleep button, a Ringer On/Off switch, a Volume Up button and a Volume Down button, together with the Home button below the screen. The iPhone 5s and the iPhone 5c have the same controls as each other, but the iPhone 5s has a fingerprint scanner built into the Home button, whereas the iPhone 5c does not.

Most stores and carriers insert a SIM card in your iPhone for you. But in some cases, you may need to insert a suitable SIM card yourself.

## Turn On Your iPhone and Meet Its Hardware Controls

**1** Press and hold the Power/Sleep button on top of the iPhone for a couple of seconds.

As the iPhone starts, the Apple logo appears on the screen.

Above the iPhone's screen:

**A** The front-facing camera.

**B** The receiver speaker, which plays phone calls into your ear when you hold the iPhone up to your face.

**C** Below the iPhone's screen is the Home button, which you press to display the Home screen.

**Note:** The Home button on the iPhone 5s includes a fingerprint scanner, which enables you to unlock your iPhone with your fingerprint.

At the bottom of the iPhone are:

**D** The headphone socket.

**E** The microphone.

**F** The Lightning connector.

**G** The speakers.

**2** Turn the iPhone so that you can see its left side.

**3** Move the Ringer On/Off switch to the rear, so that the orange background appears, when you want to turn off the ringer.

**Note:** Turn the ringer off when you do not want the iPhone to disturb you or the peace. Move the Ringer On/Off switch back to the front when you want to turn the ringer back on.

**4** Press the Volume Up (+) button to increase the ringer volume.

**Note:** When the Camera app is displayed, you can press the Volume Up (+) button to take a picture with the camera.

**5** Press the Volume Down (−) button to decrease the ringer volume.

**6** When the lock screen appears, tap the **slide to unlock** prompt, and then drag your finger to the right.

The iPhone unlocks, and the Home screen appears.

## TIP

**How do I insert a SIM card in my iPhone?**

If the store or carrier has not inserted a SIM card, insert the SIM removal tool (**A**) in the SIM hole (**B**) on the right side of the iPhone. Push gently until the tray (**C**) pops out, and then pull it with your fingernails. Insert the SIM in the tray (**D**), and then push the tray in fully.

# Download, Install, and Set Up iTunes

To sync your iPhone with your computer, you use Apple's iTunes application. iTunes comes preinstalled on every Mac but not on PCs; to get iTunes for Windows, you download it from the Apple website and then install it on your PC.

If you do not have a computer, or you do not want to sync your iPhone with your computer, you can set up and sync your iPhone using Apple's iCloud service, as described later in this chapter.

## Download, Install, and Set Up iTunes

1 On your PC, open the web browser, Internet Explorer in this example.

2 Click the Address box, type **www.apple.com/itunes/download**, and then press `Enter`.

The Download iTunes Now web page appears.

3 Click the check boxes (☑ changes to ☐) unless you want to receive e-mail from Apple.

4 Click **Download Now**.

The download bar appears.

5 Click ▼.

The Save pop-up menu opens.

6 Click **Save and run**.

Internet Explorer downloads the file, and then starts running it.

The iTunes installation begins, and the Welcome to iTunes dialog opens.

7 Click **Next**, and then follow the steps of the installer.

**Note:** You must accept the license agreement to install iTunes.

**8** On the Installation Options screen, click the **Add iTunes shortcut to my desktop** check box (☑ changes to ☐) unless you want this shortcut.

**9** Select (☑) or deselect (☐) the **Use iTunes as the default player for audio files** check box, as needed.

**10** Select (☑) or deselect (☐) the **Automatically update iTunes and other Apple software** check box, as needed. This feature is usually helpful.

**11** Click **Install**.

When the installation finishes, the installer displays the Congratulations screen.

**12** Click **Open iTunes after the installer exits** (☑ changes to ☐) if you do not want iTunes to launch automatically when you close the installer.

**13** Click **Finish**.

The installer closes.

Unless you chose not to open iTunes automatically, iTunes opens.

**TIP**

**How do I set up iTunes on a Mac?**

If you have not run iTunes already, click the **iTunes** icon (●) that appears on the Dock by default. If the Dock contains no iTunes icon, click **Launchpad** (●) on the Dock, and then click **iTunes** (●) on the Launchpad screen. The iTunes Setup Assistant launches. Follow the steps to set up iTunes.

# Begin Setup and Activate Your iPhone

Before you can use your iPhone, you must begin setup and activate the device. The first stage of setup involves choosing the language to use, specifying your country or region, connecting to the Internet through either a Wi-Fi network or the cellular network, and choosing whether to use Location Services. You then activate the iPhone, registering it with Apple's servers.

At the end of the first stage of setup, you choose whether to set up the iPhone as a new iPhone, restore it from an iCloud backup, or restore it from an iTunes backup.

## Begin Setup and Activate Your iPhone

**1** Turn on the iPhone by pressing and holding the Power/Sleep button for a couple of seconds until the Apple logo appears on-screen.

**2** When the initial iPhone screen appears, tap the prompt and slide your finger to the right.

The iPhone unlocks and begins the setup routine.

The Language screen appears.

**3** Tap the language you want to use.

The Select Your Country or Region screen appears.

**4** Tap your country or region.

The Choose a Wi-Fi Network screen appears.

**5** Tap the wireless network you want to use.

**A** If your Wi-Fi network does not appear because it does not broadcast its network name, tap **Choose another network**. You can then type the network's name.

**B** If your Wi-Fi network does not appear because it is out of range, tap **Use Cellular Connection**.

**6** On the Enter Password screen, type the password.

**7** Tap **Join**.

Your iPhone joins the wireless network and connects to the Internet.

**C** The Activating Your iPhone screen appears while iOS activates your iPhone.

**8** On the Location Services screen, tap **Enable Location Services** or **Disable Location Services**, as needed. See the tip for advice.

**9** On the Set Up Your iPhone screen, tap the appropriate button:

**D** Tap **Set Up as New iPhone** to set up your iPhone from scratch using iCloud. See the next task, "Set Up Your iPhone as New Using iCloud" for details.

**E** Tap **Restore from iCloud Backup** to set up your iPhone using a backup stored in iCloud. See the task "Set Up Your iPhone from an iCloud Backup" later in this chapter, for details.

**F** Tap **Restore from iTunes Backup** to set up your iPhone using a backup stored on your computer. See the task "Set Up Your iPhone from iTunes" later in this chapter, for details.

## TIP

**Should I enable Location Services?**

Normally, enabling Location Services is helpful because it lets apps such as Maps determine your exact location, which makes them more useful. Using Location Services does mean that your iPhone continually tracks your location, but this is something the cellular network does anyway for cell phones. That said, it is a good idea to open the Location Settings screen in the Settings app and turn off the switch for any app you do not want to track you.

# Set Up Your iPhone as New Using iCloud

If you want to set up and use your iPhone without syncing it to your computer, you can set it up using Apple's iCloud online service. With this approach, you sync your data to your account on iCloud, from which you can access it using other iOS devices, a Mac, or a web browser on any computer.

To set up a new iPhone to use iCloud, follow the instructions in the previous task to begin setup, and then continue with the instructions in this task. If you have backed up your iPhone to iCloud, and want to restore it from that backup, turn to the next task instead.

## Set Up Your iPhone as New Using iCloud

1. Begin setup as explained in the previous task, "Begin Setup and Activate Your iPhone."

2. On the Set Up Your iPhone screen, tap **Set Up as New iPhone**.

   The Apple ID screen appears.

3. Tap **Sign In with Your Apple ID**.

   **Note:** If you do not yet have an Apple ID, tap **Create a Free Apple ID** and follow through the screens that appear.

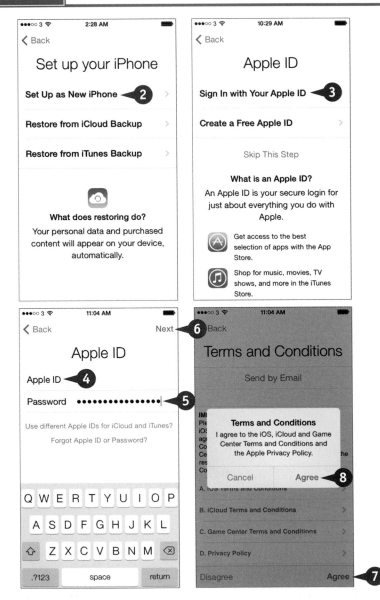

Another Apple ID screen appears.

4. Type your Apple ID.

5. Type your password.

6. Tap **Next**.

   The Terms and Conditions screen appears.

7. Tap **Agree**.

   The Terms and Conditions dialog opens.

8. Tap **Agree**.

The iCloud screen appears.

**9** Tap **Use iCloud** if you want to use iCloud.

**Note:** Normally, you will be able to get more out of your iPhone by using iCloud.

The Find My iPhone screen appears.

**10** Tap **Use Find My iPhone** or **Don't Use Find My iPhone**, as needed.

The Set Up Touch ID screen appears.

**Note:** On the iPhone 5c, which does not offer the Touch ID feature, the Passcode Lock screen appears. Go to step **16**.

**11** Tap **Set Up Now**.

**Note:** Tap **Set Up Later** if you do not want to set up Touch ID now. Normally, it is a good idea to set up Touch ID to secure your iPhone 5s.

The Set Up Fingerprints screen appears.

**12** Place your finger or thumb on the Home button. Use the digit you will normally use for the Home button.

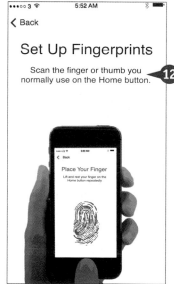

## TIP

**What is the Find My iPhone service, and should I use it?**

The Find My iPhone service enables you to track your iPhone if you mislay it or someone takes it. You can play a tone on your iPhone to help you locate it, lock your iPhone with a passcode, or erase its contents remotely. See Chapter 14 for instructions on using Find My iPhone.

continued ▶

When you set up your iPhone using iCloud, use an e-mail address that you intend to keep for the long term. This is especially true if you use the same e-mail address for the Apple ID you use for the App Store; each app you buy is tied to that e-mail address, so if you change the address, you will need to authenticate again for each app update.

When setting up your iPhone using iCloud, you can set up the Touch ID feature and a passcode to secure your iPhone 5s; for an iPhone 5c, you can set a passcode. You can also enable the Siri voice-controlled assistant.

## Set Up Your iPhone as New Using iCloud (continued)

The Place Your Finger screen appears.

**13** Place your finger on the Home button for a moment and then lift it. Repeat this several times. The iPhone may prompt you to adjust your grip or fill in the edges of your finger.

The Success screen appears.

**14** Tap **Continue**.

The Touch ID for Purchases screen appears.

**15** Tap **Use Touch ID for Purchases** if you want to use Touch ID to authorize purchases on the App Store and iTunes Store. If not, tap **Set Up Later**.

**Note:** Use a passcode to protect your iPhone. On the iPhone 5s, the passcode gives you a second means of unlocking the phone if Touch ID does not work.

On the iPhone 5s or the iPhone 5c, the Create a Passcode screen appears.

**16** Tap a four-digit passcode.

**Note:** If you use a weak passcode, such as 1111, your iPhone displays a warning dialog.

The Create a Passcode screen prompts you to reenter your passcode.

**17** Type your passcode again.

The Set Up Siri screen appears.

**18** Tap **Use Siri** or **Don't use Siri**, as appropriate.

**Note:** You can turn Siri on or off at any point after setup.

The Diagnostics screen appears.

**19** Tap **Automatically Send** or **Don't Send**, as needed.

**Note:** To learn which details the diagnostics and usage reports contain, tap **About Diagnostics and Privacy**.

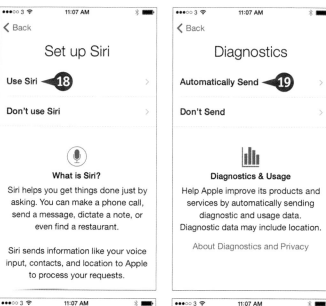

The Registration screen appears.

**20** Set the **Register with Apple** switch to On ( ) if you want to register your iPhone with Apple or to Off ( ) if you do not want to register it.

**21** Tap **Next**.

The Welcome to iPhone screen appears.

**22** Tap **Get Started**.

The Home screen appears, and you can begin using your iPhone.

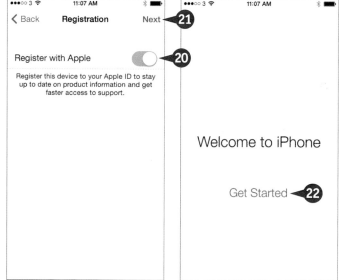

**TIP**

**What is iCloud Keychain, and should I use it?**

iCloud Keychain gives you an easy way to store your passwords and credit card information securely on your iPhone, other iOS devices, and Mac. Instead of having to remember the password for each website, or look at a credit card when you need to enter its details, you can have iCloud Keychain automatically provide the details.

iCloud Keychain encrypts your data, but you must use a complex passcode to keep it secure. A standard four-digit numeric passcode is not strong enough to keep your iCloud Keychain secure against serious attacks.

# Set Up Your iPhone from an iCloud Backup

Instead of setting up your iPhone as new using iCloud, you can set it up by restoring it from an iCloud backup. This backup can be from either another iPhone or iOS device or from the same iPhone. For example, if you are upgrading to the iPhone 5s, you can restore the backup of your previous iPhone.

When you restore your iPhone from an iCloud backup, you choose which backup to use — normally, the most recent one. iOS automatically restores your settings, downloads your apps from the App Store, and then installs them on the iPhone.

## Set Up Your iPhone from an iCloud Backup

1 Begin setup as explained in the task "Begin Setup and Activate Your iPhone," earlier in this chapter.

2 On the Set Up Your iPhone screen, tap **Restore from iCloud Backup**.

The iCloud Sign In screen appears.

3 Type your Apple ID.

4 Type your password.

5 Tap **Next**.

The Terms and Conditions screen appears.

6 Tap **Agree**.

The Terms and Conditions dialog opens.

7 Tap **Agree**.

The Choose Backup screen appears.

8 Tap the backup you want to use.

Ⓐ If the backup you want to use does not appear, tap **Show all backups** to display other backups, and then tap the appropriate backup.

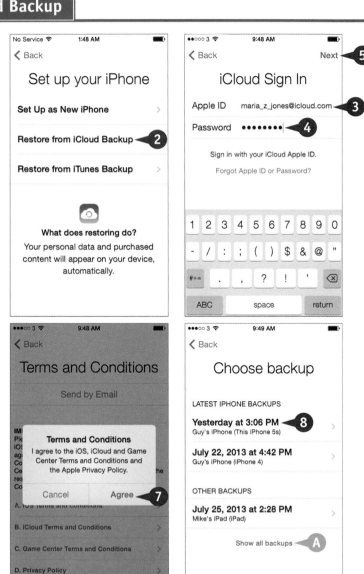

The Restore from iCloud screen appears while iOS restores the backup to your iPhone.

After iOS completes the restoration, your iPhone restarts.

A screen for signing in to iCloud appears.

**9** Type your password.

**10** Tap **Next**.

The Find My iPhone in iOS 7 screen appears.

**11** Tap **Continue**.

On an iPhone 5s, the Set Up Touch ID screen appears. On an iPhone 5c, go to step **13**.

**12** Follow steps **12** to **15** in the previous task to set up Touch ID with your fingerprint.

**13** Follow steps **16** and **17** in the previous task to set a passcode for your iPhone.

The Welcome to iPhone screen appears.

**14** Tap **Get Started** to start using your iPhone.

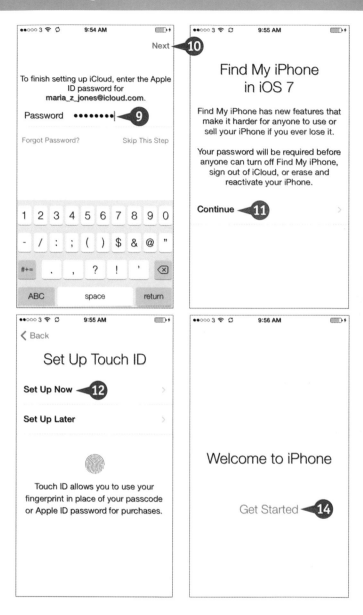

**Which iPhone backup should I use?**
Normally, it is best to use the most recent backup available for this iPhone or for the iPhone whose backups you are using. But sometimes you may find a problem exists with the latest backup. In this case, try the previous backup.

# Set Up Your iPhone from iTunes

Instead of setting up your iPhone using iCloud, as described in the previous two tasks, you can set it up using iTunes. You can either restore an iTunes backup to the device or set up the iPhone from scratch using iTunes.

When setting up your iPhone for the first time, you can restore it from an iTunes backup of another iPhone — for example, your previous iPhone. If you have already set up this iPhone, you can restore it from its own backup.

## Set Up Your iPhone from iTunes

**1** Begin setup as explained in the task "Begin Setup and Activate Your iPhone," earlier in this chapter.

**2** On the Set Up Your iPhone screen, tap **Restore from iTunes Backup**.

The Connect to iTunes screen appears.

**3** Connect your iPhone to your computer via the USB cable.

On your computer, iTunes opens or becomes active.

The Welcome to Your New iPhone screen appears.

**4** Make sure the **Restore from this backup** radio button is selected (●).

**5** In the pop-up menu, select the appropriate iPhone.

**6** Click **Continue**.

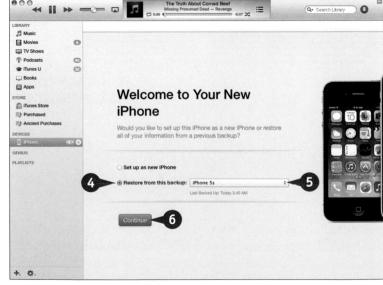

iTunes restores your iPhone from the backup.

When the restore is complete, your iPhone restarts.

Your iPhone's control screens appear in the iTunes window.

You can now choose sync settings for the iPhone as explained in the next task, "Choose Which Items to Sync from Your Computer."

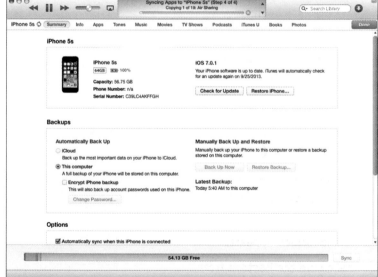

## TIP

**How do I set up my iPhone from scratch using iTunes?**

On the Set Up Your iPhone screen, tap **Restore from iTunes Backup**, and then connect your iPhone to your computer via the USB cable. When the Welcome to Your New iPhone screen appears in iTunes on your computer, click **Set up as new iPhone** (○ changes to ⦿). Click **Continue**. On the Sync with iTunes screen that appears, click **Get Started**. The iPhone's control screens appear, and you can set up sync as described in the next task, "Choose Which Items to Sync from Your Computer."

# Choose Which Items to Sync from Your Computer

After specifying that you will use iTunes to sync your iPhone, as explained in the previous task, "Set Up Your iPhone from iTunes," you use the iPhone's control screens in iTunes to choose which items to sync between your computer and your iPhone.

When setting your sync preferences, the best place to start is the Summary tab. Here, you can change your iPhone's name, choose whether to back up the iPhone to iCloud or to your computer, decide whether to encrypt the backup, and set general options for controlling syncing.

## Choose Which Items to Sync from Your Computer

### Connect Your iPhone and Choose Options on the Summary Tab

**1** Connect your iPhone to your computer via the USB cable.

The iTunes window appears.

**2** If your iPhone's control screens do not automatically appear, click the iPhone's button on the navigation bar at the top of the screen.

**Note:** Your iPhone appears in iTunes with either a default name or the name you have given it.

The iPhone's control screens appear.

**3** Click **Summary** if the Summary tab is not already displayed.

The Summary tab appears.

**4** To change the iPhone's name, click the existing name, type the new name, and press **Enter** or **Return**.

**5** In the Automatically Back Up area, click **iCloud** (○ changes to ⊙) or **This computer** (○ changes to ⊙) to specify where to back up your iPhone.

**6** If you choose to back up to this computer, click **Encrypt iPhone backup** (□ changes to ☑).

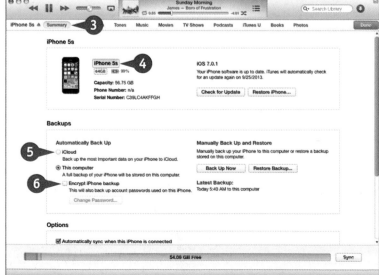

**7** In the Set Password dialog, type a password twice.

**8** On a Mac, click **Remember this password in my keychain** (☐ changes to ☑) if you want to save the password in your keychain.

**9** Click **Set Password**, and the dialog closes.

**10** Scroll down the iTunes window.

**11** Click the **Automatically sync when this iPhone is connected** check box (☐ changes to ☑) if you want to sync your iPhone automatically when you connect it.

**12** Click the **Sync only checked songs and videos** check box (☐ changes to ☑) if you want syncing to omit any song or video whose check box you have deselected (☐).

**13** Click the **Convert higher bit rate songs to AAC** check box (☐ changes to ☑) if you want to compress larger songs to fit more on your iPhone. In the pop-up menu, choose the bit rate.

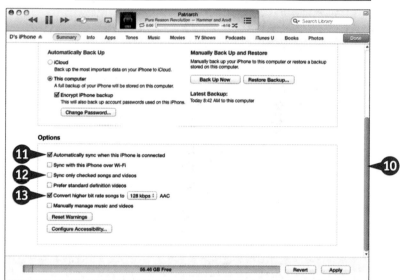

---

**TIP**

**Should I back up my iPhone to my computer or to iCloud?**

If you plan to use your iPhone mostly with your computer, back up the iPhone to the computer. Doing so makes iTunes store a full backup of the iPhone on the computer, so you can restore all the data to your iPhone, or to a replacement iPhone, if necessary. You can also encrypt the backup. To keep your data safe, you must back up your computer as well. For example, you can use Time Machine to back up a Mac.

continued ▶

Whector syncing your iPhone with your computer using iTunes, you can quickly set up the communications accounts you want the iPhone to use.

On the Info tab of the iPhone's control screens in iTunes, you can set your contacts, calendars, e-mail accounts, bookmarks, and notes to sync to your iPhone. When you need to resolve problems such as data corruption on the iPhone, you can also set iTunes to overwrite particular items on the iPhone during the next sync.

## Choose Which Items to Sync from Your Computer (continued)

### Sync Your Communications Information to Your iPhone

1 Click the **Info** tab.

2 Click **Sync Contacts** (☐ changes to ☑).

**Note:** In Windows, select the program that contains the contacts — for example, Outlook.

3 To sync only some contacts, click **Selected groups** (○ changes to ◉).

4 Click each contacts group to sync (☐ changes to ☑).

5 Click **Add contacts created outside of groups on this iPhone to** (☐ changes to ☑).

6 Click ⬍ and then click the contacts group to which you want to add contacts created outside the iPhone.

7 Click **Sync Calendars** (☐ changes to ☑).

8 To sync only some calendars, click **Selected calendars** (○ changes to ◉).

9 Click each calendar to sync (☐ changes to ☑).

10 To limit the number of days of calendar data, click **Do not sync events older than 30 days** (☐ changes to ☑).

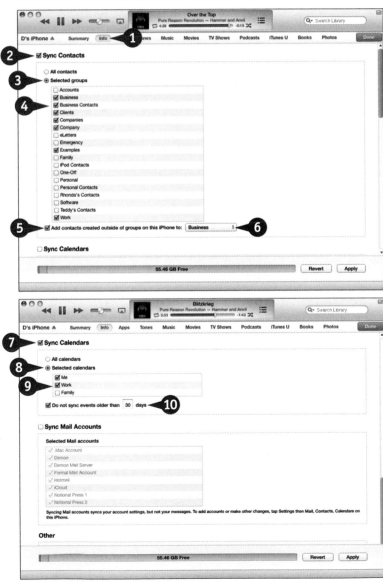

**11** Click **Sync Mail Accounts**
(☐ changes to ☑).

**Note:** In Windows, click **Sync selected mail accounts from** (☐ changes to ☑). Click the drop-down menu, and then click the program.

**12** Click each mail account you want to sync (☐ changes to ☑).

**13** Click **Sync Safari bookmarks** (☐ changes to ☑) if you want to sync your Safari bookmarks.

**14** Click **Sync notes** (☐ changes to ☑) if you want to sync your notes.

**15** In the Advanced area, click any item you want to overwrite on the iPhone (☐ changes to ☑).

**Note:** Normally, when you first set up an iPhone to sync items such as notes, bookmarks, or e-mail accounts, you do not need to overwrite the data on the iPhone. You need to overwrite the data on the iPhone only if it becomes corrupted. After syncing and overwriting the data, iTunes clears these check boxes (☑ changes to ☐) so that it does not overwrite the data again unless you select the check boxes.

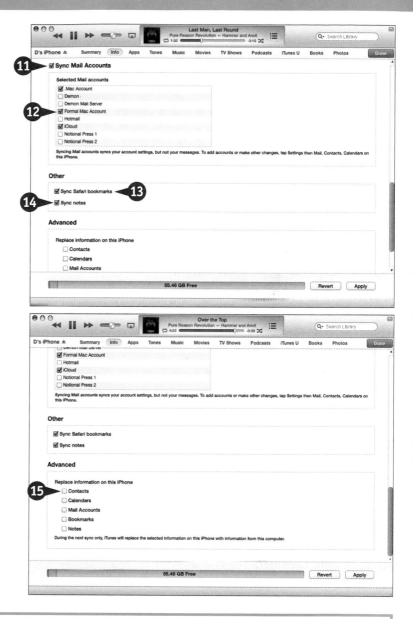

## TIP

**Why does the Info tab not appear on the iPhone's control screens?**

If your Mac is running OS X Mavericks, the Info tab does not appear on the iPhone's control screens. This is because OS X Mavericks is designed to sync data through iCloud and similar online services.

To sync your e-mail, contacts, calendars, reminders, and notes, set up your Internet accounts on your iPhone as explained in Chapter 4.

continued ▶

# Choose Which Items to Sync from Your Computer (continued)

When syncing your iPhone with your computer using iTunes, you can choose which apps to install on your iPhone from those you have purchased from the App Store.

Similarly, you can choose which music to sync by choosing playlists, artists, genres, and albums on the Albums tab. And if you have ringtones on your computer, you can sync them to your iPhone by using the Tones tab.

## Choose Which Items to Sync from Your Computer (continued)

### Choose Which Apps to Sync

**1** Click **Apps**.

The Apps tab appears.

**A** You can click ↕ and choose how to sort the apps: Click **Sort by Name**, **Sort by Kind**, **Sort by Category**, **Sort by Date**, or **Sort by Size**, as needed.

**2** Click **Install** for each app you want to sync to the iPhone (Install changes to Will Install).

**3** Scroll down the screen and click **Automatically sync new apps** (☐ changes to ☑) if you want to sync new apps automatically. This is usually helpful.

### Choose Which Music and Tones to Sync

**1** Click **Music**.

The Music tab appears.

**2** Click **Sync Music** (☐ changes to ☑).

**B** If the amount of music selected is too much to fit on your iPhone, the Over Capacity warning appears.

**3** To load a selection of music instead of your entire music library, click **Selected playlists, artists, albums, and genres** (○ changes to ⊙) instead of **Entire music library**.

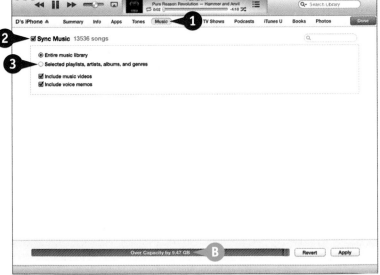

The controls in the lower part of the tab appear.

**C** Click **Automatically fill free space with songs** (☐ changes to ☑) if you want to put as much music as possible on your iPhone.

**4** In the Playlists area, click the check box (☐ changes to ☑) for each playlist to include.

**5** In the Artists area, click the check box (☐ changes to ☑) for each artist to include.

**6** In the Genres area, click the check box (☐ changes to ☑) for each genre to load.

**7** In the Albums area, click the check box (☐ changes to ☑) for each album to load.

**8** Click **Tones**.

The Tones tab appears.

**9** Click **Sync Tones** (☐ changes to ☑).

**10** Click **All tones** (○ changes to ◉) or **Selected tones** (○ changes to ◉), as needed.

**11** If you choose Selected Tones, click the check box (☐ changes to ☑) for each tone to load.

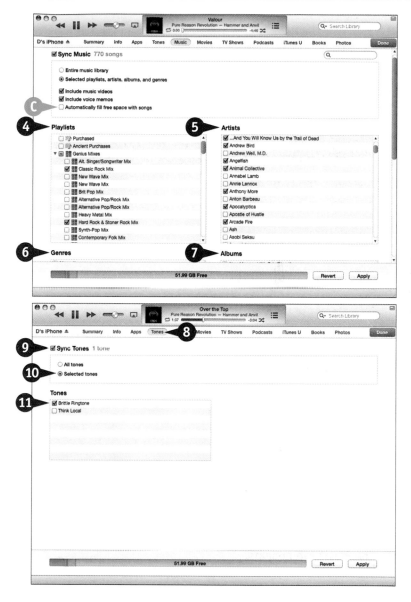

## TIP

**Should I sync my entire music library to my iPhone?**

This depends on how big your music library is, how high your iPhone's capacity is, and how much other data you need to put on the iPhone. Normally, it is best to put a selection of your favorite music, and perhaps your newest music, on your iPhone and leave plenty of space for other content. Leave the **Automatically fill free space with songs** check box deselected (☐) to prevent iTunes from filling all the free space, because this may prevent you from shooting video, taking photos, or recording audio.

continued ▶

# Choose Which Items to Sync from Your Computer (continued)

The wide range of content you can sync to your iPhone using iTunes includes movies, TV shows, podcasts, iTunes U lessons, books, and photos. To choose which items to sync, you click the appropriate tab, and then make your selection using the controls that appear on it. For each category of content, you can choose between syncing all the items and only selected ones.

After choosing all the content you want to sync to your iPhone, you click **Apply** or **Sync**. iTunes then syncs all the content to your iPhone across the USB connection.

## Choose Which Items to Sync from Your Computer (continued)

### Sync Movies, TV Shows, Podcasts, and iTunes U Lessons

1. Click a tab, **Movies**, for example.

2. Click **Sync Movies** (☐ changes to ☑).

3. Click **Automatically include** (☐ changes to ☑) to have iTunes load some movies automatically.

4. Click ↕ and choose what to include — for example, click **all unwatched** or **10 most recent**.

5. Specify other items to sync (☐ changes to ☑).

### Sync Books

1. Click the **Books** tab.

2. Click **Sync Books** (☐ changes to ☑).

3. To sync only some books, click **Selected books** (○ changes to ⦿).

4. Click each book or PDF file to sync (☐ changes to ☑).

Ⓐ You can click ↕ and click **Only Books** or **Only PDF Files** to shorten the list.

5. Click **Sync Audiobooks** (☐ changes to ☑).

6. Choose which audiobooks to sync.

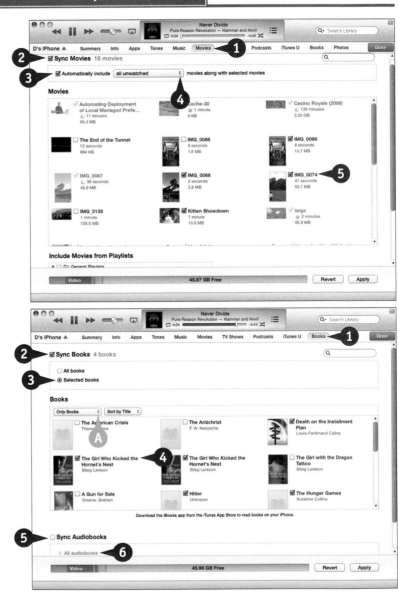

## Sync Photos

1 Click **Photos**.

2 Click **Sync Photos from** (☐ changes to ☑).

**Note:** In Windows, click **Sync Photos with** (☐ changes to ☑), and then choose the folder in the drop-down list.

3 In the pop-up menu, choose the source of the photos — for example, iPhoto.

4 Choose which photos to sync. For example, click **Selected albums, Events, and Faces, and automatically include** (○ changes to ⊙), and then choose which albums, events, and faces to include.

## Apply Your Changes and Sync

1 Click **Apply** or **Sync**.

iTunes syncs the items to your iPhone.

B The readout shows you the sync progress.

C If you need to stop the sync, click ⊗.

2 When the sync finishes, disconnect your iPhone.

### TIP

**How can I fit more content on my iPhone?**

You cannot increase your iPhone's storage capacity — with some other phones, you can install a memory card — so the way to fit more content on is to prune and compress the existing content.

Video and music files tend to take the most space. For video, your only option is to remove files you do not need on your iPhone. For music, click the **Convert higher bit rate songs** check box (☐ changes to ☑) on the Summary tab and choose a low bit rate, such as 128 Kbps, to reduce the size of music files while retaining acceptable audio quality.

# Sync Your iPhone with iTunes via Wi-Fi

The normal way to sync your iPhone with iTunes is by using the USB cable to connect the iPhone to your computer. But if you connect both your computer and your iPhone to the same network, you can sync the iPhone with iTunes wirelessly. This is called syncing "over the air."

To use wireless sync, you must first enable it in iTunes. You can then have the iPhone sync automatically when connected to a power source and to the same wireless network as the computer. You can also start a sync manually from the iPhone, even if it is not connected to a power source.

## Sync Your iPhone with iTunes via Wi-Fi

### Set Your iPhone to Sync with iTunes via Wi-Fi

1 Connect your iPhone to your computer with the USB cable.

The iTunes window appears.

2 Click the button for your iPhone.

**Note:** Your iPhone appears in iTunes with the name you gave it.

The iPhone's control screens appear.

3 Click **Summary**.

The Summary tab appears.

4 Click **Sync with this iPhone over Wi-Fi** (☐ changes to ☑).

5 Click **Apply**.

iTunes applies the change.

6 Disconnect your iPhone from your computer.

### Perform a Manual Sync via Wi-Fi

1 Press the Home button.

The Home screen appears.

2 Tap **Settings**.

The Settings screen appears.

3 Tap **General**.

The General screen appears.

**4** Tap **iTunes Wi-Fi Sync**.

The iTunes Wi-Fi Sync screen appears.

**5** Tap **Sync Now**.

The sync runs.

**A** The Sync symbol ( ☉ ) appears in the status bar.

**B** The readout shows which part of the sync is currently running.

**6** When the sync completes, tap **General**.

The General screen appears.

**TIP**

**Can I sync my iPhone automatically via Wi-Fi?**

To sync your iPhone automatically via Wi-Fi, connect your iPhone to a power source — for example, the iPhone power adapter. Make sure your computer is on and connected to your network, and that iTunes is running. Your iPhone automatically connects to your computer across the wireless network. iTunes syncs the latest songs, videos, and data.

# Transfer Files Using iTunes File Sharing

When you need to transfer files to the iPhone, you can use the File Sharing feature built into iTunes. This feature enables you to transfer files to the iPhone's storage area devoted to a particular app. For example, when you need to use a file with the DocsToGo app on the iPhone, you transfer to the DocsToGo area using File Sharing.

Only some apps can transfer files, and you must install an app capable of transferring files via File Sharing before you can use File Sharing as described in this task.

## Transfer Files Using iTunes File Sharing

**1** Connect the iPhone to your PC or Mac.

iTunes launches or becomes active, and the iPhone appears in the navigation bar.

**2** Click your iPhone.

The iPhone's control screens appear, with the Summary screen at the front.

**3** Click **Apps**.

The Apps screen appears.

**4** Scroll down.

The File Sharing area appears.

**5** Click the app to which you want to add the file.

**6** Click **Add**.

The Add dialog opens on the Mac, or the Open dialog appears in Windows.

**7** Click the file you want to copy to the iPhone.

**Note:** You can copy multiple files at once by selecting them. For example, click the first file, and then Shift+click the last file to select a range of files.

**8** Click **Open** in Windows or **Add** on a Mac.

iTunes copies the file or files to the iPhone.

---

**TIP**

**How do I copy a file from the iPhone to my computer?**

**1** Open File Sharing as discussed in this task.

**2** In the Apps area, click the app that contains the file.

**3** In the Documents area, click the file.

**4** Click **Save to**. The Open dialog appears.

**5** Click the folder to save the file in.

**6** Click **Select Folder** in Windows or **Choose** on a Mac. iTunes copies the file.

# Explore the iPhone's User Interface and Launch Apps

After you set up your iPhone with iCloud or iTunes, you are ready to start using the device. When you press the Home button to wake the iPhone from sleep, it displays the lock screen. You then unlock the iPhone to reach the Home screen, which contains icons for running the apps installed on the iPhone.

You can quickly launch an app by tapping its icon on the Home screen. From the app, you can return to the Home screen by pressing the Home button. You can then launch another app as needed.

## Explore the iPhone's User Interface and Launch Apps

**1** Press the Home button.

The iPhone's screen lights up and shows the lock screen.

**2** On an iPhone 5s, touch your finger to the Home button to unlock the iPhone using Touch ID. On an iPhone 5c, tap the slider, drag it to the right, and then enter your passcode if you have set one.

The iPhone unlocks, and the Home screen appears.

**A** The iPhone has two or more Home screens, depending on how many apps are installed. The gray dots at the bottom of the Home screen show how many Home screens you have. The white dot shows the current Home screen.

**3** Tap **Notes**.

The Notes app opens.

**Note:** If you chose to sync notes with your iPhone, the synced notes appear in the Notes app. Otherwise, the list is empty until you create a note.

**4** Tap **New**.

A new note opens, and the on-screen keyboard appears.

**5** Type a short note by tapping the keys.

**B** If a pop-up bubble suggests a correction or word completion, tap **space** to accept it. Tap × on the bubble to reject it.

**6** Tap **Done**.

The on-screen keyboard closes.

**7** Tap **Notes**.

**C** The Notes list appears, with your note in it.

**8** Press the Home button.

The Home screen appears.

**9** Tap and drag to the left to display the second Home screen.

**Note:** You can also tap at the right end of the row of dots on the Home screen to move one screen to the right. Tap at the left end to move one screen to the left.

You can now launch another app by tapping its icon.

**10** Press the Power/Sleep button.

Your iPhone goes to sleep.

**TIP**

**Where do I get more apps to perform other tasks?**
You can find an amazingly wide selection of apps — both free and ones you pay for — on Apple's App Store. See Chapter 7 for instructions on finding and downloading the apps you need.

# Use Notification Center

As your communications hub, your iPhone handles many different types of alerts for you: missed phone calls, text messages, reminders, meetings, and so on.

To help you keep on top of all these alerts, your iPhone integrates them into Notification Center, together with information about the current weather and stock prices. You can quickly access Notification Center from the Home screen or any other screen. After you display Notification Center, you can respond to an alert, view your upcoming appointments, check on the weather, or look at your current stock prices.

## Use Notification Center

### Open Notification Center

**1** Tap at the top of the screen and swipe your finger down.

Notification Center appears.

**A** The Today tab shows you a list of today's commitments.

**B** A summary of the weather and your appointments appears at the top of the screen.

**C** Your calendar appears below that.

**2** Scroll down the screen.

**D** Your Stocks list appears, showing current data.

**E** A summary of your commitments for tomorrow appears at the bottom of the screen.

**3** Tap **all**.

The full list of notifications appears.

**F** Tap a notification to access the app to which it belongs.

**G** You can tap **missed** to display your list of missed items.

**4** Tap and drag up from the bottom of the screen.

Notification Center closes.

## Open the Weather App from Notification Center

1 In Notification Center, tap the weather item at the top of the screen.

The Weather app opens, displaying the current weather.

You can then swipe your finger to the left or right across the timeline to display other hourly details.

Swipe your finger left or right below the timeline to view the weather for another location.

## Open the Stocks App from Notification Center

1 In Notification Center, tap **Stocks**.

The Stocks app opens, displaying the current stock prices, market capitalizations, and charts.

**Note:** You can customize Notification Center to show the notifications you want to see. See Chapter 2 for details.

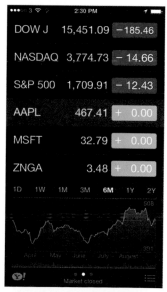

---

### TIP

**What happens if I receive a notification when my iPhone is locked?**
What happens when you receive a notification while the screen is locked depends on the type of notification. For most types of notifications, your iPhone displays an alert on the lock screen to alert you to the notification. Unlocking your iPhone while the alert is showing takes you directly to the notification in whatever app it belongs to — for example, to an instant message in the Messages app.

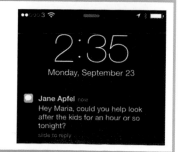

# Use Control Center

Control Center puts your iPhone's most essential controls right where you need them. From Control Center, you can turn Airplane mode, Wi-Fi, Bluetooth, Do Not Disturb mode, and Orientation Lock on or off; control music playback and volume, and direct your iPhone's audio output to AirPlay devices; change the setting for the AirDrop sharing feature; and quickly access the Flashlight, Clock, Calculator, and Camera apps.

Control Center appears as a pane that you open by swiping upward from the bottom of the screen. After using Control Center, you can drag the pane closed or simply tap the screen above it.

## Use Control Center

### Open Control Center

1 Tap and swipe up from the very bottom of the screen.

Control Center opens.

**Note:** You can open Control Center from most apps and screens. You may find some exceptions — for example, where iOS interprets an upward swipe as an action within the app.

### Control Essential Settings

1 Tap **Airplane Mode** (✈) to turn Airplane mode on or off.

2 Tap **Wi-Fi** (📶) to turn Wi-Fi on or off.

3 Tap **Bluetooth** (✳) to turn Bluetooth on or off.

4 Tap **Do Not Disturb** (🌙) to turn Do Not Disturb mode on or off.

5 Tap **Orientation Lock** (🔒) to turn Orientation Lock on or off.

## Choose an AirPlay Device

**1** In Control Center, tap **AirPlay**.

The AirPlay dialog opens.

**2** Tap the AirPlay speaker or Apple TV you want to use.

**3** If you choose an AirPlay TV, set the **Mirroring** switch to On ( ) or Off ( ), as needed.

**4** Tap **Done**.

The AirPlay dialog closes.

## Open Flashlight, Clock, Calculator, or Camera

**1** In Control Center, tap the appropriate icon:

**A** Tap **Flashlight** (  ) to turn on the Flashlight.

**B** Tap **Clock** (  ) to display the Clock app.

**C** Tap **Calculator** (  ) to display the Calculator app.

**D** Tap **Camera** (  ) to display the Camera app.

The Flashlight turns on, or the app opens.

**TIP**

### Can I use Control Center in landscape mode as well?

Yes, Control Center works in landscape orientation. Simply swipe up from the bottom of the screen in an app that supports the rotated orientation. Control Center has a different landscape layout, but the controls work the same way.

# CHAPTER 2

# Personalizing Your iPhone

To make your iPhone work the way you prefer, you can configure its many settings. In this chapter, you learn how to control iCloud sync, notifications, audio preferences, screen brightness, and other key aspects of the iPhone's behavior.

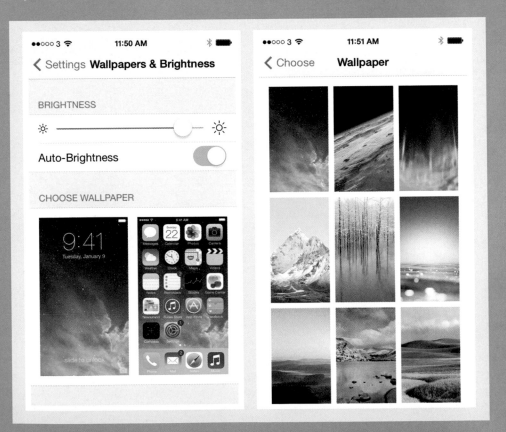

# Find the Settings You Need

To configure the iPhone, you work with its settings using the Settings app. This app contains settings for the iPhone's system software, the apps the iPhone includes, and third-party apps you have added. To reach the settings, you first display the Settings screen and then the category of settings you want to configure. Some apps provide access to settings through the apps themselves. So if you cannot find the settings for an app on the Settings screen, look within the app. In this task, you learn how to open the Settings screen and see the main categories of settings it contains.

## Find the Settings You Need

### Display the Settings Screen

**1** Press the Home button.

The Home screen appears.

**2** Tap **Settings**.

The Settings screen appears.

**3** Tap and drag up to scroll down the screen.

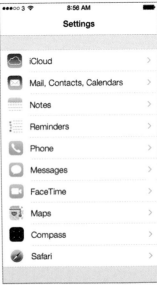

## Display a Settings Screen

**1** On the Settings screen, tap the button for the settings you want to display. For example, tap **Sounds** to display the Sounds screen.

**2** Tap **Settings** when you are ready to return to the Settings screen.

## Display the Settings for an App

**1** On the Settings screen, scroll down toward the bottom.

**2** Tap the button for the app whose settings you want to display. For example, tap **DEVONthink** to display the DEVONthink settings.

**3** Tap **Settings** when you are ready to return to the Settings screen.

**4** Press the Home button.

The Home screen appears again.

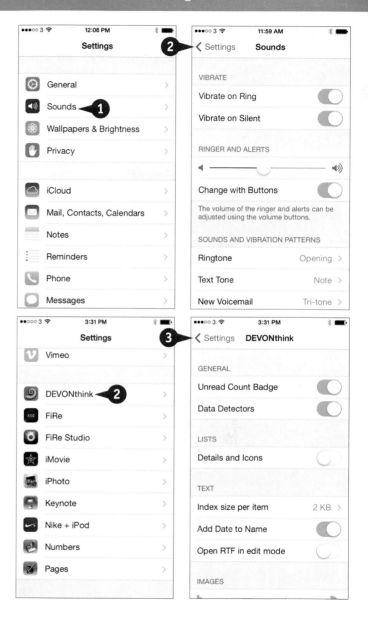

---

**TIP**

**Why do only some apps have an entry in the Settings app?**

The Settings app contains entries for only those apps that have settings you can configure directly through iOS, the iPhone's operating system. Other apps include settings that you configure directly from within the app. This approach is more convenient for apps that have settings you are likely to change frequently.

# Choose Which iCloud Items to Sync

Apple's iCloud service adds powerful online sync features to your iPhone. With iCloud, you can sync your e-mail account, contacts, calendars, reminders, Safari bookmarks, shared photos, and iWork documents and data, so you can access them from any of your devices. You can also use the Find My iPhone feature to locate your iPhone when it goes missing.

To use iCloud, you set your iPhone to use your Apple ID, and then choose which features to use. If you set up your iPhone using iCloud, your account is already active, but you may want to choose different settings for iCloud.

## Choose Which iCloud Items to Sync

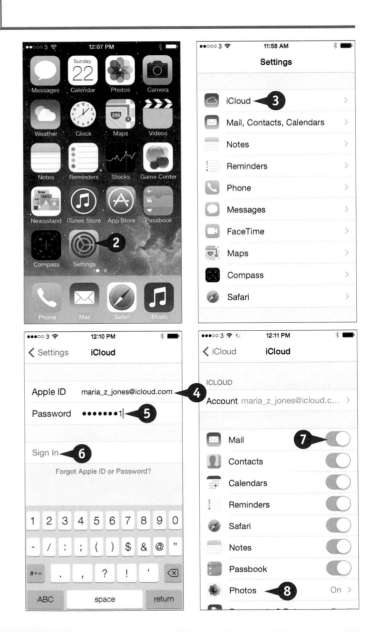

**1** Press the Home button.

The Home screen appears.

**2** Tap **Settings**.

The Settings screen appears.

**3** Tap **iCloud**.

The iCloud screen appears.

**4** Type your Apple ID.

**Note:** If you do not yet have an Apple ID, tap **Get a Free Apple ID**, farther down the iCloud screen, and then follow the prompts.

**5** Type your password.

**6** Tap **Sign In**.

**Note:** If the Allow iCloud to Use the Location of Your iPhone? dialog appears, tap **OK** if you want to use the Find My iPhone feature. This is normally helpful.

**7** On the iCloud screen, set the switches for **Mail**, **Contacts**, **Calendars**, **Reminders**, **Safari**, **Notes**, and **Passbook** to On ( ) or Off ( ), as needed.

**8** Tap **Photos**.

The Photos screen appears.

**9** Set the **My Photo Stream** switch to On (⬤) to use Photo Stream.

**10** Set the **Photo Sharing** switch to On (⬤) to use photo sharing.

**11** Tap **iCloud**.

The iCloud screen appears.

**12** Tap **Documents & Data**.

The Documents & Data screen appears.

**13** Set the **Documents & Data** switch to On (⬤) to store documents and data in iCloud.

**14** Set switches to control which apps can store documents and data in iCloud.

**15** Tap **iCloud**.

The iCloud screen appears.

**16** Set the **Find My iPhone** switch to On (⬤) if you want to use the Find My iPhone feature.

**17** Tap **Settings**.

The Settings screen appears.

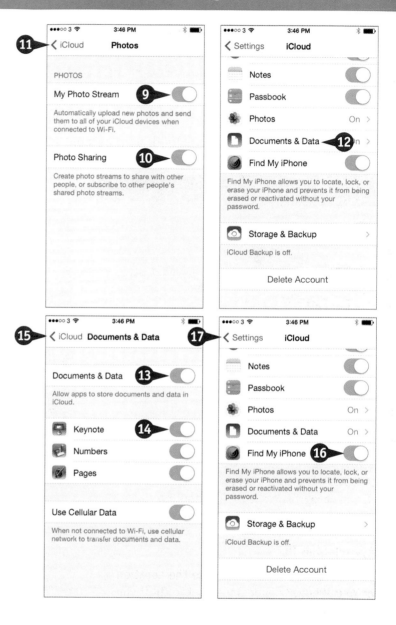

## TIP

**How much space does iCloud provide?**

iCloud provides 5GB of space for a free account; content and apps you acquire from Apple do not count against this space, nor do your Photo Stream photos or songs included in iTunes Match. You can buy more space by tapping **Storage & Backup**, tapping **Manage Storage** on the Storage & Backup screen, and then tapping **Change Storage Plan** on the Manage Storage screen.

# Choose Which Apps Can Give Notifications

Some iPhone apps can notify you when you have received messages or when updates are available. You can choose which apps give which notifications, or prevent apps from showing notifications altogether. You can also choose the order in which the notifications appear in the Notification Center and control which notifications appear on the lock screen.

iPhone apps use three types of notifications: badges on app icons, banners at the top of the screen, and alert dialogs. See the tip for details.

## Choose Which Apps Can Give Notifications

**1** Press the Home button.

The Home screen appears.

**2** Tap **Settings**.

The Settings screen appears.

**3** Tap **Notification Center**.

The Notification Center screen appears.

**4** Set the **Notifications View** switch to On (○) if you want notifications on the lock screen.

**5** Set the **Today View** switch to On (○) if you want Today View on the lock screen.

**Note:** Today View shows current weather, upcoming Calendar events, and reminders.

**6** In the Today View list, choose what to include by setting each switch to On (○) or Off (○).

**7** In the Notifications View list, tap **Sort Manually** to use manual sorting. Tap **Sort By Time** to sort the apps by the times of their notifications.

**8** In the Include list, tap the app for which you want to choose notification options.

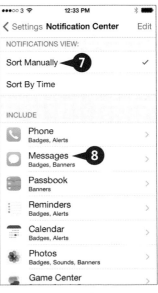

**9** In the Alert Style area, tap **Alerts** to display alerts, **Banners** to display banners, or **None** to suppress alerts.

**10** Set the **Badge App Icon** switch to On (◉) to show badges or Off (◯) to hide them.

**11** Tap **Alert Sound**, choose a sound on the Alert Sound screen, and then tap **Messages** to return.

**12** Set the **Show In Notification Center** switch to On (◉) or Off (◯) to control whether the app's notifications appear in Notification Center.

**13** Tap **Include**, tap the number of recent items to display, and then tap the app's name button to return.

**14** Set the **Show on Lock Screen** switch and **Show Preview** switch to On (◉) or Off (◯), as needed.

**15** Tap to show alerts from everyone or only your contacts.

**16** Tap **Notification Center**.

**17** Tap **Edit** to switch to Edit mode.

**18** Drag a handle (≡) to move an app up or down the list. Drag an app to the Do Not Include list to remove it from Notification Center.

**19** Tap **Done**.

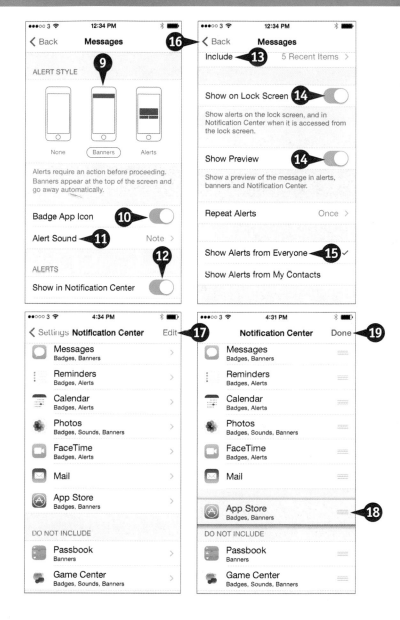

## TIP

**What are the three kinds of notifications?**

A *badge* is a red circle or rounded rectangle that appears on the app's icon on the Home screen and shows a white number indicating how many notifications there are. A *banner* is a pop-up notification that appears briefly at the top of the screen and then disappears automatically. An *alert* is a dialog that appears in front of the running app; you need to dismiss the alert before you can take other actions on your iPhone. Whichever notification type you choose, you can also have your iPhone play a sound to get your attention.

# Choose Sounds Settings

To control how the iPhone gives you audio feedback, choose options on the Sounds screen in Settings. Here, you can choose whether to have the iPhone vibrate always to signal incoming calls, or vibrate only when the ringer is silent. You can set the volume for the ringer and for alerts, choose your default ringtone and text tone, and choose whether to receive alerts for voice mail, e-mail, and calendar items.

Playing lock sounds helps confirm that you have locked or unlocked the iPhone as you intended. Playing keyboard clicks confirms each key press on the iPhone's keyboard.

## Choose Sounds Settings

**1** Press the Home button.

The Home screen appears.

**2** Tap **Settings**.

The Settings screen appears.

**3** Tap **Sounds**.

The Sounds screen appears.

**4** Set the **Vibrate on Ring** switch to On (⬤) or Off ( ⬤ ), as needed.

**5** Set the **Vibrate on Silent** switch to On (⬤) or Off ( ⬤ ), as needed.

**6** Tap and drag the **Ringer and Alerts** slider to set the volume.

**Ⓐ** When the **Change with Buttons** switch is On (⬤), you can change the Ringer and Alerts volume by pressing the volume buttons on the side of the iPhone.

**7** Tap **Ringtone**.

The Ringtone screen appears.

**8** Tap the ringtone you want to hear.

**9** Tap **Vibration**.

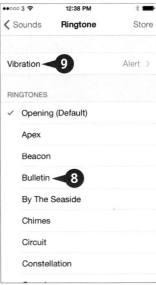

The Vibration screen appears.

**10** Tap the vibration pattern you want.

**11** If you prefer a custom vibration, tap **Create New Vibration** in the Custom area.

The New Vibration screen appears.

**12** Tap a rhythm.

**13** Tap **Stop**.

**14** Tap **Play** to play back the vibration.

**15** Tap **Save**.

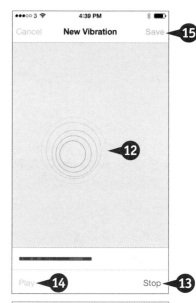

**16** In the New Vibration dialog, type a name.

**17** Tap **Save**.

**18** On the Ringtone screen, tap **Sounds**.

The Sounds screen appears.

**19** Repeat steps **7** to **18** to set other tones, such as text tones.

**20** Set the **Lock Sounds** switch to On (⬤◯) or Off (◯ ), as needed.

**21** Set the **Keyboard Clicks** switch to On (⬤◯) or Off (◯ ), as needed.

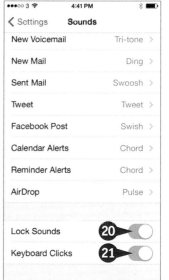

---

**TIP**

**How do I use different ringtones for different callers?**

The ringtone and text tone you set in the Ringtone area of the Sounds screen are your standard tone for phone calls, FaceTime calls, and messaging calls. To set different tones for a contact, press the Home button, tap **Phone**, and then tap **Contacts**. In the Contacts list, tap the contact, tap **Edit**, and then tap **Ringtone**. On the Ringtone screen, tap the ringtone and then tap **Done**. You can also change other settings, such as the ringtone's vibration for the contact. Tap **Done** when you finish.

# Set Screen Brightness and Wallpaper Backgrounds

To make the screen easier to see, you can change its brightness. You can also have the iPhone's Auto-Brightness feature automatically set the screen's brightness to a level suitable for the ambient brightness that the iPhone's light sensor detects.

To make the screen attractive to your eye, you can choose which picture to use as the wallpaper that appears in the background. You can use either a static wallpaper or a dynamic, changing wallpaper. You can set different wallpaper for the lock screen — the screen you see when the iPhone is locked — and for the Home screen.

## Set Screen Brightness and Wallpaper Backgrounds

**1** Press the Home button.

The Home screen appears.

**2** Tap **Settings**.

The Settings screen appears.

**3** Tap **Wallpapers & Brightness**.

The Wallpapers & Brightness screen appears.

**4** Tap the **Brightness** slider and drag it left or right to set brightness.

**5** Set the **Auto-Brightness** switch to On ( ⬤ ) or Off ( ⬤ ), as needed.

**6** Tap **Choose Wallpaper**.

**Note:** The Choose Wallpaper button is a single button, even though it looks like two buttons.

The Wallpaper screen appears, showing the list of picture categories.

**7** Tap **Dynamic** or **Stills** in the Apple Wallpaper area. This example uses **Stills**.

**A** To choose a picture from a different picture category, tap that category. For example, tap **Camera Roll** to display pictures you have taken with the iPhone's camera, saved from e-mail or multimedia messages, or web pages.

The Wallpaper category screen appears.

**8** Tap the wallpaper you want.

The Wallpaper Preview screen appears.

**9** Tap **Set**.

**10** Tap **Set Lock Screen**, **Set Home Screen**, or **Set Both**. Tap **Cancel** if you do not want to proceed.

**11** Tap **Choose**.

**12** Tap **Wallpaper**.

**13** Tap **Settings**.

**14** Press the Home button.

The Home screen appears.

**B** If you changed the Home screen wallpaper, the new wallpaper appears.

## TIP

**How do I use only part of a picture as the wallpaper?**

The Apple wallpapers are the right size for the screen, so you do not need to resize them. But when you use a photo for the wallpaper, you usually need to choose which part of it to display. When you choose a photo as wallpaper, the iPhone displays the screen for moving and scaling the photo. Pinch in or out to zoom the photo out or in, and tap and drag to move the picture around. When you have chosen the part you want, tap **Set**.

# Choose Privacy and Location Settings

Your iPhone contains a huge amount of information about you, the people you communicate with, what you do, and where you go. To keep this information safe, you need to choose suitable privacy and location settings.

Privacy settings enable you to control which apps may access your contacts, calendars, reminders, and photos. You can also choose which apps can use your iPhone's location services, and which track the iPhone's location via the Global Positioning System, or GPS.

## Choose Privacy and Location Settings

**1** Press the Home button.

The Home screen appears.

**2** Tap **Settings**.

The Settings screen appears.

**3** Tap **Privacy**.

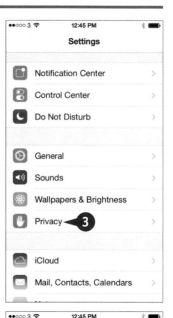

The Privacy screen appears.

**4** Tap **Location Services**.

The Location Services screen appears.

**5** If you need to turn location services off completely, set the **Location Services** switch to Off ( ).

**6** Set the switch for an app to On ( ) or Off ( ), as needed. For example, set the **Passbook** switch to On ( ).

**7** Tap **Find My iPhone**.

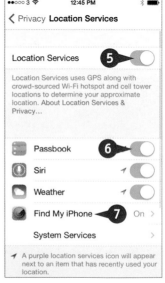

The Find My iPhone screen appears.

⑧ Set the **Find My iPhone** switch to On ( ⬤ ) if you want to be able to locate your iPhone should it go missing.

⑨ Set the **Status Bar Icon** switch to On ( ⬤ ) if you want to see an arrow in the status bar when the iPhone is being tracked.

⑩ Tap **Back**.

⑪ Scroll down to the bottom of the Location Services screen and tap **System Services**.

The System Services screen appears.

⑫ Set the switch for a system service to On ( ⬤ ) or Off ( ⚪ ), as needed.

⑬ Tap **Back**.

The Location Services screen appears.

⑭ Tap **Privacy**.

The Privacy screen appears.

⑮ Tap **Contacts**.

⑯ Set the switches to choose which apps can access your contacts.

⑰ Tap **Privacy**, and then repeat steps **15** and **16** for Calendars, Reminders, and Photos.

## TIP

**Why do some apps need to use location services?**

Some apps and system services need to use location services to determine where you are. For example, the Maps app requires location services to display your location, and the Compass service needs your location to display accurate compass information.

If you allow the Camera app to use location services, it stores GPS data in your photos. You can then sort the photos by location in applications such as iPhoto on OS X. Other apps use location services to provide context-specific information, such as information about nearby restaurants. It is a good idea to review which apps are using location services and to turn off any that do not have a compelling reason for doing so.

# Configure Spotlight Search and Find What You Need

Your iPhone can put a huge amount of data in the palm of your hand, and you may often need to search to find what you need.

To make your search results more accurate and helpful, you can configure your iPhone's Spotlight Search feature. You can turn off searching for items you do not want to see in your search results, and you can change the order in which Spotlight displays the items it finds.

## Configure Spotlight Search and Find What You Need

### Configure Spotlight Search

1 Press the Home button.

The Home screen appears.

2 Tap **Settings**.

The Settings screen appears.

3 Tap **General**.

The General screen appears.

4 Tap **Spotlight Search**.

The Spotlight Search screen appears.

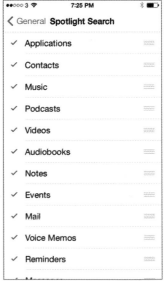

**5** Tap to remove the check mark from each item you do not want to search.

**6** Tap a movement handle and drag an item up or down the search order.

**Note:** Spotlight displays the search results in descending order, starting with the first item on the list.

**7** Tap **General** to go back to the General screen.

**8** Tap **Settings** to go back to the Settings screen.

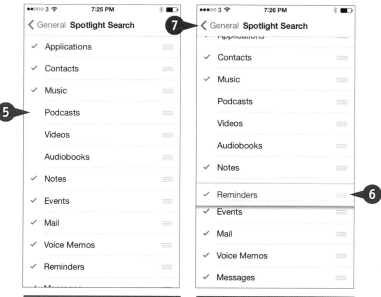

## Search for Items Using Spotlight

**1** Press the Home button.

The Home screen appears.

**2** Tap near the top of the screen and pull down.

The Search iPhone panel appears.

The keyboard appears.

**3** Type your search term.

A list of results appears.

**4** Tap the result you want to view.

---

**TIP**

**Which items should I make Spotlight search?**

This depends on what you need to be able to search for. For example, if you do not need to search for music, videos, or podcasts, remove the check marks for the Music, Podcasts, and Videos item on the Spotlight Search screen to exclude them from Spotlight searches. For normal use, you may want to leave all the check marks in place but move the items most important to you to the top of the Spotlight Search list.

# Choose Locking and Control Center Settings

To avoid unintentional taps on the screen, your iPhone automatically locks itself after a period of inactivity. After locking itself, your iPhone turns off its screen and goes to sleep to save battery power.

You can choose how long your iPhone waits before locking itself. Setting your iPhone to lock quickly helps preserve battery power, but you may prefer to leave your iPhone on longer so that you can continue work. You can then lock your iPhone manually. You can also choose whether to make the Control Center feature accessible from the lock screen.

## Choose Locking and Control Center Settings

**1** Press the Home button.

The Home screen appears.

**2** Tap **Settings**.

The Settings screen appears.

**3** Tap **General**.

The General screen appears.

**4** Tap and drag up to scroll down the screen.

**5** Tap **Auto-Lock**.

The Auto-Lock screen appears.

**6** Tap the interval — for example, **1 Minute**.

**7** Tap **General**.

The General screen appears.

**8** Tap **Settings**.

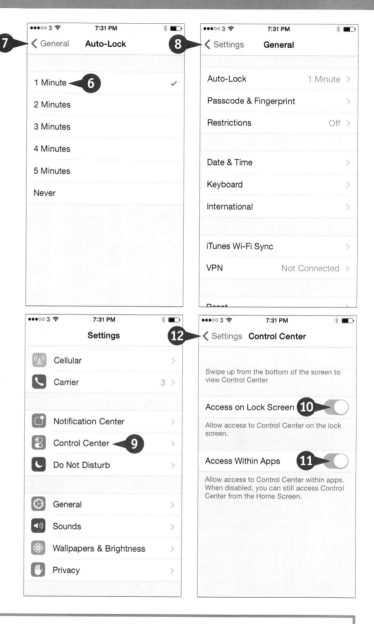

The Settings screen appears.

**9** Tap **Control Center**.

The Control Center screen appears.

**10** Set the **Access on Lock Screen** switch to On ( ) or Off ( ), as needed.

**11** Set the **Access Within Apps** switch to On ( ) or Off ( ), as needed.

**12** Tap **Settings**.

The Settings screen appears.

## TIPS

**How do I put the iPhone to sleep manually?**

You can put the iPhone to sleep at any point by pressing the Power/Sleep button for a moment.

Putting the iPhone to sleep as soon as you stop using it helps to prolong battery life. If you apply a passcode, as discussed later in this chapter, putting the iPhone to sleep also starts protecting your data sooner.

**When should I use the Never setting for Auto-Lock?**

Choose the Never setting for Auto-Lock if you need to make sure the iPhone never goes to sleep. For example, if you are playing music with the lyrics displayed, turning off auto-locking may be helpful.

# Set Up and Use Do Not Disturb Mode

When you do not want your iPhone to disturb you, turn on its Do Not Disturb mode. You can configure Do Not Disturb mode to turn on and off automatically at set times each day — for example, on at 10 p.m. and off at 7 a.m. You can turn Do Not Disturb mode on and off manually from Control Center.

You can allow particular groups of contacts to bypass Do Not Disturb mode so they can contact you even when Do Not Disturb is on. You can also allow repeated calls to ring when Do Not Disturb is on.

## Set Up and Use Do Not Disturb Mode

### Configure Do Not Disturb Mode

**1** Press the Home button.

The Home screen appears.

**2** Tap **Settings**.

The Settings screen appears.

**3** Tap **Do Not Disturb**.

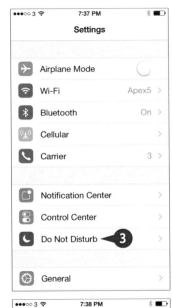

The Do Not Disturb screen appears.

**4** To turn on Do Not Disturb from this screen, set the **Manual** switch to On ( ).

**Note:** You can turn Do Not Disturb on and off more easily from Control Center.

**5** If you want to schedule your quiet hours, set the **Scheduled** switch to On ( ).

**6** Tap **From, To**.

The Quiet Hours screen appears.

**7** Tap **From**.

**8** Use the spin wheels to set the From time.

**9** Tap **To**.

**10** Set the To time.

**11** Tap **Back**.

**12** Tap **Allow Calls From**.

The Allow Calls From screen appears.

**13** Tap the group you will allow to call you during your quiet hours.

**14** Tap **Back**.

**15** Set the **Repeated Calls** switch to On ( ⬤ ) or Off ( ◯ ), as needed.

**16** In the Silence area, tap **Always** or **Only while iPhone is locked**, as needed.

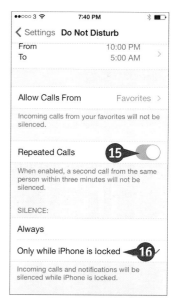

## Turn Do Not Disturb Mode On or Off Manually

**1** Press the Home button.

The Home screen appears.

**2** Tap and drag up to scroll down the screen.

Control Center opens.

**3** Tap **Do Not Disturb** to turn Do Not Disturb on ( 🌙 changes to 🌙 ) or off ( 🌙 changes to 🌙 ).

---

**TIP**

**How can I tell whether Do Not Disturb is on?**

When Do Not Disturb is on, a crescent moon symbol ( Ⓐ ) appears in the status bar to the left of the battery readout.

# Secure Your iPhone with a Passcode or Touch ID

You can lock the iPhone with a passcode that takes effect when you lock your iPhone or it locks itself. When you unlock the iPhone, you must provide the passcode. On the iPhone 5s, you can set Touch ID to require your fingerprint, or one of several fingerprints, to unlock the device. For added security, you can set the iPhone to automatically erase its data after ten failed attempts to enter the passcode. You can also choose between a four-digit password and a longer password with numbers, letters, and other characters.

## Secure Your iPhone with a Passcode or Touch ID

**1** Press the Home button.

The Home screen appears.

**2** Tap **Settings**.

The Settings screen appears.

**3** Tap **General**.

The General screen appears.

**4** Scroll down, and then tap **Passcode & Fingerprint** on the iPhone 5s. On the iPhone 5c, tap **Passcode Lock**.

The Passcode & Fingerprint screen or the Passcode Lock screen appears.

**5** To follow this example, make sure the **Simple Passcode** switch is On ( ). If not, set it to On ( changes to ).

**6** Tap **Turn Passcode On**.

The Set Passcode screen appears.

**Note:** The iPhone shows dots instead of your passcode digits in case someone is watching.

**7** Type your passcode.

The iPhone displays the Set Passcode screen again, this time with the message "Re-enter your passcode."

**8** Type the passcode again.

58

**9** On the Passcode & Fingerprint screen or the Passcode Lock screen, tap **Require Passcode**.

**10** On the Require Passcode screen, tap the button for the length of time you want — for example, **After 1 minute** or **Immediately**.

**11** Tap **Back**.

The Passcode & Fingerprint screen or the Passcode Lock screen appears.

**A** On an iPhone 5s, you can tap **Fingerprints** to display the Fingerprints screen. Here, you can set the **Passcode Unlock** switch and the **iTunes & App Store** switch to choose what the fingerprint scanner permits, or tap **Add a fingerprint** to add another fingerprint.

**12** Set the **Voice Dial** switch to On (🔵) or Off (⚪), as needed.

**13** In the Allow Access When Locked area, set the **Passbook** switch and the **Reply with Message** switch to Off (⚪) or On (🔵), as needed.

**Note:** Allowing access to Passbook when your iPhone is locked enables you to reach boarding passes and similar documents more quickly when you need them.

**14** If you want the iPhone to erase all its data after ten failed passcode attempts, set the **Erase Data** switch to On (🔵).

The iPhone displays a confirmation dialog.

**15** Tap **Enable**.

## TIPS

**How can I make my passcode even more secure?**
If you feel a four-digit passcode is not secure enough, set the **Simple Passcode** switch on the Passcode Lock screen to Off (⚪). When you tap **Turn Passcode On**, the Set Passcode screen lets you set a passcode of any length.

**What Require Passcode setting should I choose?**
Choose **Immediately** for greatest security. Choose **After 1 minute** for good security but more convenience.

# Configure Restrictions and Parental Controls

Like any other computer that can access the Internet, the iPhone can reach vast amounts of content not suitable for children or business contexts.

You can restrict the iPhone from accessing particular kinds of content. You can use the restrictions to implement parental controls — for example, preventing the iPhone's user from buying content in apps or watching adult-rated movies.

## Configure Restrictions and Parental Controls

**1** Press the Home button.

The Home screen appears.

**2** Tap **Settings**.

The Settings screen appears.

**3** Tap **General**.

The General screen appears.

**4** Scroll down, and then tap **Restrictions**.

The Restrictions screen appears.

**5** Tap **Enable Restrictions**.

The Set Passcode screen appears.

**Note:** The passcode you set to protect restrictions is different from the passcode you use to lock the iPhone. Do not use the same code.

**6** Type the passcode.

**Note:** The iPhone shows dots instead of your passcode digits in case someone is watching.

The iPhone displays the Set Passcode screen again, this time with the message "Re-enter your Restrictions Passcode."

**7** Type the passcode again.

The Restrictions screen appears with the controls in the Allow area now available.

**8** In the Allow area, set each switch to On (🔘) or Off (⚪), as needed.

**9** Scroll down to the Allowed Content area.

**10** If you need to change the country used for rating content, tap **Ratings For**. On the Ratings For screen, tap the country, and then tap **Restrictions**.

**11** Choose settings for Music, Podcasts & iTunes U, Movies, TV Shows, and Apps. For example, tap **Movies**.

The Movies screen appears.

**12** Tap the highest rating you will permit.

**13** Tap **Restrictions**.

**14** Move the **In-App Purchases** switch to Off to prevent the user buying items from within apps.

**15** Choose other settings in the Privacy area.

**16** Choose settings for Accounts, Find My Friends, Cellular Data Use, Background App Refresh, and Volume Limit.

**17** Set the **Multiplayer Games** switch and the **Adding Friends** switch to On (🔘) or Off (⚪), as needed.

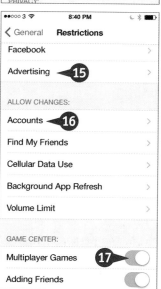

---

## TIPS

**What are in-app purchases?**

In-app purchases are items that you can buy directly from within apps. These are a popular and easy way for developers to sell extra features for apps, especially low-cost apps or free apps. They are also an easy way for the iPhone's user to spend money.

**What do the Privacy settings in Restrictions do?**

The Privacy settings in Restrictions enable you to control which apps can access the iPhone's location information, contacts, and other apps, and whether the user can change the settings.

# Choose Date, Time, and International Settings

To keep yourself on time and your data accurate, you need to make sure the iPhone is using the correct date and time.

To make dates, times, and other data appear in the formats you prefer, you may need to change the iPhone's International settings.

## Choose Date, Time, and International Settings

### Choose Date and Time Settings

**1** Press the Home button.

The Home screen appears.

**2** Tap **Settings**.

The Settings screen appears.

**3** Tap **General**.

The General screen appears.

**4** Scroll down, and then tap **Date & Time**.

The Date & Time screen appears.

**5** Set the **24-Hour Time** switch to On ( ⬤ ) if you want to use 24-hour times.

**6** To set the date and time manually, set the **Set Automatically** switch to Off ( ⬤ ).

**7** Use the controls to set the date and time.

**8** Tap **General**.

The General screen appears.

62

## Choose International Settings

1 From the General screen, tap **International**.

The International screen appears.

2 Tap **Region Format**.

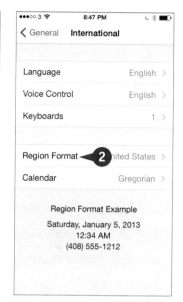

The Region Format screen appears.

3 Tap the region you want, placing a check mark next to it.

4 Tap **International**.

The International screen appears.

**Note:** From the International screen, you can also change the language used for the iPhone's user interface and the language used for voice control.

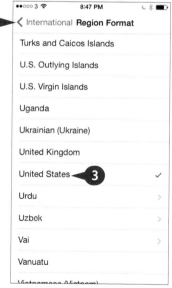

## TIPS

**How does the iPhone set the date and time automatically?**

The iPhone sets the date and time automatically by using time servers, computers on the Internet that provide date and time information to computers that request them. The iPhone automatically determines its geographical location so that it can request the right time zone from the time server.

**Why do my contacts' phone numbers appear in a different format from the region format example?**

Your cellular carrier can override the setting that controls the format for phone numbers. You cannot change this, but you can change your carrier.

# Accessorize Your iPhone

Your iPhone is as sleek and beautiful as it is powerful and practical. You will probably want to keep your iPhone protected and in good condition even as you take it everywhere with you and use it all day long.

To get the most out of your iPhone, you can protect it with a case and keep it charged with a dock or stand, a car charger, or simply an extra USB charger. You can connect a wireless keyboard, mirror your iPhone's display on an HDTV or a projector, connect your iPhone to a camera, and even print from it.

### Protect Your iPhone with an iPhone Case

To protect your iPhone, put it in a case that will prevent its body and screen from becoming scratched or collecting dust. Many cases are available, made of various materials and offering different features such as a clip for connecting to your belt or the ability to prop up your iPhone in different positions for work or play. You can even get waterproof cases.

### Charge Your iPhone with an iPhone Dock

If you need to be able to park your iPhone neatly on your desk and easily charge it, consider getting an iPhone dock. Some docks also provide an audio line-out port for connecting the iPhone to powered speakers or your stereo so you can play music; other docks come built into powered speakers. You may also be able to use other accessories with the dock, such as the Apple Digital AV Adapter and the iPhone Camera Connection Kit.

### Type Fast with a Wireless Keyboard

If you need to enter a lot of text on your iPhone, buy a Bluetooth keyboard. For example, the Apple Wireless Keyboard gives you the added convenience of actually typing with a physical keyboard while using the iPhone. Some other wireless keyboards come built into iPhone cases that enable you to prop up the iPhone at a helpful angle as you type on the keyboard.

## Show Your iPhone's Content on a Large Screen

The Lightning Digital Apple TV Adapter enables you to mirror your iPhone out to a larger HDTV or a projector, so a larger audience can view your content. This is great for presentations you create in Keynote on your iPhone, or for teaching a class lesson from an app. You connect one end of the adapter to the iPhone's Lightning port and the other end to the HDMI port of the HDTV using a third-party HDMI cable.

## Get an Extra USB Power Adapter

If you regularly use your iPhone both at home and at work, you may decide to get an extra USB power adapter so you can have one at home and one at work and keep your iPhone well charged.

If you need to charge your iPhone in the car, look for a power adapter with a 12-volt adapter.

If you travel with your iPhone, look for a travel adapter that will work in all the countries you visit.

## Print from Your iPhone with an AirPrint-Enabled Printer

If you need to print documents — such as e-mail messages, web pages, photos, or business documents — from your iPhone, get an AirPrint-enabled printer. Using AirPrint, you can print from your iPhone using Wi-Fi, so you need neither connect any cables nor install any software. To find a list of AirPrint-enabled printers, go to http://store.apple.com.

# CHAPTER 3

# Working with Voice and Accessibility

**Your iPhone includes the Siri personal assistant, powerful voice-related accessibility features, and in-car integration.**

# Give Commands with Siri

Often, speaking is even easier than using your iPhone's touch screen — especially when you are out and about or on the move. The iPhone's powerful Siri feature enables you to take essential actions by using your voice to tell your iPhone what you want. Siri requires a fast Internet connection because the speech recognition runs on servers in Apple's data center.

You can use Siri either with the iPhone's built-in microphone or with the microphone on a headset. Unless you are in a quiet environment, or you hold your iPhone close to your face, a headset microphone gives much better results than the built-in microphone.

## Open Siri

From the Home screen or any app, press the Home button or the headset clicker button for several seconds. If you have chosen to allow Siri access when your iPhone is locked, you can also activate Siri from the lock screen.

The Siri screen appears. A tone indicates that Siri is ready to take your commands.

## Send an E-Mail Message

Say "E-mail" and the contact's name, followed by the message. Siri creates an e-mail message to the contact and enters the text. Review the message, and then tap **Send** to send it.

If you prefer, you can start the message by saying "E-mail" and the contact's name, and then pausing. Siri then prompts you for the subject and text of the message in turn.

## Send a Text Message

Say "Tell" and the contact's name. When Siri responds, say the message you want to send. For example, say "Tell Chris Smith" and then "I'm stuck in traffic but I'll be there in an hour." Siri creates a text message to the contact, enters the text, and sends the message.

You can also say "tell" and the contact's name followed immediately by the message. For example, "Tell Bill Sykes the package will arrive at 10 a.m."

## Set a Reminder for Yourself

Say "Remind me" and the details of what you want Siri to remind you of. For example, say "Remind me to take my iPad to Acme Industries tomorrow morning." Siri listens to what you say and creates a reminder. Check what Siri has written, and then tap **Confirm** if it is correct.

## Set an Alarm

Say "Set an alarm for 5 a.m." and check the alarm that Siri displays.

You can turn the alarm off by tapping its switch (changes to ).

## Set Up a Meeting

Say "Meet with" and the contact's name, followed by brief details of the appointment. For example, say "Meet with Don Williamson for lunch at noon on Friday." Siri listens, sends a meeting invitation to the contact if it finds an e-mail address, and adds the meeting to your calendar.

# Dictate Text Using Siri

One of Siri's strongest features is the capability to transcribe your speech quickly and accurately into correctly spelled and punctuated text. Using your iPhone, you can dictate into any app that supports the keyboard, so you can dictate e-mail messages, notes, documents, and more. To dictate, simply tap the microphone icon (🎤), speak after Siri beeps, and then tap **Done**.

To get the most out of dictation, it is helpful to know the standard terms for dictating punctuation, capitalization, symbols, layout, and formatting.

## Insert Punctuation

To insert punctuation, use standard terms: "comma," "period" (or "full stop"), "semicolon," "colon," "exclamation point" (or "exclamation mark"), "question mark," "hyphen," "dash" (for a short dash, –), or "em dash" (for a long dash, —).

You can also say "asterisk" (*), "ampersand" (&), "open parenthesis" and "close parenthesis," "open bracket" and "close bracket," and "underscore" (_).

## Insert Standard Symbols

To insert symbols, use these terms: "at sign" (@), "percent sign" (%), "greater-than sign" (>) and "less-than sign" (<), "forward slash" (/) and "backslash" (\), "registered sign" (®), and "copyright sign" (©).

## Insert Currency Symbols

To insert currency symbols, say the currency name and "sign." For example, say "dollar sign" to insert $, "cent sign" to insert ¢, "euro sign" to insert €, "pound sterling sign" to insert £, and "yen sign" to insert ¥.

## Control Layout

You can control layout by creating new lines and new paragraphs as needed. A new paragraph enters two line breaks, creating a blank line between paragraphs.

To create a new line, say "new line." To create a new paragraph, say "new paragraph."

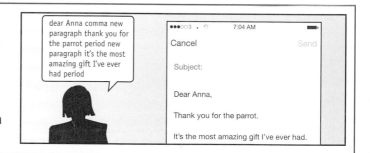

## Control Capitalization

You can apply capitalization to the first letter of a word or to a whole word. You can also switch capitalization off temporarily to force lowercase:

- Say "cap" to capitalize the first letter of the next word.

- Say "caps on" to capitalize all the words until you say "caps off."

- Say "no caps" to prevent automatic capitalization of the next word — for example, "no caps Monday" produces "monday" instead of "Monday."

- Say "no caps on" to force lowercase of all words until you say "no caps off."

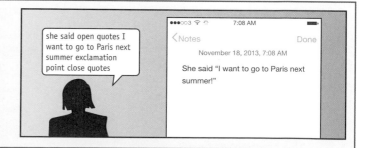

## Insert Quotes and Emoticons

To insert double quotes, say "open quotes" and "close quotes." To insert single quotes, say "open single quotes" and "close single quotes."

To enter standard emoticons, say "smiley face," "frown face," and "wink face."

# Gather and Share Information with Siri

You can use Siri to research a wide variety of information online — everything from sports and movies to restaurants worth visiting or worth avoiding. You can also use Siri to perform hands-free calculations.

When you need to share information quickly and easily, you can turn to Siri. By giving the right commands, you can quickly change your Facebook status or post on your wall. Similarly, you can send tweets on your Twitter account.

## Find Information about Sports

Launch Siri and ask a question about sports. For example:

- "Siri, when's the next White Sox game?"
- "Did the Lakers win their last game?"
- "When's the end of the NBA season?"
- "Can you show me the roster for the Maple Leafs?"

## Find Information about Movies

Launch Siri and ask a question about movies. For example:

- "Siri, where is the movie *Battle of the Year* playing in Indianapolis?"
- "What's the name of Blake Lively's latest movie?"
- "Who's the star of *The Bling Ring*?"
- "Is *World War Z* any good?"

## Find a Restaurant

Launch Siri, and then tell Siri what type of restaurant you want. For example:

- "Where's the best Mexican food in Coeur d'Alene?"
- "Where can I get sushi in Albuquerque?"
- "Is there a brew-pub in Minneapolis?"
- "Is there any dim sum within 50 miles of here?"

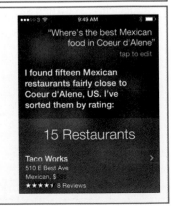

## Address a Query to the Wolfram Alpha Computational Knowledge Engine

Launch Siri, and then say "Wolfram" and your query. For example:

- "Wolfram, what is the cube of 27?"

- "Wolfram, minus 20 Centigrade in Kelvin."

- "Wolfram, tangent of 60°."

- "Wolfram, give me the chemical formula of formaldehyde."

## Update Your Facebook Status or Post a Comment on Your Wall

Launch Siri and give the appropriate command:

- "Update my Facebook status," and then give details when Siri prompts you.

- "Post on my Facebook wall," and then dictate the post when Siri prompts you.

If the post turns out to your liking, tap **Post**.

## Send a Tweet

Launch Siri, and then say "Tweet" and the text of the tweet.

Tap **Add Location** if you want to add your current location to the tweet.

When you are satisfied with the tweet, tap **Send**.

# Configure Siri to Work Your Way

To get the most out of Siri, spend a few minutes configuring Siri. You can set the language Siri uses and choose when Siri should give you voice feedback. You can also decide whether to use the Raise to Speak option, which activates Siri when you raise your iPhone to your face.

Most importantly, you can tell Siri which contact record contains your information, so that Siri knows your name, address, phone numbers, e-mail address, and other essential information.

## Configure Siri to Work Your Way

**1** Press the Home button.

The Home screen appears.

**2** Tap **Settings**.

The Settings screen appears.

**3** Tap **General**.

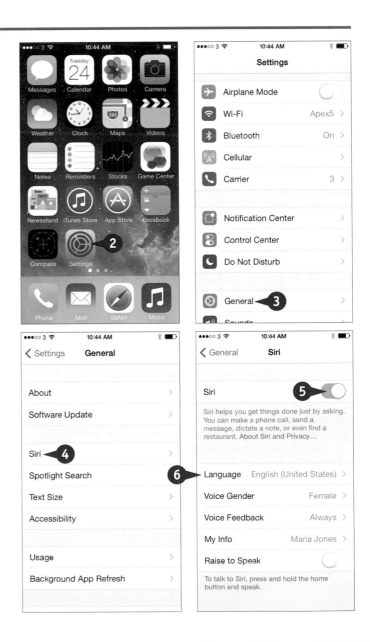

The General screen appears.

**4** Tap **Siri**.

The Siri screen appears.

**5** Make sure the **Siri** switch is in the On position ( ⬤ ) if you want to use Siri.

**Note:** When Siri is off, you can use the Voice Control feature to take actions such as dialing numbers and controlling music playback.

**6** Tap **Language**.

The Language screen appears.

**7** Tap the language you want to use, placing a check mark next to it.

**8** Tap **Siri**.

The Siri screen appears.

**9** Tap **Voice Gender** to display the Voice Gender screen, tap **Male** or **Female**, and then tap **Siri** to return to the Siri screen.

**10** Tap **Voice Feedback**.

The Voice Feedback screen appears.

**11** Tap **Handsfree Only** or **Always**, as needed, to choose when to receive voice feedback.

**12** Tap **Siri**.

The Siri screen appears.

**13** Tap **My Info**.

The Contacts list appears.

**14** Tap the contact record that contains your information.

**15** On the Siri screen, make sure the **Raise to Speak** switch is set to On ( ) if you want Siri to become active when you raise your iPhone to your face.

## TIP

**Does Apple store the details of what I ask Siri?**

Yes, but not in a way that will come back to haunt you. When you use Siri, your iPhone passes your input to servers in Apple's data center in North Carolina, U.S.A, for processing. The servers analyze your request and tell Siri how to respond to it. Apple's data center stores the details of your request and may analyze them to determine what people use Siri for and work out ways of making Siri more effective. Apple does not associate your Siri data with other data Apple holds about you — for example, the identity and credit card data you used to pay for iTunes Match.

# Use VoiceOver to Identify Items On-Screen

If you have trouble identifying the iPhone's controls on-screen, you can use the VoiceOver feature to read them to you. VoiceOver changes your iPhone's standard finger gestures so that you tap to select the item whose name you want it to speak, double-tap to activate an item, and flick three fingers to scroll.

VoiceOver can make your iPhone easier to use. Your iPhone also includes other accessibility features, which you can learn about in the next task, "Use Other Accessibility Features."

## Use VoiceOver to Identify Items On-Screen

**1** Press the Home button.

The Home screen appears.

**2** Tap **Settings**.

The Settings screen appears.

**3** Tap **General**.

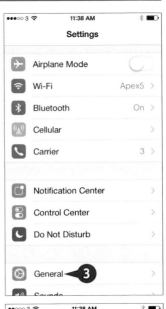

The General screen appears.

**4** Tap **Accessibility**.

The Accessibility screen appears.

**5** Tap **VoiceOver**.

**Note:** You cannot use VoiceOver and Zoom at the same time. If Zoom is on when you try to switch VoiceOver on, your iPhone prompts you to choose which of the two to use.

**6** Tap the **VoiceOver** switch and move it to On ( ⬤ changes to ⬤ ).

**7** Tap **VoiceOver Practice**.

A selection border appears around the button, and VoiceOver speaks its name.

**8** Double-tap **VoiceOver Practice**.

**9** Practice tapping, double-tapping, triple-tapping, and swiping. VoiceOver identifies each gesture and displays an explanation.

**10** Tap **Done** to select the button, and then double-tap **Done**.

**11** Swipe up with three fingers.

The screen scrolls down.

**12** Tap **Speaking Rate** to select it, and then swipe up or down to adjust the rate.

**13** Move the **Speak Hints** switch to On ( ⬤ changes to ⬤ ) if you want VoiceOver to speak hints about using VoiceOver.

**14** Farther down the screen, tap **Typing Feedback** to select it, and then double-tap.

**15** Tap the feedback type you want: **Nothing**, **Characters**, **Words**, or **Characters and Words**.

**TIP**

**Is there an easy way to turn VoiceOver on and off?**
Yes. You can set your iPhone to toggle VoiceOver on or off when you press the Home button three times in rapid sequence. From the Accessibility screen, tap **Accessibility Shortcut** to display the Accessibility Shortcut screen. Tap **VoiceOver** (Ⓐ), placing a check mark next to it, and then tap **Accessibility**.

# Use Other Accessibility Features

If you have trouble using your iPhone in its default configuration, you may do well to explore the other accessibility features that your iPhone offers apart from VoiceOver. These include zooming in the screen, displaying text at a larger size, changing the screen to reverse video, playing audio in mono, and speaking automatic corrections made while you type.

## Use Other Accessibility Features

**1** Press the Home button.

The Home screen appears.

**2** Tap **Settings**.

The Settings screen appears.

**3** Tap **General**.

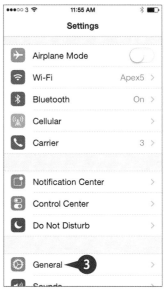

The General screen appears.

**Note:** Apart from the accessibility features explained in this task, your iPhone supports physical accessibility features such as Switch Control and AssistiveTouch. Switch Control enables you to control your iPhone through a physical switch you connect to it. AssistiveTouch lets you use an adaptive accessory to touch the screen.

**4** Tap **Accessibility**.

The Accessibility screen appears.

**5** Tap **Zoom**.

The Zoom screen appears.

**6** Tap the **Zoom** switch and move it to On ( ⬜ changes to 🔵 ).

**7** Double-tap the screen with three fingers to zoom in.

**8** Double-tap again with three fingers to zoom out.

**9** Tap **Accessibility**.

The Accessibility screen appears.

**10** Tap **Larger Type**.

The Larger Type screen appears.

**11** Tap the **Larger Dynamic Type** switch and move it to On ( ⬜ changes to 🔵 ).

**12** Tap the text size you want.

**13** Tap **Accessibility**.

The Accessibility screen appears.

**14** Tap the **Invert Colors** switch and move it to On ( ⬜ changes to 🔵 ).

The screen changes to reverse video.

**15** Tap the **Speak Auto-text** switch and move it to On ( ⬜ changes to 🔵 ) if you want your iPhone to speak text corrections.

**16** Tap **General**.

---

## TIP

**Is there an easy way to turn the Zoom feature on and off?**

Yes. You can set your iPhone to toggle Zoom on or off when you press the Home button three times in rapid sequence. From the Accessibility screen, tap **Accessibility Shortcut** to display the Accessibility Shortcut screen. Tap **Zoom** (Ⓐ), placing a check mark next to it, and then tap **Accessibility**. You can also use the Home triple-press to toggle the Invert Colors feature, the Switch Control feature, or the AssistiveTouch feature.

# Use Your iPhone in Your Car

If you take your iPhone everywhere with you, you will most likely want to use it in your car. You can choose from a wide range of technology for using your iPhone in your car. Your choices range from simply playing music through your existing stereo via a cable or radio transmitter, to connecting the iPhone to a car unit that supports an iPhone-compatibility standard, such as iOS in the Car.

With an iOS in the Car–compatible system, you can display your iPhone's content on your in-car device, enabling you to play music, make phone calls, view maps, hear and dictate messages, and take other actions.

## Connect Your iPhone to Your Car Stereo via a Cable

If your car does not have an iOS in the Car–compatible system, and you are not able to add such a system, you can connect your iPhone to your car stereo via a cable so that you can play music from your iPhone through the car stereo. You can connect your iPhone's headphone socket to a standard line-in socket on the stereo using a cable with 3.5mm connectors, which allows you to control the volume from the iPhone. Alternatively, you can use a Lightning-to–30-pin connector to get line-out audio from the iPhone, and then connect the 30-pin connector to the audio input.

You control the music from the iPhone, so it is helpful to have a mount or holder with which to secure the iPhone.

## Connect Your iPhone to Your Car Stereo via a Radio Transmitter

If your car has neither an iOS in the Car–compatible system nor an audio input jack, you can play music from your iPhone through your car stereo by using a wireless transmitter. You connect the wireless transmitter to the iPhone, usually via the Lightning socket, and tune the radio on your car stereo to the frequency on which the transmitter is broadcasting. Provided you pick a frequency with no nearby radio stations, you can get good reception and decent music quality.

With this arrangement, you control the music from the iPhone, so it is helpful to have a mount or holder to secure the iPhone. Some transmitters include stands for mounting the iPhone and electrical connections for charging the iPhone from your car's accessory socket.

## Connect Your iPhone to Your Car's iOS in the Car Unit

If your vehicle has an iOS in the Car–compatible unit, you can connect your iPhone to it by inserting the iPhone in its dock. When you insert the iPhone, the iOS in the Car unit automatically detects the device and establishes communication with it. You can then use iPhone functions such as playing music, displaying maps, making hands-free phone calls, or having your messages read to you.

## Play Music through Your Car's Stereo

After connecting your iPhone to your iOS in the Car unit, you can play music from the iPhone through your car's stereo. The iOS in the Car unit mirrors the iPhone's screen, so you can easily see the music you are playing. You can control playback by using the controls built into the unit or built into your car — for example, using controls built into the steering wheel.

## Display Maps on Your Car's Display

After connecting your iPhone to your iOS in the Car unit, you can use your iPhone's Maps app to navigate. For example, you can ask Siri for directions from one place to another, and then get turn-by-turn guidance for the journey.

# CHAPTER 4

# Setting Up Communications

In this chapter, you learn how to add your e-mail accounts to the Mail app and control how Mail displays your messages. This chapter also shows you how to control the way the iPhone displays your contacts, import contacts from a SIM card, and choose options for your calendars and notes.

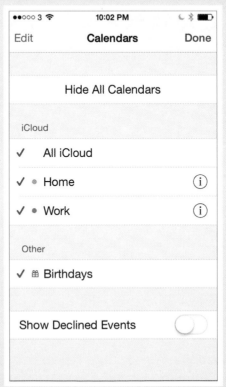

# Set Up Your Mail Accounts

The easiest way to set up an e-mail account on your iPhone is to synchronize the details from your PC or Mac, as discussed in Chapter 1. But if the e-mail account is not set up on the computer with which you synchronize the iPhone, you can set up the account directly on the iPhone as explained in this task.

To set up an e-mail account, you need to know the e-mail address and password, as well as the e-mail provider. You may also need to know the addresses of the mail servers the account uses. For Microsoft Exchange, you must know the domain name as well.

## Set Up Your Mail Accounts

**1** Press the Home button.

The Home screen appears.

**2** Tap **Settings**.

The Settings screen appears.

**Note:** If you have not yet set up an e-mail account on the iPhone, you can also open the Add Account screen by tapping **Mail** on the iPhone's Home screen.

**3** Tap and drag up to scroll down until the fourth group of buttons appears.

**4** Tap **Mail, Contacts, Calendars**.

The Mail, Contacts, Calendars screen appears.

**5** Tap **Add Account**.

**Note:** This example uses a Gmail account. Setting up a Yahoo! account or an AOL account uses the same fields of information. For an iCloud account, you enter only the e-mail address and password. See the tip for instructions on changing the name of the iCloud account after you set it up.

The Add Account screen opens.

**6** Tap the kind of account you want to set up.

The screen for setting up that type of account appears.

**7** Tap **Name** and type your name as you want it to appear in messages you send.

**8** Tap **Email** and type the e-mail address.

**9** Tap **Password** and type the password.

**10** Tap **Description** and type a descriptive name.

**11** Tap **Next**.

The configuration screen for the account appears.

**12** Make sure the **Mail** switch is set to On (⬤ ).

**13** Set the **Contacts** switch, **Calendars** switch, **Notes** switch, and any other switches to On (⬤ ) or Off (⬤ ), as needed.

**14** Tap **Save**.

**A** The account appears on the Mail, Contacts, Calendars screen.

## TIP

**How do I change the name for an iCloud account?**

When you set up an iCloud account, the iCloud screen prompts you for only your Apple ID (which is your e-mail address) and password. The account appears with that e-mail address in the Accounts list on the Mail, Contacts, Calendars screen. To change the name, press the Home button and then tap **Settings**. Scroll down to display the fourth group of buttons and tap **Mail, Contacts, Calendars**. Tap the iCloud account and then tap **Account**. Tap **Description** and type the name to identify the account. Tap **Done** and then tap **Mail, Contacts, Calendars**.

# Control How the iPhone Displays Your E-Mail

To make your iPhone's Mail app easy to use, you can choose settings that suit the way you work. You can choose how many lines to include in the message preview, decide whether to display the To and Cc label, and control whether Mail prompts you before deleting a message. To make messages easy to read, you can change the minimum font size. You can also choose whether to load remote images in messages and whether to increase the indentation on messages you reply to or forward.

## Control How the iPhone Displays Your E-Mail

**1** Press the Home button.

The Home screen appears.

**2** Tap **Settings**.

The Settings screen appears.

**3** Tap and drag up to scroll down until the fourth group of buttons appears.

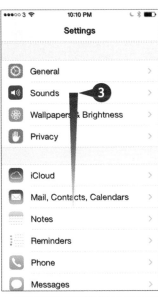

**4** Tap **Mail, Contacts, Calendars**.

The Mail, Contacts, Calendars screen appears.

**5** If necessary, tap and drag up to scroll down the screen.

The Mail options appear.

**6** Tap **Preview**.

The Preview screen appears.

**7** Tap the number of lines you want to see in previews.

**8** Tap **Mail, Contacts, Calendars**.

**9** Set the **Show To/Cc Label** switch to On ( ) or Off ( ).

**10** Tap **Flag Style** and then tap **Color** or **Shape** to control how message flags appear.

**11** Set the **Ask Before Deleting** switch to On ( ) or Off ( ).

**12** Set the **Load Remote Images** switch to On ( ) or Off ( ).

**13** Tap **Increase Quote Level**.

The Increase Quote Level screen appears.

**14** Set the **Increase Quote Level** switch to On ( ) or Off ( ).

**15** Tap **Mail, Contacts, Calendars**.

**16** Tap **Settings**.

The Settings screen appears.

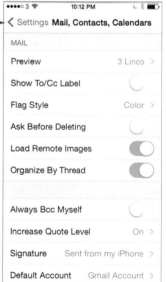

## TIPS

**Why turn off Load Remote Images?**

Loading a remote image lets the sender know that you have opened the message. When Mail requests the remote image, the server that provides the image can log the date and time and your Internet connection's IP address, which reveals your approximate location.

**What is Always Bcc Myself useful for?**

Most e-mail services automatically put a copy of each message you send or forward into a folder with a name such as Sent. If your e-mail service does not use a Sent folder, set the **Always Bcc Myself** switch to On ( ) to send a bcc copy of each message to yourself. You can then file these messages in a folder to keep a record of your sent messages.

# Organize Your E-Mail Messages by Thread

The Mail app gives you two ways to view e-mail messages. You can view the messages as a simple list, or you can view them with related messages organized into *threads*, which are sometimes called *conversations*.

Having Mail display your messages as threads can help you navigate your Inbox quickly and find related messages easily. You may find threading useful if you tend to have long e-mail conversations, because threading reduces the number of messages you see at once.

## Organize Your E-Mail Messages by Thread

### Set Mail to Organize Your Messages by Thread

1 Press the Home button.

The Home screen appears.

2 Tap **Settings**.

The Settings screen appears.

3 Tap and drag up to scroll down until the fourth group of buttons appears.

4 Tap **Mail, Contacts, Calendars**.

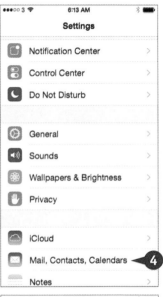

The Mail, Contacts, Calendars screen appears.

5 Tap and drag up to scroll down the screen.

The Mail options appear.

6 Set the **Organize By Thread** switch to On (  ).

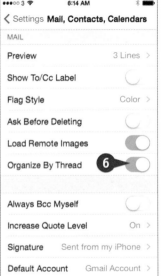

## Read Messages Organized into Threads

**1** Press the Home button.

The Home screen appears.

**2** Tap **Mail**.

The Mailboxes screen appears.

**3** Tap the mailbox you want to open.

The Inbox for the account appears.

**A** Two chevrons on the right indicate a threaded message.

**4** Tap the threaded message.

A screen showing the threaded message appears.

**5** Tap the message you want to display.

**Is there a quick way to enter my name and information at the end of a message?**

Yes. You can create one or more e-mail signatures, which are sections of predefined text that Mail can insert at the end of messages. From the Home screen, tap **Settings**, and then tap **Mail, Contacts, Calendars**. Scroll down and tap **Signature** to display the Signature screen. Tap **All Accounts** to use the same signature for each account, or tap **Per Account** to use a different signature for each account. Then type the text to use.

# Set Your Default E-Mail Account

If you set up two or more e-mail accounts on your iPhone, make sure that you set the right e-mail account to be the default account. The default account is the one from which the Mail app sends messages unless you choose another account, so choosing the appropriate account is important.

You can quickly set your default e-mail account on the Mail, Contacts, Calendars screen in the Settings app.

## Set Your Default E-Mail Account

**1** Press the Home button.

The Home screen appears.

**2** Tap **Settings**.

The Settings screen appears.

**3** Tap and drag up to scroll down until the fourth group of buttons appears.

**4** Tap **Mail, Contacts, Calendars**.

The Mail, Contacts, Calendars screen appears.

**5** Tap and drag up to scroll down until the fourth group of buttons appears.

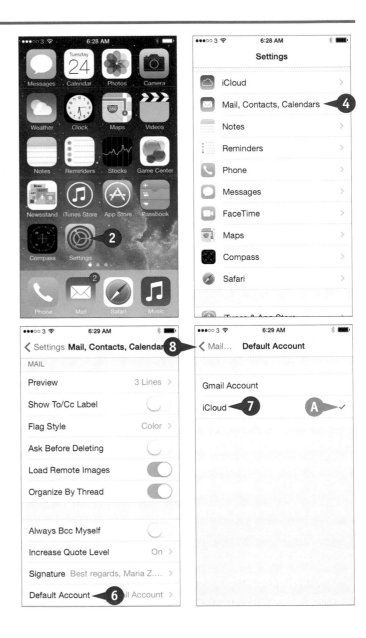

**6** Tap **Default Account**.

The Default Account screen appears.

**7** Tap the account you want to make the default.

**A** A check mark appears next to the account you tapped.

**8** Tap **Mail, Contacts, Calendars**.

**Note:** To change the e-mail account for a new message, tap and hold the **From** button, and then tap the address on the list that appears.

# Choose How Your iPhone Displays Your Contacts

To swiftly and easily find the contacts you need, you can set your iPhone to sort and display the contacts in your preferred order.

Your iPhone can sort contacts either by first name or by last name. Whichever way you sort the contacts, your iPhone can display them in alphabetical order either by first name or by last name. By entering data only in the Company field for a business, you can make business names sort correctly whether you sort people's names by first name or last name.

## Choose How Your iPhone Displays Your Contacts

**1** Press the Home button.

**2** On the Home screen, tap **Settings**.

**3** On the Settings screen, tap and drag up until the fourth group of buttons appears.

**4** Tap **Mail, Contacts, Calendars**.

**5** On the Mail, Contacts, Calendars screen, tap and drag up to display the Contacts area.

**6** Tap **Sort Order**.

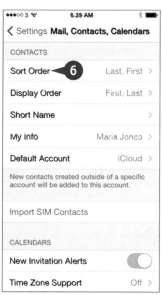

**7** On the Sort Order screen, tap **First, Last** or **Last, First**.

**8** Tap **Mail, Contacts, Calendars**.

**9** On the Mail, Contacts, Calendars screen, tap **Display Order**.

**10** On the Display Order screen, tap **First, Last** or **Last, First**.

**11** Tap **Mail, Contacts, Calendars**.

**12** On the Mail, Contacts, Calendars screen, tap **Short Name**.

**13** On the Short Name screen, set the **Short Name** switch to On (⬤).

**14** Tap the format to use. For example, tap **First Name Only**.

**15** Set the **Prefer Nicknames** switch to On (⬤) to display nicknames for contacts who have them.

# Import Contacts from a SIM Card

If you have stored contacts on a SIM card, you can import them into your iPhone. For example, you may have contacts stored on a SIM card from your previous cell phone. If the SIM card is the same size as the iPhone's SIM card, you can insert the SIM card in the iPhone temporarily and import the contacts. Another approach is to insert the iPhone's SIM card in an unlocked cell phone, copy the contacts to the SIM card, and then put the SIM card back in the iPhone.

## Import Contacts from a SIM Card

**1** Press the Home button.

The Home screen appears.

**2** Tap **Settings**.

The Settings screen appears.

**3** Tap and drag up to scroll down until the fourth group of buttons appears.

**4** Tap **Mail, Contacts, Calendars**.

The Mail, Contacts, Calendars screen appears.

**5** Tap and drag up to scroll down all the way to the bottom of the screen.

The bottom part of the Mail, Contacts, Calendars screen appears.

**6** Tap **Import SIM Contacts**.

**7** If the Import SIM Contacts to Account dialog appears, tap the account to use.

Your iPhone imports the contacts from the SIM.

**8** Tap **Settings**.

# Choose Alert Options for Calendar Events

B y synchronizing your calendars from your PC or Mac with your iPhone, you can keep details of your events in the palm of your hand.

To keep yourself on schedule, you can set the iPhone to alert you to new invitations you receive. You can also set default alert times to give you the warning you need before a regular event, an all-day event, or a birthday.

## Choose Alert Options for Calendar Events

**1** Press the Home button.

**2** On the Home screen, tap **Settings**.

The Settings screen appears.

**3** Tap **Mail, Contacts, Calendars**.

The Mail, Contacts, Calendars screen appears.

**4** Tap and drag up to the bottom of the screen.

**5** Set the **New Invitation Alerts** switch to On ( ) or Off ( ).

**6** Set the **Shared Calendar Alerts** switch to On ( ) or Off ( ).

**7** Tap **Default Alert Times**.

The Default Alert Times screen appears.

**8** Tap the event type to set the default alert time for. For example, tap **Events**.

The Events screen, Birthdays screen, or All-Day Events screen appears.

**9** Tap the amount of time for the warning.

**10** Tap **Back**.

**11** On the Default Alert Times screen, set default alert times for other event types by repeating steps **8** to **10**.

**12** Tap **Mail, Contacts, Calendars**.

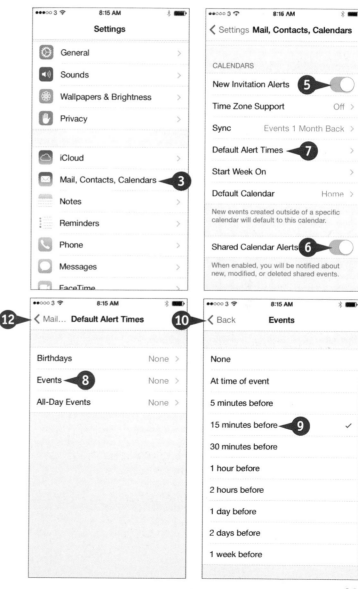

# Choose Your Default Calendar and Time Zone

When you use multiple calendars on your iPhone, you should set your default calendar. This is the calendar that receives events you create outside any specific calendar. For example, if you have a Work calendar and a Home calendar, you can set the Home calendar as the default calendar.

If you travel to different time zones, you may need to specify which time zone to show event dates and times in. Otherwise, Calendar uses the time zone for your current location.

## Choose Your Default Calendar and Time Zone

**1** Press the Home button.

The Home screen appears.

**2** Tap **Settings**.

The Settings screen appears.

**3** Tap and drag up to scroll down until the fourth group of buttons appears.

**4** Tap **Mail, Contacts, Calendars**.

The Mail, Contacts, Calendars screen appears.

**5** Tap and drag up to scroll down all the way to the bottom of the screen.

The bottom part of the Mail, Contacts, Calendars screen appears.

**6** Tap **Time Zone Support**.

The Time Zone Support screen appears.

**7** Set the **Time Zone Support** switch to On ( ⬤ ).

**8** Tap **Time Zone**.

The Time Zone screen appears.

**9** Type the first letters of a city in the time zone.

**10** Tap the search result you want.

The Time Zone Support screen appears.

**11** Tap **Mail, Contacts, Calendars**.

The Mail, Contacts, Calendars screen appears.

**12** Tap **Default Calendar**.

The Default Calendar screen appears.

**13** Tap the calendar you want to make the default.

**A** A check mark appears next to the calendar.

**14** Tap **Mail, Contacts, Calendars**.

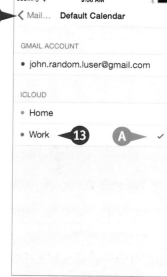

## TIP

**How do I choose which calendars to display in the Calendar app?**

You choose the calendars in the Calendar app, not in the Settings app. Press the Home button to display the Home screen, tap **Calendar**, and then tap **Calendars**. On the Calendars screen, tap to place a check mark on each calendar you want shown. Tap to remove a check mark from a calendar you want to hide. Tap **Done** when you are finished.

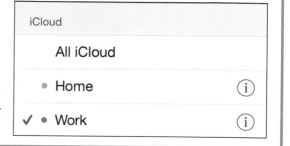

# Set Your Default Account for Notes

As described earlier in this chapter, you can set up multiple e-mail accounts on your iPhone. Each e-mail account can synchronize notes if the server offers this feature.

When you have set up multiple e-mail accounts with notes, you should set the default account for notes. The default account is the account in which your iPhone stores new notes unless you specify storing them elsewhere.

## Set Your Default Account for Notes

**1** Press the Home button.

The Home screen appears.

**2** Tap **Settings**.

The Settings screen appears.

**3** Tap and drag up to scroll down until the fourth group of buttons appears.

**4** Tap **Notes**.

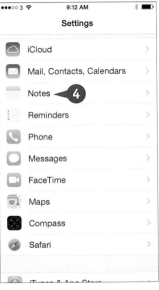

The Notes screen appears.

**5** Tap **Default Account**.

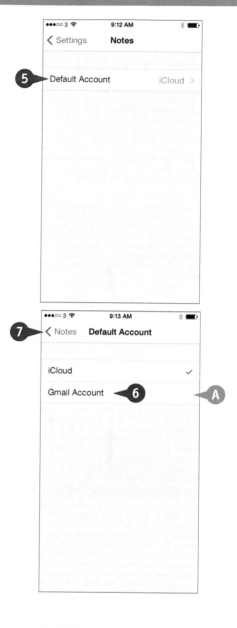

The Default Account screen appears.

**6** Tap the account you want to make the default.

Ⓐ A check mark appears next to the account you tapped.

**7** Tap **Notes**.

The Notes screen appears.

**Why does the Default Account setting not appear on the Notes screen on my iPhone?**
The Default Account setting appears on the Notes screen in the Settings app when you have set up two or more e-mail accounts to synchronize notes. If you add multiple e-mail accounts to the iPhone, but set up only one account to synchronize notes, the Default Account setting does not appear because the only Notes account is the default account.

# CHAPTER 5

# Using Your iPhone to Make Calls

**You can make calls by holding the iPhone to your face, by using the speakerphone, or by using a headset.**

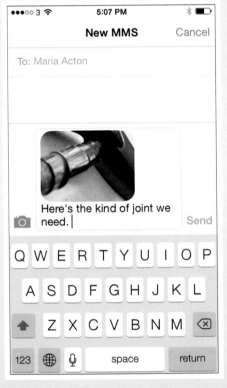

# Make Phone Calls

With your iPhone, you can make phone calls anywhere you have a connection to the cellular network. You can make a phone call by dialing the phone number using the iPhone's keypad, but you can place calls more easily by tapping the appropriate phone number for a contact, using the Recents screen, or using the Favorites list.

When you need other people near you to be able to hear the phone call you are making, you can switch on your iPhone's speaker.

## Make Phone Calls

### Open the Phone App

1 Press the Home button.

The Home screen appears.

2 Tap **Phone**.

The Phone app opens and displays the screen you used last — for example, the Contacts screen.

**Note:** You can also place a call to a phone number that the iPhone has identified — for example, by tapping an underlined phone number on a web page.

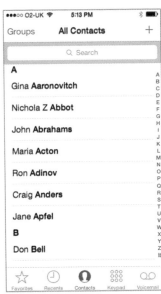

### Dial a Call Using the Keypad

1 Tap **Keypad**.

The Keypad screen appears.

**Note:** On the Keypad screen, you can tap **Call** without dialing a number to display the last number dialed.

2 Tap the number keys to dial the number.

Ⓐ You can tap **Add to Contacts** to add this number to your Contacts list.

3 Tap **Call**.

Your iPhone makes the call.

## Dial a Call to a Contact

**1** Tap **Contacts**.

The Contacts list appears.

**2** Tap the contact you want to call.

The contact's info appears.

**3** Tap the phone number you want to call.

Your iPhone makes the call.

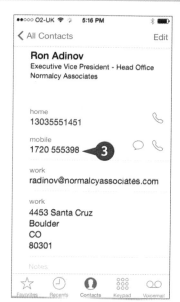

## End a Phone Call

**1** Tap **End**.

Your iPhone ends the call.

The Call Ended screen appears for a moment.

Your iPhone then displays the screen from which you placed the call.

TIP

### Can I use the iPhone as a speaker phone?

Yes. Tap **Speaker** on the screen that appears while you are making a phone call. The iPhone starts playing the phone call through the speaker on the bottom instead of the small speaker at the top.

Tap **Speaker** again when you want to switch off the speaker.

# Use the Headset to Make and Take Calls

Your iPhone includes a headset that you can use not only for listening to music but also for making and taking phone calls. The control box on the headset's wire includes a microphone, a clicker switch for answering and hanging up phone calls, and Volume Up and Volume Down buttons.

Using the headset is convenient not only when you are out and about but also when you are listening to music. Your iPhone automatically pauses the music when you receive a phone call.

## Use the Headset to Make and Take Calls

### Make a Call Using the Headset

**1** Connect the headset to your iPhone if it is not already connected.

**Note:** You can dial a call by activating Siri and speaking the number or the contact's name. See Chapter 3 for instructions on using Siri.

**2** Press the Home button.

The Home screen appears.

**3** Tap **Phone**.

The Phone app opens.

**4** Dial the call as usual using one of the techniques described in this chapter. For example, tap **Contacts**, tap the contact, and then tap the phone number.

**5** If you need to change the volume, press the Volume Up button or the Volume Down button on the headset control box.

**6** Press the clicker button on the headset when you are ready to end the call.

102

## Take a Call Using the Headset

① Connect the headset to your iPhone if it is not already connected.

When you receive an incoming call, the phone ring plays in the headset and the screen comes on if it is off.

The screen shows the caller's name and phone details — for example, Mobile or the phone number.

**Note:** If you are listening to music when you receive a call, your iPhone automatically fades and pauses the music. The same goes for video.

② Press the clicker button on the headset to take the call.

Ⓐ The screen shows the caller's name and the call's duration.

③ If you need to change the volume, press the Volume Up button or the Volume Down button on the headset control box.

④ Press the clicker button on the headset when you are ready to end the call.

The Call Ended screen appears briefly.

The previous screen then reappears.

**TIP**

**How do I access the phone controls during a call I accepted with the headset?**

To access the phone controls while the iPhone is locked, tap and drag the **slide to unlock** prompt to the right. The Home screen appears with a green bar at the top. Tap this bar (Ⓐ) to display the call screen.

# Use a Wireless Headset or Car Kit

Instead of using the headset that came with your iPhone, you can use a Bluetooth headset. Similarly, you can use a car kit with a Bluetooth connection when using your iPhone in your vehicle.

You must first pair the Bluetooth headset or car kit with your iPhone, as discussed in Chapter 6.

## Use a Wireless Headset or Car Kit

**1** Turn on the wireless headset or connection, and make sure it works.

**2** Press the Home button.

The Home screen appears.

**3** Tap **Phone**.

The Phone app opens.

**4** Dial the call as usual using one of the techniques described in this chapter. For example, tap **Contacts**, tap the contact, and then tap the phone number.

**Note:** You can also tell Siri to place the call for you.

Your iPhone starts to place the call.

A screen for choosing the audio device appears.

**5** Tap the headset or other device you want to use.

The call begins.

**Note:** If you are playing audio or video on a Bluetooth headset when you receive a call, your iPhone automatically pauses the audio or video and plays the ringtone on the headset.

# Mute a Call or Put a Call on Hold

When you are on a call, you may need to mute your iPhone's microphone so that you can confer with people near you without the person at the other end of the phone call hearing.

You may also need to put a call on hold so that you can make another call or take a break from the call.

## Mute a Call or Put a Call on Hold

**1** Establish the phone call as usual. For example, call a contact.

**2** Tap **mute**.

The text of the Mute button changes to gray on a white background, and the iPhone mutes the call.

**3** When you are ready to unmute the call, tap **mute** again.

**4** To put the call on hold, tap and hold **mute** for several seconds.

The Hold button appears in place of the Mute button, and turns blue.

**5** When you are ready to take the call off hold, tap **hold**.

**Note:** After placing a call on hold, you can make another call if necessary.

# Make a Conference Call

As well as making phone calls to one other phone at a time, your iPhone can make conference calls to multiple phones. To make a conference call, you call the first participant, and then add each other participant in turn.

During a conference call, you can talk in private to individual participants. You can also drop a participant from the call.

## Make a Conference Call

**1** Press the Home button.

The Home screen appears.

**2** Tap **Phone**.

The Phone app opens.

**3** Tap **Contacts**.

The Contacts screen appears.

**4** Tap the contact you want to call first.

The contact's record appears.

**5** Tap the phone number to use.

**Note:** You can also add a contact to the call by using Favorites, Recents, or Keypad.

Your iPhone makes the call.

**6** Tap **add call**.

The Contacts screen appears.

**7** Tap the contact you want to add.

The contact's record appears.

**8** Tap the phone number to use.

**A** The iPhone places the first call on hold and makes the new call.

**9** Tap **merge calls**.

The iPhone merges the calls and displays Conference at the top of the screen. You can now speak to both participants.

**B** You can add further participants by tapping **add call**, specifying the contact or number, and then merging the calls.

**10** To speak privately to a participant, tap ⓘ.

The Conference screen appears, showing a list of the participants.

**11** Tap **Private** next to the participant.

The iPhone places the other callers on hold.

**12** When you are ready to resume the conference call, tap **Back**, and then tap **merge calls**.

The iPhone merges the calls, and all participants can hear each other again.

**13** When you finish the call, tap **End**.

The iPhone ends the call.

**TIP**

**How do I drop a participant from a conference call?**
Tap ⓘ to display the Conference screen, and then tap **End** (Ⓐ) next to the participant you want to drop.

# Save Time with Call Favorites and Recents

You can dial phone numbers easily from your Contacts list, but you can save further time and effort by using the Favorites and Recents features built into the Phone app.

Favorites are phone numbers that you mark as being especially important to you. Recents are phone numbers you have called and received calls from recently.

## Save Time with Call Favorites and Recents

### Add a Contact to Your Favorites List

**1** Press the Home button.

The Home screen appears.

**2** Tap **Phone**.

The Phone app opens.

**3** Tap **Contacts**.

The Contacts list appears.

**4** Tap the contact you want to add.

The contact's record appears.

**5** Tap **Add to Favorites**.

The Add to Favorites dialog opens.

**6** Tap the phone number or e-mail address you want to add to your Favorites list.

The Add to Favorites As dialog opens.

**7** Tap **Voice Call** to create a favorite for voice calls.

**Ⓐ** You can tap **FaceTime** to create a favorite for FaceTime video calling or tap **FaceTime Audio** to create a favorite for audio-only calls with FaceTime.

## Call a Favorite

**1** In the Phone app, tap **Favorites**.

The Favorites list appears.

**2** Tap the Favorite you want to call.

Your iPhone places the call.

**B** To display the contact's record, tap ⓘ instead of tapping the contact's button. You can then tap a different phone number for the contact if necessary.

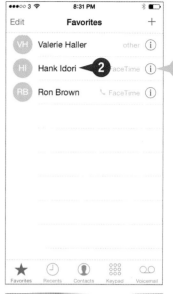

## Call a Recent

**1** In the Phone app, tap **Recents**.

The Recents screen appears. Red entries indicate calls you missed.

**C** Tap **Missed** if you want to see only recent calls you missed.

**2** Tap the recent you want to call.

Your iPhone places the call.

**D** If you want to clear the Recents list, tap **Edit** and **Clear**. In the dialog that opens, tap **Clear All Recents**.

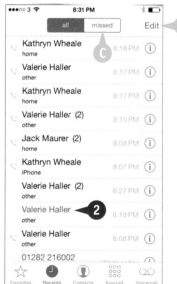

### TIP

**How do I remove a contact from my Favorites?**

Tap **Favorites** to display the Favorites list, and then tap **Edit**. Tap ⊖ next to the contact. You can also rearrange your favorites by tapping ☰ and dragging up or down. Tap **Done** when you have finished changing your favorites.

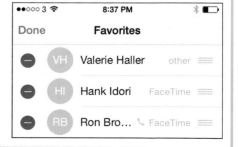

# Set Up and Use Visual Voicemail

Your iPhone includes the Visual Voicemail system, which enables you to see a list of your voice mails and listen to those you want to hear instead of having to listen to them all in sequence.

Before you can use Visual Voicemail, you may need to perform a one-time setup routine that includes setting a passcode. You should also record a custom greeting so that callers are certain they have reached the correct voice mail box. You can re-record the greeting any time you need to change it.

## Set Up and Use Visual Voicemail

### Set Up Visual Voicemail and Record Your Greeting

1 Press the Home button.

The Home screen appears.

2 Tap **Phone**.

The Phone app opens.

3 Tap **Voicemail**.

**Note:** The first time you access Visual Voicemail on a newly activated iPhone, you usually need to perform a setup routine. Tap **Set Up Now** and follow the prompts for assigning a passcode or password.

4 Tap **Greeting**.

The Greeting screen appears.

5 Tap **Custom**.

6 Tap **Record**.

7 Speak your greeting, and then tap **Stop**.

8 Tap **Play**, and verify that your greeting is as you want it.

**Note:** To rerecord your greeting, tap **Record**.

9 Tap **Save**.

Voicemail saves the greeting, and then displays the Voicemail screen.

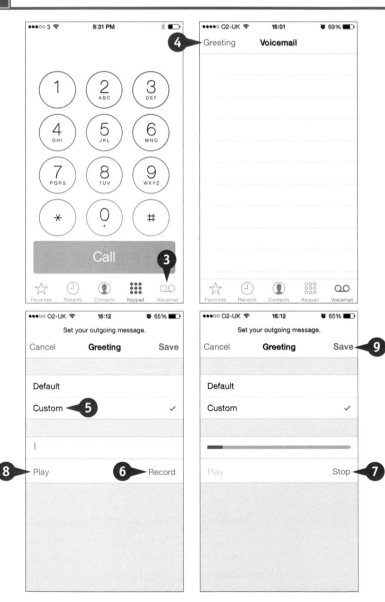

## Use Visual Voicemail

**1** In the Phone app, tap **Voicemail**.

The Voicemail screen appears.

**A** A blue dot indicates a message you have not yet listened to.

**2** Tap a message to display its playback controls.

**3** Tap **Play** (▶) to play the message.

**B** You can tap **Speaker** to play the message through your iPhone's speaker.

**C** You can tap ⓘ to see the contact's details.

**D** You can tap **Call Back** to call the phone that left the message.

**E** You can tap **Delete** to delete the message.

**4** Tap the message again to hide its playback controls.

**5** Tap **Edit** to display the controls for deleting messages.

**6** Tap ⊖.

The rectangular Delete button appears to the right of the message.

**7** Tap **Delete**.

Visual Voicemail deletes the message.

**8** Tap **Done**.

Visual Voicemail displays the list of messages again.

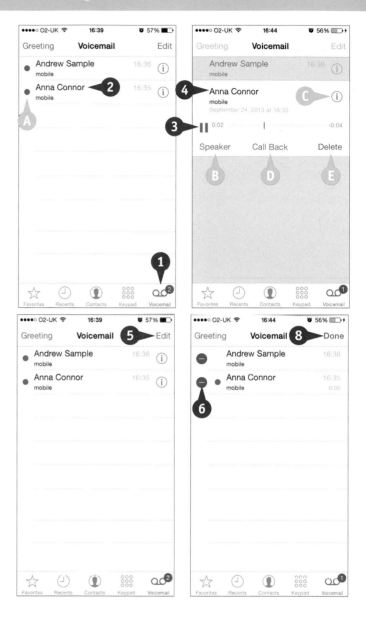

### TIP

**How do I turn on Visual Voicemail instead of regular voice mail?**

If your iPhone does not display the Visual Voicemail screen when you tap the Voicemail button, but instead dials a voice mail service, your carrier does not provide Visual Voicemail. In this case, the only way to turn on Visual Voicemail is to switch to a carrier that does provide Visual Voicemail.

# Send Text and Multimedia Messages

When you need to communicate quickly with another phone user, but do not need to speak to him, you can send an instant message. Your iPhone can send instant messages using the Short Message Service, abbreviated to SMS; the Multimedia Messaging Service, MMS; or Apple's iMessage service.

An SMS message consists of only text, whereas an MMS message can contain text, videos, photos, sounds, or other data. An iMessage can contain text, multimedia content, or both. The Messages app automatically chooses the appropriate type — SMS, MMS, or iMessage — for the messages you create and the ways you send them.

## Send Text and Multimedia Messages

**1** Press the Home button.

The Home screen appears.

**2** Tap **Messages**.

The Messages screen appears.

**3** Tap **New Message** (🖉).

**Note:** Before sending an SMS or MMS message, make sure the recipient's phone number can receive such messages. Typically, you do not receive an alert if the message cannot be delivered.

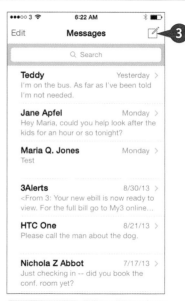

The New Message screen appears.

**4** Tap ⊕.

The Contacts list appears.

**5** Tap the contact to whose phone you want to send the message.

**Note:** If the contact's record contains only one phone number, the iPhone may add the contact's name to the New Message screen without displaying the contact's record.

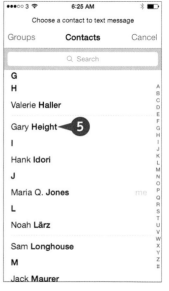

The contact's record opens.

**6** Tap the phone number to use.

The contact's name appears in the To field of the New Message screen.

**7** Tap in the text field, and then type your message.

**8** To add a photo, tap 📷.

**9** In the dialog that opens, tap **Choose Existing**. In this dialog, you can tap **Take Photo or Video** to take a photo or video with the camera (see Chapter 13), and then send it with the message.

The Photos screen appears.

**10** Navigate to the photo you want to use.

**11** Tap the photo.

The photo opens.

**12** Tap **Choose**.

The photo appears in the message.

**Note:** You can attach another photo or video by repeating steps **8** to **12**.

**13** Tap **Send**.

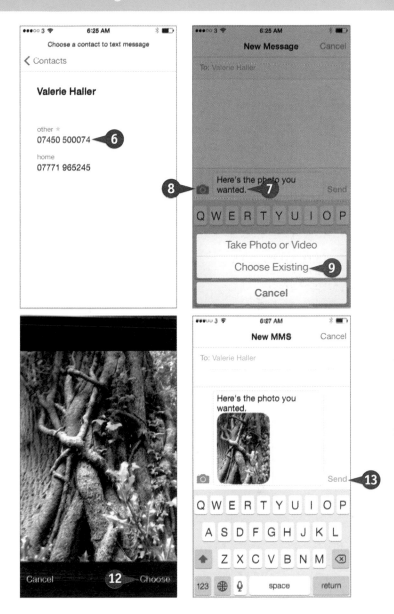

## TIP

**Is there another way to send a photo or video?**

Yes. You can start from the Camera app or the Photos app. This way of sending a photo or video is handy when you are taking photos or videos or when you are browsing your photos or videos. Tap the photo or video you want to share, and then tap **Share** (📤). On the Share screen, tap **Message**. Your iPhone starts an MMS message containing the photo or video. You can then address and send the message.

# Manage Your Instant Messages

Messages is great for communicating quickly and frequently with your nearest, dearest, and your colleagues, so it may not take long before the interface is so full of messages that it becomes hard to navigate.

To keep your messages under control, you can forward messages to others and delete messages you do not need to keep. You can either delete messages from a conversation, leaving the conversation's other messages, or delete the entire conversation.

## Manage Your Instant Messages

### Delete an Entire Conversation

**1** Press the Home button.

The Home screen appears.

**2** Tap **Messages**.

The Messages screen appears.

**3** Tap **Edit**.

The Messages screen switches to Edit mode.

**4** Tap ⊖ for the conversation you want to delete.

**Note:** You can also tap a conversation and swipe left to display the Delete button. This is faster than tapping Edit and then tapping ⊖.

The Delete button appears.

**5** Tap **Delete**.

Messages deletes the conversation.

**6** When you finish deleting conversations, tap **Done**.

Messages turns off Edit mode.

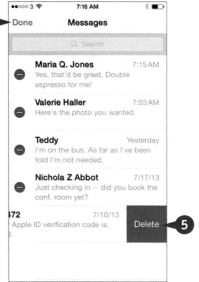

## Forward or Delete One or More Messages from a Conversation

**1** On the Messages screen, tap the conversation that contains the message or messages you will forward.

The conversation appears.

**2** Tap and hold a message.

A pop-up menu appears.

**3** Tap **More**.

A selection button ( ) appears to the left of each message.

**4** Tap ( changes to ) for each message you want to affect.

**5** Tap **Forward** ( ).

Messages starts a new message containing the message or messages you selected.

**Note:** Instead of forwarding the messages, you can tap **Delete** ( ) to delete them from the conversation. Alternatively, tap **Delete All** to delete all the messages.

**6** Address the message.

**7** Type any extra text needed.

**8** Tap **Send** to send the message.

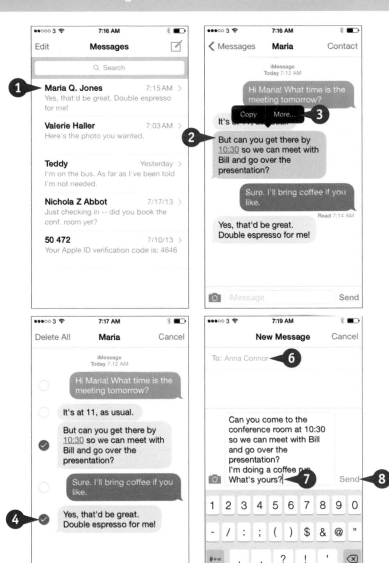

### Can I resend a message?

You can resend a message in either of these ways:

- If a red icon with an exclamation point appears next to the message, the message has not been sent. Tap the icon to try sending the message again.
- If the message has been sent, you can forward it as described in this task. Alternatively, tap and hold the message text, and then tap **Copy** to copy it. Tap and hold in the message text field, and then tap **Paste** to paste the text. Tap **Send** to send the message.

# Chat Face to Face Using FaceTime

By using your iPhone's FaceTime feature, you can enjoy video chats with any of your contacts who have an iPhone 4 or later, an iPad 2 or later, an iPad mini, a fourth-generation or later iPod touch, or the FaceTime for OS X application.

To make a FaceTime call, you and your contact must both have Apple IDs. Your iPhone must be connected to either a wireless network or the cellular network. Using a wireless network is preferable because you typically get better performance and do not use up your cellular data allowance.

## Chat Face to Face Using FaceTime

### Receive a FaceTime Call

1 When your iPhone receives a FaceTime request, and the screen shows who is calling, aim the camera at your face, and then tap **Answer**.

**Note:** If your iPhone is locked, drag the slider to answer.

When the connection is established, your iPhone displays the caller full screen, with your video inset.

2 Tap the screen.

The controls and status bar appear.

3 If you need to mute your microphone, tap **Mute** (🎤).

Ⓐ The background behind the Mute icon turns gray, and the Mute icon appears on your inset video.

4 Tap **Mute** (🎤) when you want to turn muting off again.

5 Tap **End** when you are ready to end the FaceTime call.

## Make a FaceTime Call

**1** Press the Home button.

The Home screen appears.

**2** Tap **Phone**.

The Phone app opens.

**3** Tap **Contacts**.

The Contacts list appears.

**4** Tap the contact you want to call with FaceTime.

The contact's record opens.

**5** Tap **FaceTime**.

The Phone app starts a FaceTime call, showing your video preview.

**6** When your contact answers, smile and speak.

**7** If you need to show your contact something using the rear-facing camera, tap **Switch Cameras** (📷).

Ⓑ Your inset video shows the picture that is being sent to your contact.

**8** When you need to switch back to showing yourself, tap **Switch Cameras** (📷).

**9** When you are ready to end the call, tap **End**.

---

**TIP**

### Are there other ways of starting a FaceTime call?

Yes. You can start a FaceTime call in these ways:

• During a phone call, tap the **FaceTime** icon.

• In the Contacts app, tap the contact to display the contact record, and then tap **FaceTime**.

• Ask Siri to call a contact via FaceTime. For example, press and hold the Home button to summon Siri, and then say "FaceTime John Smith."

# CHAPTER 6

# Networking and Social Networking

**You can control which cellular and wireless networks your iPhone uses and enjoy social networking wherever you go.**

# Turn Cellular and Wi-Fi Access On and Off

Normally, you will want to keep your iPhone connected to the cellular network so that you can make or receive phone calls and access the Internet. But when you do not need or may not use the cellular network, you can turn on the iPhone's Airplane Mode feature to cut off all connections.

Turning on Airplane Mode turns off Wi-Fi connections as well, but you can also turn Wi-Fi on and off separately when you need to.

## Turn Cellular and Wi-Fi Access On and Off

**1** Press the Home button.

The Home screen appears.

**2** Tap **Settings**.

The Settings screen appears.

**3** To turn Airplane Mode on, set the **Airplane Mode** switch to On ( ).

**Note:** When your iPhone has a wireless network connection, it uses that connection instead of the cellular connection. This helps keep down your cellular network usage and often gives a faster connection.

**A** The iPhone turns off all cellular and Wi-Fi connections. An airplane icon appears in the status bar.

**4** To turn on Wi-Fi, tap **Wi-Fi**.

The Wi-Fi screen appears.

**5** Set the **Wi-Fi** switch to On ( ).

The list of available networks appears, and you can connect as described in the task "Connect to Wi-Fi Networks," later in this chapter.

# Monitor Your Cellular Network Usage

Most iPhone contracts include a certain amount of cellular network usage every month. If you use your iPhone extensively, you may need to monitor your usage of the cellular network to avoid incurring extra charges.

## Monitor Your Cellular Network Usage

**1** Press the Home button.

The Home screen appears.

**2** Tap **Settings**.

The Settings screen appears.

**3** Tap **Cellular**.

The Cellular screen appears.

**Ⓐ** The readouts in the Call Time area show the amount of time you have spent making calls in the current billing period and your phone's lifetime.

**Ⓑ** The readouts in the Cellular Data Usage area show your cellular data usage for the current period and how much roaming data you have used.

**Note:** To reset your usage statistics, tap **Reset Statistics** at the bottom of the Cellular screen.

# Control Cellular Data and Background Refresh

To control your iPhone's use of cellular data, you can turn cellular data on and off on the Cellular screen in the Settings app.

Often you will get better results by controlling which apps can use cellular data. You can consult the readouts on the Cellular screen to find out which apps and services use the most data, and then turn off greedy apps. You can also use the Background App Refresh feature to control which apps refresh their content via Wi-Fi or cellular connections when running in the background instead of as the foreground app.

## Control Cellular Data and Background Refresh

**1** Press the Home button.

The Home screen appears.

**2** Tap **Settings**.

The Settings screen appears.

**3** Tap **Cellular**.

The Cellular screen appears.

**4** If you need to turn cellular data off altogether, set the **Cellular Data** switch to Off (  ). Normally, you will want to leave this switch set to On (  ).

**5** In the Use Cellular Data For area of the Cellular screen, set each app's switch to On (  ) or Off (  ), as needed.

**Note:** If you set the **Cellular Data** switch to Off (  ), the app switches are dimmed and unavailable in the Use Cellular Data For area of the Cellular screen.

**6** To see which system services have been using cellular data, tap **System Services**.

The System Services screen appears.

**7** Browse the list to identify any services that hog cellular data.

**8** Tap **Cellular**.

The Cellular screen appears.

**9** Tap **Settings**.

The Settings screen appears.

**10** Tap **General**.

The General screen appears.

**11** Tap **Background App Refresh**.

The Background App Refresh screen appears.

**12** Set the **Background App Refresh** switch to On ( ) or Off ( ), as needed.

**13** Set each individual app switch to On ( ) or Off ( ), as needed.

**14** Tap **General**.

The General screen appears.

**15** Tap **Settings**.

The Settings screen appears.

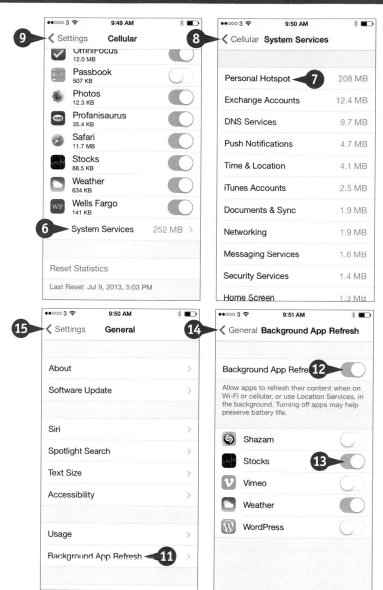

## TIP

**Which apps should I allow to use Background App Refresh?**

Normally, you should restrict Background App Refresh to those apps for which it is important to have updated information immediately available each time you access the app. For example, if you use your iPhone for navigation, getting updated map and GPS information in the background is a good idea, whereas updating magazine subscriptions is usually a waste of cellular data.

# Connect Your iPhone to a Different Carrier

Your iPhone's SIM card makes it connect automatically to a particular carrier's network, such as the AT&T network or the Verizon network. When you go outside your carrier's network, you can connect the iPhone manually to a different carrier's network. For example, if you travel to the United Kingdom, you can connect your iPhone to carriers such as O2, Vodafone, 3, or EE.

To connect to a different carrier's network, you may need to set up an account with that carrier or pay extra charges to your standard carrier.

## Connect Your iPhone to a Different Carrier

1 Press the Home button.

The Home screen appears.

2 Tap **Settings**.

The Settings screen appears.

3 Tap **Carrier**.

The Network Selection screen appears.

4 Set the **Automatic** switch to Off ( ).

The list of available carriers appears.

5 Tap the carrier you want to use.

A A check mark appears next to the carrier.

**Note:** When you want to switch back to your regular carrier, set the **Automatic** switch on the Network Selection screen to On ( ).

# Turn Data Roaming On or Off

When you need to use your iPhone in a location where your carrier does not provide Internet service, you can turn on the iPhone's Data Roaming feature. Data roaming enables you to access the Internet using other carriers' networks. You can incur extra charges when using data roaming, especially when you use it in another country. For this reason, you may prefer to keep data roaming off most of the time and turn it on only when you need it. Normally, you will want to use data roaming only when no wireless network connection is available.

## Turn Data Roaming On or Off

**1** Press the Home button.

The Home screen appears.

**2** Tap **Settings**.

The Settings screen appears.

**3** Tap **Cellular**.

The Cellular screen appears.

**A** You can also turn off cellular data altogether by setting the **Cellular Data** switch to Off (  ). Do this when you need to ensure all apps use Wi-Fi rather than cellular connections.

**4** Set the **Data Roaming** switch to On (  ).

**Note:** When you need to turn data roaming off again, set the **Data Roaming** switch on the Cellular screen to Off (  ).

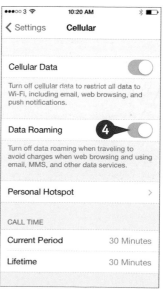

# Connect Bluetooth Devices to Your iPhone

To extend your iPhone's functionality, you can connect devices to it that communicate using the wireless Bluetooth technology.

For example, you can connect a Bluetooth headset and microphone so that you can listen to music and make and take phone calls. Or you can connect a Bluetooth keyboard so that you can quickly type e-mail messages, notes, or documents.

## Connect Bluetooth Devices to Your iPhone

### Set Up a Bluetooth Device

1. Press the Home button.

   The Home screen appears.

2. Tap **Settings**.

   The Settings screen appears.

3. Tap **Bluetooth**.

The Bluetooth screen appears.

4. Set the **Bluetooth** switch to On ( ).

A. The Devices list appears, and the iPhone scans for Bluetooth devices.

5. Turn on the Bluetooth device and make it discoverable.

**Note:** Read the Bluetooth device's instructions to find out how to make the device discoverable via Bluetooth.

**B** The Bluetooth device appears in the Devices list, marked Not Paired.

**6** Tap the device's button.

**Note:** When pairing with a Bluetooth device, you may need to enter a code on either the device or your iPhone.

The iPhone pairs with the device and then connects to it.

**C** The Devices list shows the device as Connected.

## Choose the Device for Playing Audio or Taking a Call

**1** Tap at the bottom of the screen and swipe up. This example uses the Music app.

Control Center opens.

**2** Tap **AirPlay**.

The AirPlay dialog opens.

**3** Tap the device you want to use.

**4** Tap **Done**.

The AirPlay dialog closes.

**5** Tap the app above Control Center.

Control Center closes.

## TIP

**How do I stop using a Bluetooth device?**

When you no longer need to use a particular Bluetooth device, tell your iPhone to forget it. Press the Home button, and then tap **Settings**. Tap **Bluetooth**, and then tap the device's info button ( ⓘ ). On the device's screen, tap **Forget this Device** (**A**), and then tap **Forget Device** in the confirmation dialog.

# Share Items via AirDrop

AirDrop is a technology for sharing files swiftly and easily with iOS devices near your iPhone and Macs running OS X 10.7, Lion, or later versions. AirDrop uses Wi-Fi or Bluetooth to transfer files wirelessly without the iOS devices having to be on the same wireless network. For example, you can use AirDrop to share a photo, a contact record, or an item from Passbook. You can use AirDrop in any app that displays a Share button ($\hat{\sqcup}$).

You can turn AirDrop on when you need it and off when you do not. When AirDrop is on, you can choose between accepting items only from your contacts or from everyone.

## Share Items via AirDrop

### Turn AirDrop On or Off

**1** Swipe up from the bottom of the screen.

Control Center opens.

**A** The readout shows AirDrop's status: *AirDrop*, indicating the feature is off; *AirDrop: Contacts Only*; or *AirDrop, Everyone*.

**2** Tap **AirDrop**.

The AirDrop dialog opens.

**3** Tap **Off**, **Contacts Only**, or **Everyone**, as needed.

The AirDrop dialog closes.

**B** The AirDrop readout shows the AirDrop setting you chose.

**4** Tap the screen above Control Center.

Control Center closes.

## Share an Item via AirDrop

**1** Open the app that contains the item. For example, tap **Photos** on the Home screen.

**2** Navigate to the item you want to share. For example, tap a photo to open it.

**3** Tap **Share** (□).

The Share screen appears.

**C** In some apps, you can select other items to share at the same time. For example, in Photos, you can select other photos.

**4** In the AirDrop area, tap the device to which you want to send the item.

## Receive an Item via AirDrop

**D** When someone tries to send you an item via AirDrop, your iPhone displays a pop-up message.

**1** Tap **Accept** or **Decline**, as appropriate.

**E** If you tap **Accept**, your iPhone receives the item and stores it in the appropriate app.

---

## TIPS

**Which devices can use AirDrop?**

AirDrop works on the iPhone 5s, iPhone 5c, iPhone 5, fifth-generation iPad, fourth-generation iPad, iPad mini, and fifth-generation iPod touch. Earlier iOS devices do not have the wireless hardware needed for AirDrop.

**Does AirDrop pose a security threat to my iPhone and data?**

AirDrop encrypts files so it can transfer them securely. When using AirDrop, you choose which files — if any — you want to share from your iPhone; other devices cannot use AirDrop to grab files from your iPhone. Similarly, when someone tries to send you a file via AirDrop, you can choose whether to accept or reject it.

# Share Your iPhone's Internet Access Using Personal Hotspot

Your iPhone can not only access the Internet itself from anywhere it has a suitable connection to the cellular network, but it can also share that Internet access with your computer and other devices. This feature is called Personal Hotspot.

For you to use Personal Hotspot, your iPhone's carrier must permit you to use it. Most carriers charge an extra fee per month on top of the standard iPhone charge.

## Share Your iPhone's Internet Access Using Personal Hotspot

### Set Up Personal Hotspot

**1** Press the Home button.

The Home screen appears.

**2** Tap **Settings**.

The Settings screen appears.

**3** Tap **Personal Hotspot**.

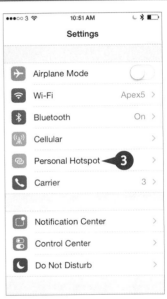

The Personal Hotspot screen appears.

**4** Tap **Wi-Fi Password**.

The Wi-Fi Password screen appears.

**5** Tap ⊗ to clear the default password.

**6** Type the password you want to use.

**7** Tap **Done**.

The Personal Hotspot screen appears again.

**8** Set the **Personal Hotspot** switch to On ( 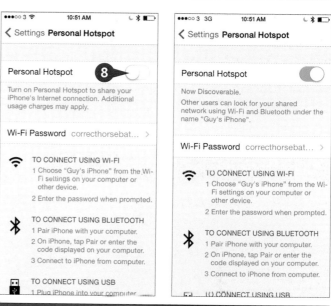 ).

The Personal Hotspot screen shows the message Now Discoverable and displays information for connecting computers and devices to the hotspot.

**Note:** When Personal Hotspot is active — when a computer or device is using the connection — Personal Hotspot appears in a blue bar across the lock screen and the Home screen to remind you. The bar shows the number of connections.

You can now connect your PC or Mac to the iPhone's Internet connection.

## Connect a PC to Personal Hotspot via USB

**1** Turn on Personal Hotspot on your iPhone as described earlier.

**2** Connect the iPhone to the PC via USB.

**Note:** The first time you use Personal Hotspot with your computer, Windows detects the iPhone's Internet connection as a new network connection and installs software for it. If the Driver Software Installation dialog opens, click **Close**.

The Set Network Location dialog opens.

**3** Click **Home network** or **Public network**, as appropriate.

## TIPS

**Which devices can I connect to Personal Hotspot?**
You can connect almost any Wi-Fi–capable computer or device to Personal Hotspot. Personal Hotspot works like other wireless access points, which makes it easy to connect your devices.

**Should I use USB or Wi-Fi to connect my computer to Personal Hotspot?**
If your PC or Mac is close to the iPhone, using the USB cable is usually easiest. But Wi-Fi gives you greater range and allows you to connect multiple computers to Personal Hotspot at once.

continued ▶

You can connect up to five computers or other devices, such as iPads or other tablet computers, to the Internet by using Personal Hotspot on your iPhone. Because the devices share the connection, the more devices you use, the slower the connection speed will appear to be on each device. Connecting more devices also typically increases the amount of data transferred across the iPhone's Internet connection and so consumes your data allowance faster.

## Share Your iPhone's Internet Access Using Personal Hotspot (continued)

The Set Network Location dialog updates its screen.

**4** Click **Close**.

Your PC starts using the iPhone's Internet connection.

### Connect a Mac via Personal Hotspot

**1** Turn on Personal Hotspot on your iPhone as described earlier.

**2** Connect the iPhone to the Mac via USB.

**Note:** If your Mac displays the A New Network Interface Has Been Detected dialog, click **Network Preferences** to open Network Preferences.

**3** Control +click or right-click **System Preferences** ( ) in the Dock.

The System Preferences context menu opens.

**4** Click **Network**.

The Network preferences pane of System Preferences opens.

**5** Click **iPhone USB**.

**6** Click **Apply**.

## Stop Using Personal Hotspot

**1** Press the Home button.

The Home screen appears.

**2** Tap **Settings**.

The Settings screen appears.

**3** Tap **Personal Hotspot**.

The Personal Hotspot screen appears.

**4** Set the **Personal Hotspot** switch to Off ( ).

---

**TIP**

### Can I use Personal Hotspot as my main Internet connection?

Yes. But make sure that your data plan provides enough data for your computer use as well as your iPhone use. If it does not, you may incur extra charges, and you will do better to use Personal Hotspot only when your main Internet connection is not available.

The Internet connection speeds you get from a connection to your iPhone's Personal Hotspot are usually slower than a broadband Internet connection such as a DSL or cable connection. But if your Internet use is light, you may find these speeds adequate.

# Connect to Wi-Fi Networks

Your iPhone can connect to the Internet via either the cell phone network or a Wi-Fi network. To conserve your data allowance, use a Wi-Fi network instead of the cell phone network whenever you can.

The first time you connect to a Wi-Fi network, you must provide the network's password. After that, the iPhone stores the password, so you can connect to the network without entering the password again.

## Connect to Wi-Fi Networks

### Connect to a Network Listed on the Wi-Fi Screen

**1** Press the Home button.

The Home screen appears.

**2** Tap **Settings**.

The Settings screen appears.

**3** Tap **Wi-Fi**.

The Wi-Fi screen appears.

**4** If Wi-Fi is off, set the **Wi-Fi** switch to On ( ).

The Choose a Network list appears. A lock icon ( ) indicates the network has security such as a password.

**5** Tap the network you want to connect to.

**Note:** If the network does not have a password, your iPhone connects to it without prompting you for a password.

The Enter Password screen appears.

**6** Type the password.

**7** Tap **Join**.

Your iPhone connects to the wireless network.

**A** The Wi-Fi screen appears again, showing a check mark next to the network the iPhone has connected to.

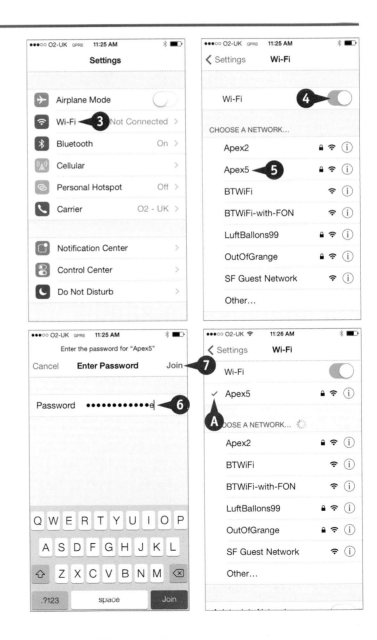

134

## Connect to a Network Not Listed on the Wi-Fi Screen

**1** On the Wi-Fi screen, tap **Other**.

The Other Network screen appears.

**2** Type the network name.

**3** Tap **Security**.

The Security screen appears.

**4** Tap the security type — for example, **WPA**.

**5** Tap **Back**.

The Other Network screen appears.

**6** Type the password.

**7** Tap **Join**.

Your iPhone joins the network.

**8** Tap **Settings**.

The Settings screen appears.

**B** The Wi-Fi signal icon ( 📶 ) in the status bar and on the Wi-Fi screen shows the strength of the Wi-Fi signal. The more bars that appear, the stronger the signal is.

---

## TIPS

**What does the Ask to Join Networks switch control?**
Your iPhone automatically connects to networks it "knows" — those it has connected to before. Set the **Ask to Join Networks** switch to On ( 🔵 ) if you want your iPhone to prompt you when unknown networks are available.

**How do I stop using a particular wireless network?**
Tap the info button ( ⓘ ) to the right of the network's name on the Wi-Fi screen. On the network's screen, tap **Forget this Network**. In the dialog that opens, tap **Forget**.

# Log In to Wi-Fi Hotspots

When you are in town or on the road, you can log in to Wi-Fi hotspots to enjoy fast Internet access without using your iPhone's data allowance.

You can find Wi-Fi hotspots at many locations, including coffee shops and restaurants, hotels, and airports. Some municipal areas, and even some parks and highway rest stops, also provide public Wi-Fi. Some Wi-Fi hotspots charge for access, whereas others are free to use.

## Log In to Wi-Fi Hotspots

**1** Press the Home button.

The Home screen appears.

**2** Tap **Settings**.

The Settings screen appears.

**3** Tap **Wi-Fi**.

The Wi-Fi screen appears.

**4** If Wi-Fi is off, set the **Wi-Fi** switch to On ( ).

The list of wireless networks appears.

**5** Tap the Wi-Fi hotspot you want to join.

**Note:** If the iPhone prompts you to enter a username and password, enter those the hotspot operator has given you. Many Wi-Fi hotspots use a login page instead of a username and password.

**A** The iPhone joins the hotspot. The Wi-Fi screen displays a check mark next to the hotspot.

**6** If Safari opens and displays a login page, type the login information for the hotspot, and then tap the button for logging in.

After connecting to the hotspot, you can use the Internet. For example, you can browse the web using Safari or send and receive e-mail using Mail.

---

## TIP

**What precautions should I take when using Wi-Fi hotspots?**

The main danger is that you may connect to a malevolent network.

To stay safe, connect only to hotspots provided by reputable establishments — for example, national hotel or restaurant chains — instead of hotspots run by unknown operators.

When you finish using a Wi-Fi hotspot that you do not plan to use again, tell the iPhone to forget the network using the technique described in the previous task, "Connect to Wi-Fi Networks."

Forgetting the network avoids this problem: After you have connected the iPhone to a wireless network, it will connect to another network that has the same name, security type, and password, even if that network is not the same network. This feature normally saves time, but it also enables an imposter to set up a fake hotspot that pretends to be a genuine hotspot you have previously used.

# Set Up Your Social Networking Accounts

**Y**our iPhone has built-in support for several types of social networks, including Facebook, Twitter, Flickr, and Vimeo. iOS makes it easy to post updates, photos, and videos to your accounts on these social networks. For example, you can quickly create a Facebook post or a Twitter tweet from the Notifications screen, or you can share a photo from the Photos app or the Camera app.

Before you can use a social network, you must enter the details of your account, as described in this task.

## Set Up Your Social Networking Accounts

### Open the Settings App and Locate the Social Network Buttons

**1** Press the Home button.

The Home screen appears.

**2** Tap **Settings**.

The Settings screen appears.

**3** Scroll down until you see the area containing the buttons for the social networks.

### Set Up Your Twitter Account

**1** On the Settings screen, tap **Twitter**.

The Twitter screen appears.

**2** Type your username.

**Note:** To create a new Twitter account, tap **Create New Account** and follow the resulting screens.

**3** Type your password.

**4** Tap **Sign In**.

Twitter verifies your username and password, and then sets up your account on the iPhone.

**5** In the Allow These Apps to Use Your Account area, set each switch to On (🔘) or Off ( ⬭ ), as needed.

**6** Tap **Settings**.

The Settings screen appears.

138

## Set Up Your Facebook Account

**1** On the Settings screen, tap **Facebook**.

**2** On the Facebook screen, type your username.

**Note:** To create a new Facebook account, tap **Create New Account** and follow the resulting screens.

**3** Type your password.

**4** Tap **Sign In**.

**5** On the information screen, tap **Sign In**.

Facebook verifies your username and password. The Facebook screen appears, with your account enabled.

**6** In the Allow These Apps to Use Your Account area, set each switch to On (○) or Off ( ), as needed.

**7** Tap **Settings**.

The Settings screen appears.

**8** Set the **Vibrate** switch and **Play Sound** switch to control which chat and message alerts you get.

**9** Set the **Record HD Video** switch to On (○) or Off ( ), as needed.

**10** Tap **Facebook**.

The Facebook screen appears.

**11** Tap **Settings**.

The Settings screen appears.

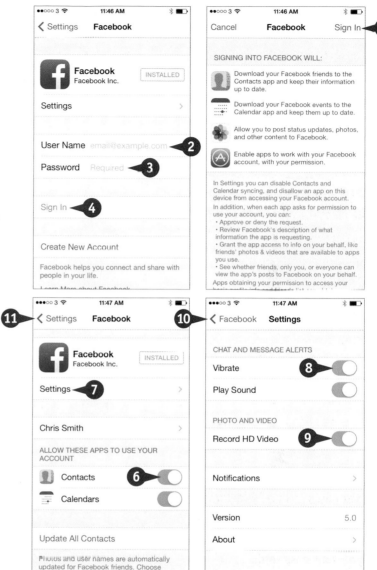

**TIP**

**How do I set up my Flickr account and Vimeo account?**

To set up a Flickr account or Vimeo account, tap **Flickr** or **Vimeo** on the Settings screen. If the Install button appears, the app is not yet installed, so you need to tap **Install** to install it. You can then return to the Settings app, type your username and password, and tap **Sign In**.

# Share Your Updates Using Twitter

Your iPhone's apps are fully integrated with Twitter, the online microblogging service. If you need to send a short textual tweet, you can use the Twitter app, creating the tweet from within the app itself. If you need to send a photo, you can start from the Photos app, and create a tweet in moments.

## Share Your Updates Using Twitter

### Send a Text Tweet

**1** Press the Home button.

The Home screen appears.

**2** Tap **Twitter**.

**Note:** If Twitter does not appear on the Home screen, tap **Settings**, tap **Twitter**, and then tap **Install**.

The Twitter app opens.

**3** Tap **New Tweet** (☑).

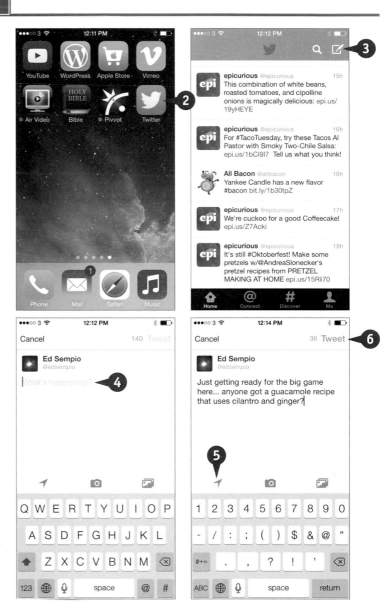

The New Tweet screen appears.

**4** Type the text of the tweet.

**Note:** You can also tap the microphone icon (🎤) to activate Siri, and then dictate the text of the tweet.

**5** Tap ✈ if you want to add your location to the tweet.

**6** Tap **Tweet**.

Twitter posts the tweet to your Twitter account.

## Send a Photo Tweet

**1** From the Home screen, tap **Photos**.

The Photos app opens.

**2** Navigate to the photo you want to tweet. For example, tap **Camera Roll**.

**3** Tap the photo to display it.

**4** Tap **Share** (⬆).

The Share screen appears.

**5** Tap **Twitter**.

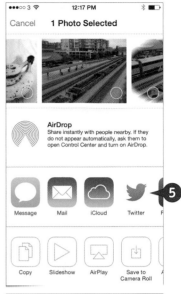

**A** The Twitter dialog opens, showing the tweet with the photo attached.

**6** Tap **Location** if you want to add the location to the tweet. In the Location dialog, check that the location is correct, and then tap **Twitter** to return to the Twitter dialog.

**7** Type the text of the tweet.

**8** Tap **Post**.

Your iPhone posts the tweet.

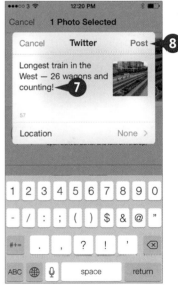

---

### TIP

**How do I read other people's tweets?**
To read other people's tweets, use the Twitter app. Press the Home button to display the Home screen, tap **Twitter**, and then tap **Home** to catch up on tweets from the Twitter accounts you are following.

# Post Updates on Facebook

If you have an account on Facebook, the world's biggest social network, you can post updates directly from your iPhone with a minimum of fuss.

You can work either from within the Facebook app or from apps that contain content suitable for Facebook posts. For example, you can post a photo from the Photos app to Facebook, as described in this task.

## Post Updates on Facebook

### Post an Update Using the Facebook App

1. Press the Home button.

   The Home screen appears.

2. Tap **Facebook**.

   **Note:** If Facebook does not appear on the Home screen, tap **Settings**, tap **Facebook**, and then tap **Install**.

   The Facebook app opens.

3. Tap **Status**.

   The Update Status screen appears.

4. Type your update.

5. Tap **Post**.

   Ⓐ The update appears on your screen.

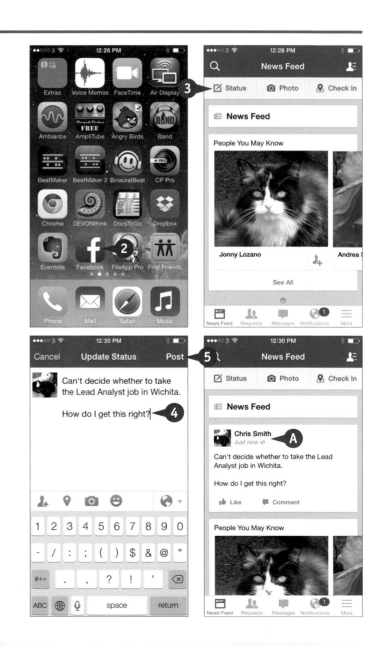

## Post a Photo Update

**1** In the Photos app, navigate to the photo you want to post. For example, tap **Moments** and then tap the moment that contains the photo.

**2** Tap the photo to display it.

**3** Tap **Share** (⬆).

The Share screen appears.

**4** Tap **Facebook**.

The Facebook dialog opens.

**5** Type the text for the update.

**6** Tap **Album**.

The Album screen appears.

**7** Tap the album to which you want to assign the photo.

**8** To add the location, tap **Location**, select the location in the Location dialog, and then tap **Facebook** to return to the Facebook dialog.

**9** Tap **Audience**.

The Audience dialog appears.

**10** Tap the Facebook audience to share the post with.

**11** In the Facebook dialog, tap **Post**.

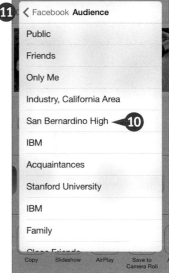

---

## TIP

**From what other apps can I post updates to Facebook?**

You can post updates to Facebook from any app to which the developer has added Facebook integration. For example, you can post a location from the Maps app or a lecture from iTunes U to Facebook.

To see whether you can post updates to Facebook from an app, tap **Share** (⬆) from the app. If Facebook appears on the Share screen, you can post an update to Facebook.

# Share Photos on Flickr

You can easily share photos from your iPhone to your account on the Flickr photo-sharing service. You can post either a single photo or multiple photos. Flickr adds the photos to your Photostream, making them available instantly.

When posting photos to Flickr, you can choose the audience for them. For example, you may want to give some photos a Public audience, whereas restricting others to Family or Friends. You may prefer to keep some photos to yourself by using the Only Me audience.

## Share Photos on Flickr

1 Press the Home button.

The Home screen appears.

2 Tap **Photos**.

The Photos screen appears.

3 Navigate to the item that contains the photo or photos you want to share. For example, tap **Albums** and then tap the album that contains the photo.

4 Tap **Select**.

**Note:** If you want to share a single photo, you can tap the photo to open it, and then tap **Share** (⬆).

The Photos app displays selection controls.

5 Tap each photo you want to share (✔ appears on each selected photo).

6 Tap **Share** (⬆).

The Share screen appears.

**7** Tap **Flickr**.

**Note:** You may need to scroll the list of apps to the left to see Flickr.

The Flickr dialog opens.

**8** Type the accompanying text for the photo or photos.

**9** Tap **Audience**.

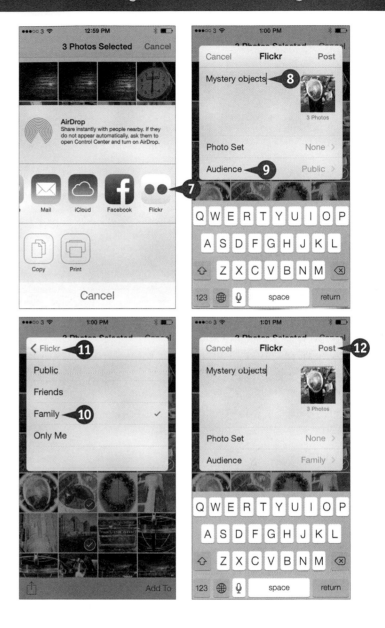

The Audience dialog opens.

**10** Tap the audience you want for the photos. For example, tap **Family**.

**11** Tap **Flickr**.

The Flickr dialog appears.

**12** Tap **Post**.

Your iPhone posts the photos to your Flickr Photostream.

## TIP

**Can I upload photos to Flickr from other apps?**
You can upload photos to Flickr from any app whose Share screen displays the Flickr icon. The easiest way to find out if an app supports uploading to Flickr is to select an item in the app and tap **Share** (⬆) to display the Share screen.

# Share Your Videos on Vimeo

If you shoot your own videos on your iPhone, you can upload them to the Vimeo video-sharing service so that other people can watch them. To use Vimeo, you must sign up for an account and install the Vimeo app on your iPhone.

Before uploading the video, set up your Vimeo account in the iPhone's Settings app, as described in the task "Set Up Your Social Networking Accounts," earlier in this chapter.

## Share Your Videos on Vimeo

**1** Press the Home button.

The Home screen appears.

**2** Tap **Photos**.

The Photos app opens.

**3** Tap the item that contains the video you want to share. For example, tap **Albums**, and then tap **Camera Roll** to share a video you have shot with the Camera app.

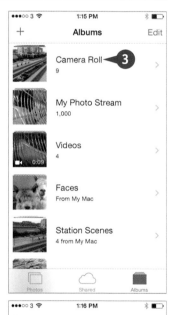

**4** Tap the video you want to share.

The video opens.

**5** Tap **Share** (⬆).

The Share screen appears.

**6** Tap **Vimeo**.

**Note:** You may need to swipe the list of apps to the left to see Vimeo.

The Vimeo dialog opens.

**7** Type any accompanying text for the video.

**8** Tap **Details**.

The Details dialog opens.

**9** In the Add Description area, type a description for the video.

**10** In the Add Tags area, type tags to associate with the video to help with searching.

**11** In the Video Size area, tap **Small**, **Medium**, or **Large (HD)**, as appropriate.

**12** In the Privacy area, tap **Public** or **Private**, as needed.

**13** Tap **Vimeo**.

The Vimeo dialog appears.

**14** Tap **Post**.

Your iPhone posts the video to Vimeo.

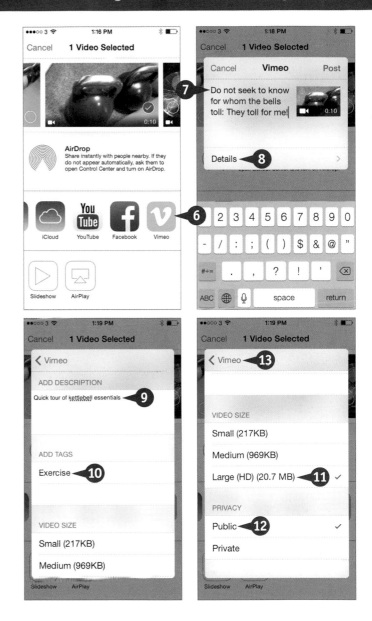

## TIP

**Can I also start uploading a video from within the Vimeo app?**
No. At this writing, the Vimeo app for iOS does not give you the option for uploading a video from within the app itself. Instead, start from the app that contains the video — for example, the Camera app or the Photos app.

# CHAPTER 7

# Working with Apps

In this chapter, you first learn to customize the Home screen, putting the icons you need most right to hand and organizing them into folders. You then grasp how to switch instantly among the apps you are running, how to find the apps you need on Apple's App Store, and how to update and remove apps. You also learn how to install apps provided by an administrator and how to work with text.

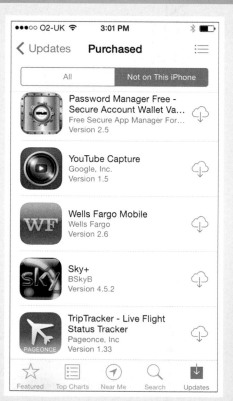

# Customize the Home Screen

From the Home screen, you run the apps on your iPhone. You can customize the Home screen to put the apps you use most frequently within easy reach. You can create further Home screens as needed and move the app icons among them. You can customize the Home screen by working on the iPhone, as described here. If you synchronize your iPhone with a computer, you can use iTunes instead. This is an easier way to make extensive changes, such as changing the order of the home screens.

## Customize the Home Screen

### Unlock the Icons for Customization

**1** Press the Home button.

The Home screen appears.

**2** Tap and drag left or right to display the Home screen you want to customize.

**Ⓐ** You can also tap the dots to move from one Home screen to another.

**3** Tap and hold the icon you want to move.

**Note:** You can tap and hold any icon until the apps start jiggling. Usually, it is easiest to tap and hold the icon you want to move, and then drag the icon.

The icons start to jiggle, indicating that you can move them.

### Move an Icon within a Home Screen

**1** After unlocking the icons, drag the icon to where you want it.

The other icons move out of the way.

**2** When the icon is in the right place, drop it.

**Ⓑ** The icon stays in its new position.

## Move an Icon to a Different Home Screen

**1** After unlocking the icons, drag the icon to the left edge of the screen to display the previous Home screen or to the right edge to display the next Home screen.

The previous Home screen or next Home screen appears.

**2** Drag the icon to where you want it.

If the Home screen contains other icons, they move out of the way as needed.

**3** Drop the icon.

The icon stays in its new position.

## Stop Customizing the Home Screen

**1** Press the Home button.

The icons stop jiggling.

**How can I put the default apps back on the Home screen?**
Press the Home button, tap **Settings**, and then tap **General**. Tap and drag up to scroll down the screen, and then tap **Reset**. On the Reset screen, tap **Reset Home Screen Layout**, and then tap **Reset Home Screen** (**A**) in the dialog that opens. Press the Home button to return to the Home screen.

This will reset your home screen layout to factory defaults.

Reset Home Screen **A**

Cancel

# Organize Apps with Folders

To organize the Home screen, you can arrange the items into folders. The iPhone's default Home screen layout includes a folder named Extras, which contains items such as the Contacts app and the Calculator app, but you can create as many other folders as you need. Like the Home screen, each folder can have multiple pages, so you can put many apps in a folder.

You create a folder by dragging one icon onto another icon. Doing this creates a folder containing both items. You can then rename the folder and add further apps to it.

## Organize Apps with Folders

### Create a Folder

**1** Display the Home screen that contains the item you want to put into a folder.

**2** Tap and hold the item until the icons start to jiggle.

**Note:** When creating a folder, you may find it easiest to first put both the items you will add to the folder on the same screen.

**3** Drag the item to the other icon you want to place in the folder you create.

The iPhone creates a folder, puts both icons in it, and assigns a default name based on the genre.

**4** Tap ⊗ in the folder name box.

The keyboard appears.

**5** Type the name for the folder.

**6** Tap outside the folder.

The iPhone applies the name to the folder.

**7** Press the Home button.

The icons stop jiggling.

## Open an Item in a Folder

**1** Display the Home screen that contains the folder.

**2** Tap the folder's icon.

The folder's contents appear, and the items outside the folder fade.

**3** If necessary, drag left or right or tap a dot to navigate to another page in the folder.

**4** Tap the item you want to open.

The item opens.

## Add an Item to a Folder

**1** Display the Home screen that contains the item.

**2** Tap and hold the item until the icons start to jiggle.

**3** Drag the icon on top of the folder and drop it there.

**Note:** If the folder is on a different Home screen from the icon, drag the icon to the left edge to display the previous Home screen or to the right edge to display the next Home screen.

The item goes into the folder.

**4** Press the Home button to stop the icons jiggling.

## TIPS

**How do I take an item out of a folder?**
Tap the folder to display its contents, and then tap and hold the item until the icons start to jiggle. Drag the item out of the folder, drag it to where you want it on the Home screen, and then drop it.

**How do I create another page in a folder?**
Open the folder, and then tap and hold an item until the icons start jiggling. Drag the item to the right of the screen. A new page appears automatically.

# Switch Quickly from One App to Another

You can run many apps on your iPhone at the same time, switching from one app to another as needed.

The most straightforward way of switching from one app to another is to press the Home button to display the Home screen, and then tap the icon for the app you want to start using. But the iPhone also has an app-switching screen that enables you to switch quickly from one running app to another running app more quickly. From the app-switching screen, you can also easily close one or more running apps.

## Switch Quickly from One App to Another

**1** Press the Home button.

The Home screen appears.

**2** Tap the app you want to launch.

The app's screen appears.

**3** Start using the app as usual.

**4** Press the Home button twice in quick succession.

**A** The app-switching screen appears.

**5** Tap and drag left or right to scroll until you see the app you want.

**6** Tap the app.

The app appears.

**7** When you are ready to switch back, press the Home button twice in quick succession.

The app-switching screen appears.

**8** Scroll left or right as needed, and then tap the app to which you want to return.

The app appears, ready to resume from where you stopped using it.

**How do I stop an app that is not responding?**

If an app stops responding, you can quickly close it from the app-switching screen. Press the Home button twice to open the app-switching screen. Scroll to the problem app, and then drag it upward so it disappears off the screen. Tap the app you want to use or press the Home button to return to the Home screen.

You can use this move to close any app that you no longer want to use, whether or not is has stopped responding.

# Find the Apps You Need on the App Store

The iPhone comes with essential apps, such as Safari for surfing the web, Mail for e-mail, and Calendar for keeping your schedule. But to get the most out of your iPhone, you will likely need to add other apps.

To get apps, you use the App Store, which provides apps that Apple has approved as correctly programmed, suitable for purpose, and not containing malevolent code. Before you can download any apps, including free apps, you must create an App Store account.

## Find the Apps You Need on the App Store

**1** Press the Home button.

The Home screen appears.

**2** Tap **App Store**.

The App Store screen appears.

**3** Tap **Categories**.

The Categories screen appears.

**4** Tap the category you want to see.

The category screen appears, showing the New list and the What's Hot list.

**5** Tap and drag to see further apps in a list, or tap and drag up to see other lists. Then tap **See All** to display your chosen list.

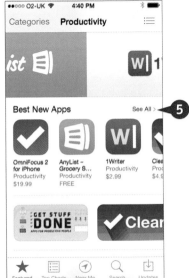

The screen shows the list you chose.

**6** Tap the app you want to view.

The app's screen appears.

**Note:** To understand what an app does and how well it does it, look at the app's rating, read the description, and read the user reviews.

**7** Tap the price button or the **Free** button.

The price button or Free button changes to an Install App button.

**8** Tap **Install App**.

**9** If the iPhone prompts you to sign in, type your password and tap **OK**.

**Note:** If you have not created an App Store account already, the iPhone prompts you to create one now.

The iPhone downloads and installs the app.

**10** Tap **Open** to launch the app.

## TIP

**Why does the App Store not appear on the Home screen or when I search?**

If the App Store does not appear on the Home screen, and if searching for it does not show a result, the iPhone has restrictions applied that prevent you from installing apps. You can remove these restrictions if you know the restrictions passcode. Press the Home button, tap **Settings**, and then tap **General**. Scroll down, and then tap **Restrictions**. Type the passcode on the Enter Passcode screen, and then tap the **Installing Apps** switch and move it to On ( changes to ).

# Update and Remove Apps

To keep your iPhone's apps running well, you should install app updates when they become available. Most updates for paid apps are free, but you must often pay to upgrade to a new version of the app. You can download and install updates using either the iPhone itself or iTunes on your computer.

When you no longer need an app you have installed on your iPhone, you can remove it. You can remove the app either by working on your iPhone or by using iTunes on your computer. You cannot remove the built-in apps.

## Update and Remove Apps

### Update an App

1 Press the Home button.

The Home screen appears.

Ⓐ The badge on the App Store icon shows the number of available updates.

2 Tap **App Store**.

The App Store screen appears.

3 Tap **Updates**.

The Updates screen appears.

4 Tap **Update All** to apply all the available updates now.

Ⓑ You can tap **Update** to update a single app.

Ⓒ Tap **Purchased** if you want to view the list of apps you have purchased.

From the Purchased screen, you can update individual apps or install apps you have bought but not yet installed on this iPhone.

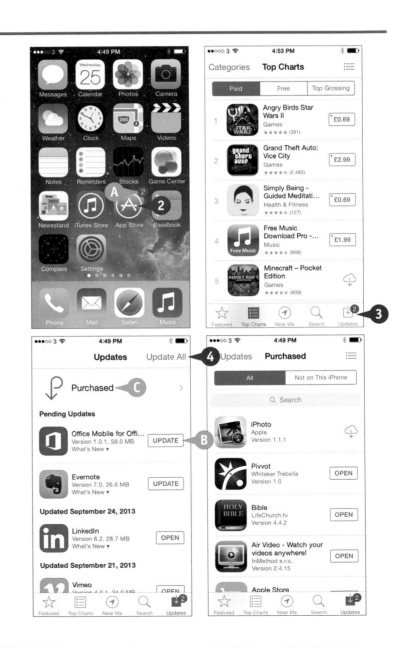

## Remove an App from the iPhone

**1** Press the Home button.

The Home screen appears.

**2** Display the Home screen that contains the app you want to delete.

**3** Tap and hold the item until the icons start to jiggle.

**4** Tap ✕ on the icon.

The Delete dialog appears.

**5** Tap **Delete**.

The iPhone deletes the app, and the app's icon disappears.

**6** Press the Home button.

The icons stop jiggling.

---

## TIPS

**How do I update an app using iTunes?**

In iTunes, click the left pop-up button and click **Apps**. In the bar at the top of the iTunes window, click **Updates**, and then click **Update All Apps**. In the Sign In to Download from the iTunes Store dialog, type your password and click **Sign In**. On the My App Updates screen, click **Download All Free Updates**, connect your iPhone, and then click **Sync** to start synchronization.

**How do I remove an app from my iPhone using iTunes?**

Connect your iPhone to your computer, and then click its button on the bar at the top of the iTunes window; if you have multiple iOS devices, click **Devices**, and then click your iPhone. Click the **Apps** tab, and then click **Remove** for the app. Click **Sync** to start synchronization.

# Install an App Provided by an Administrator

If you use an iPhone administered by a company or organization, an administrator may provide apps for you to install using iTunes. You will usually copy the app's file from a network drive, but you may also receive it attached to an e-mail message.

To install the app, you add it to iTunes on your PC or Mac, and then sync the iPhone with iTunes.

## Install an App Provided by an Administrator

1 Click **File**.

2 Click **Add File to Library** in Windows or **Add to Library** on a Mac.

The Add To Library dialog opens.

**Note:** If you receive the app's file attached to an e-mail message, save it to a folder, and then use the Add To Library dialog to add it to iTunes. In Mail on a Mac, you can simply click an attached app's file to add it to iTunes.

3 Open the folder that contains the app's file.

4 Click the app's file.

5 Click **Open**.

Ⓐ iTunes adds the app to the apps list.

6 Connect your iPhone to the PC or Mac via the USB cable.

**Note:** You can also install an app provided by an administrator by syncing wirelessly.

7 Click the button for the iPhone. If you have multiple iOS devices connected, click **Devices**, and then click the iPhone.

The iPhone's control screens appear.

**8** Click **Apps**.

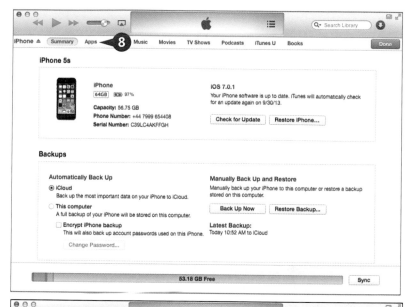

The Apps screen appears.

**9** Click **Install**.

**Note:** You can also click **Automatically sync new apps** (☐ changes to ☑) below the Apps list to make iTunes automatically sync all new apps.

**10** Click **Apply**. If you have not made changes, this button is named Sync.

iTunes installs the app on your iPhone.

**TIP**

**Is there another way to add an app's file to iTunes?**
Yes. You can quickly add an app's file to iTunes by dragging the app's file from a Windows Explorer window or a Finder window to the main part of the iTunes window — for example, the part that shows the music when iTunes is in Music view. On a Mac, you can also add the app to iTunes by dragging the app's file to the iTunes icon on the Dock and dropping it there.

# Cut, Copy, and Paste Text

You can type text easily on your iPhone's keyboard or dictate it using Siri, but if the text already exists, you can copy the text and paste it instead. For example, you can copy text from a note and paste it into an e-mail message you are composing.

If the text is in a document you can edit, you can cut the text from the document instead of copying it. If the text is in a document you cannot edit, you can copy the text but not cut it. The technique depends on whether you can edit the document.

## Cut, Copy, and Paste Text

### Select and Copy Text You Cannot Edit

**Note:** An example of text you cannot edit is a web page you open in Safari.

**1** Tap and hold in the section of text you want to copy.

A selection highlight with handles appears around the text. The Copy button appears above the selection.

**2** Drag the handles of the selection highlight around the text that you want.

**3** Tap **Copy**.

Your iPhone places the text on the Clipboard, a hidden storage area.

### Select and Copy Text You Can Edit

**Note:** An example of text you can edit is a note you create in Notes or a message you compose in Mail.

**1** Tap and hold until you see the magnifying glass and then release.

A bar appears containing the Select button and Select All button.

**2** Tap **Select**.

**Note:** Tap **Select All** to select all the text.

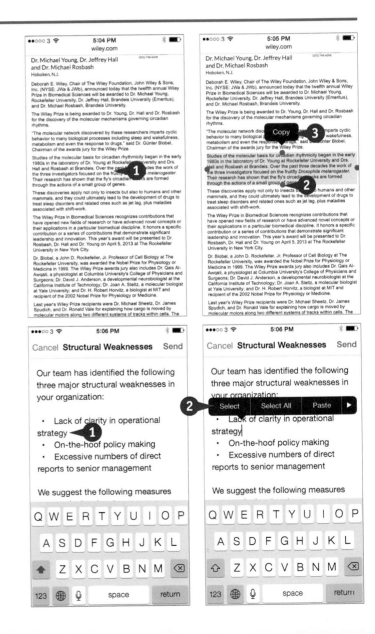

Blue selection handles appear around the current word, and further options appear on the selection bar.

③ Tap and drag the selection handles around the text that you want.

④ Tap **Copy** or **Cut**, as needed.

**Note:** This example uses Copy instead of Cut.

## Paste the Content You Have Copied or Cut

① Open the app in which you want to paste the text.

**Note:** This example shows text being pasted into a new note in the Notes app.

② Tap where you want to paste the text.

③ Tap **Paste**.

Ⓐ Your iPhone inserts the copied text in the document.

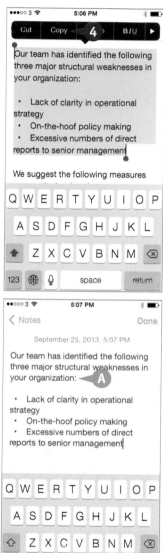

## TIPS

**How many items can I store on the Clipboard?**
You can store only one item on the Clipboard at a time. Each item you cut or copy replaces the existing item on the Clipboard. But until you replace the existing item on the Clipboard, you can paste it as many times as needed.

**Can I transfer the contents of the Clipboard to my computer?**
You cannot transfer the Clipboard's contents directly to your computer, but you can easily transfer them indirectly. For example, paste them into an e-mail message and send it to yourself, or paste them into a note in the Notes app and sync your devices.

# Bold, Italicize, Underline, and Replace Text

Some apps enable you to add text formatting such as boldface, underline, and italics to text to make parts of it stand out. For example, you can apply formatting in e-mail messages you create using the Mail app and in various apps for creating word-processing documents.

To apply formatting, you first select the text, and then choose options from the pop-up formatting bar. Some apps also offer other text commands, such as replacing a word or phrase from a menu of suggestions.

## Bold, Italicize, Underline, and Replace Text

### Apply Bold, Italics, and Underline

1 Tap and hold the text to which you want to apply bold, italics, or underline.

A pop-up bar of text options appears.

2 Tap **Select**.

Part of the text is highlighted and handles appear.

3 Drag the handles to select the text that you want to bold, italicize, or underline.

4 Tap the **B**/**U** button in the pop-up bar.

The pop-up bar displays formatting options.

5 Tap **Bold**, **Italics**, or **Underline**, as needed.

The text takes on the formatting you chose.

6 Tap outside the selected text to deselect it.

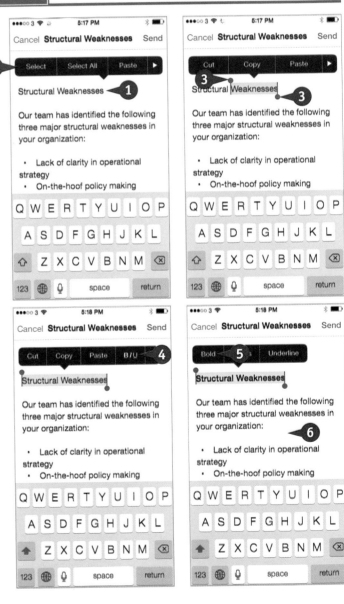

## Replace Text with Suggested Words

1 Double-tap the word you want to replace.

**Note:** You can tap and hold in the word, and then tap **Select** on the pop-up formatting bar to select the word.

Selection handles appear around the word.

The pop-up formatting bar appears.

2 Tap ▶.

The pop-up formatting bar displays other buttons.

3 Tap **Replace**.

The pop-up formatting bar displays suggested replacement words.

4 Tap the word with which you want to replace the selected word.

Your iPhone replaces the word.

**What does the Quote Level button on the pop-up formatting bar in Mail do?**

Tap the **Quote Level** button when you need to increase or decrease the quote level of your selected text. When you tap Quote Level, the pop-up formatting bar displays an Increase button and a Decrease button. Tap **Increase** to increase the quote level, indenting the text more, or **Decrease** to decrease the quote level, reducing the existing indent.

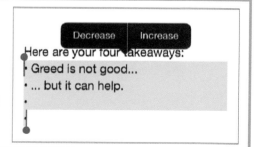

# CHAPTER 8

# Browsing the Web and Sending E-Mail

Your iPhone is fully equipped to browse the web and send e-mail via a Wi-Fi connection or cellular network.

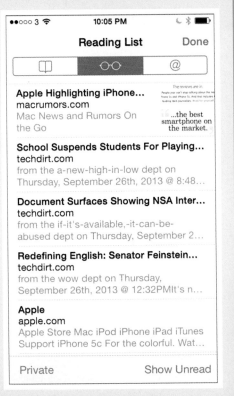

# Browse the Web with Safari

Your iPhone comes equipped with the Safari app, which you use for browsing the web. You can quickly go to a web page by entering its address in the Address box or by following a link.

Although you can browse quickly by opening a single web page at a time, you may prefer to open multiple pages and switch back and forth among them. Safari makes this easy to do.

## Browse the Web with Safari

### Open Safari and Navigate to Web Pages

**1** Press the Home button.

The Home screen appears.

**2** Tap **Safari**.

Safari opens and loads the last web page that was shown.

**3** Tap the Address box.

Safari selects the current contents of the Address box, and the keyboard appears.

**4** Tap ⊗ if you need to delete the contents of the Address box.

**5** Type the address of the page you want to open.

**A** You can also tap a search result that Safari displays below the Address box.

**6** Tap **Go**.

Safari displays the page.

**7** Tap a link on the page.

Safari displays that page.

**B** After going to a new page, tap ‹ to display the previous page. You can then tap › to go forward again to the page you just went back from.

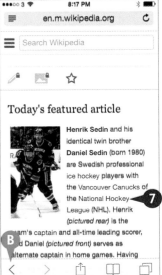

## Open Multiple Pages and Navigate among Them

**1** Tap **Pages** (⬜).

Safari displays the list of open pages, each bearing a Close button ( ✕ ).

**2** Tap **New Page** (⬛).

Safari opens a new page and displays your bookmarks.

**3** Tap the Address box, and then go to the page you want.

**Note:** You can also go to a page by using a bookmark, as described in the next task, "Access Websites Quickly with Your Bookmarks."

The page appears.

**4** To switch to another page, tap **Pages** (⬜).

Safari displays the list of pages.

**5** Tap the page you want to see.

**C** You can tap the **Close** button ( ✕ ) to close a page.

## TIP

### How do I search for information?

Tap the Address box to select its current contents, and then type your search terms (**A**). Safari searches as you type; you can type further to narrow down the results, and stop as soon as you see suitable results. Tap the result you want to see (**B**), and then tap a link on the results page that Safari opens.

# Access Websites Quickly with Your Bookmarks

Typing web addresses can be laborious, even with the help of the iPhone's keyboard adds, so you will probably want to use bookmarks to access websites you visit often.

By syncing your existing bookmarks from your computer or online account, as described in Chapter 1, you can instantly provide your iPhone with quick access to the web pages you want to visit most frequently. You can also create bookmarks on your iPhone, as discussed in the next task, "Create Bookmarks."

## Access Websites Quickly with Your Bookmarks

### Open the Bookmarks Screen

**1** Press the Home button.

The Home screen appears.

**2** Tap **Safari**.

Safari opens.

**3** Tap **Bookmarks** (📖).

The Bookmarks screen appears.

### Explore Your History

**1** On the Bookmarks screen, tap **History**.

A list of the web pages you have recently visited appears.

**A** The headings break up your history list into straightforward time sections, such as This Evening or Wednesday Afternoon, to help you locate what you are looking for.

**2** Tap **Bookmarks** to return to the Bookmarks screen.

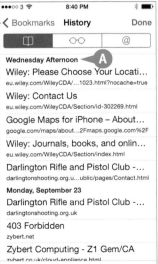

## Explore a Bookmarks Category

**1** On the Bookmarks screen, tap the bookmarks folder or category you want to see. This example uses the **Mac** folder.

The contents of the folder or category appear. For example, the contents of the Bookmarks Bar folder appear.

**2** Tap the item you want to view.

The bookmarked web page appears.

**3** Tap the button in the upper left corner one or more times to go back. For example, tap **Bookmarks** to return to the Bookmarks screen.

## Open a Bookmarked Page

**1** When you find the bookmark for the web page you want to open, tap the bookmark.

**B** The web page opens.

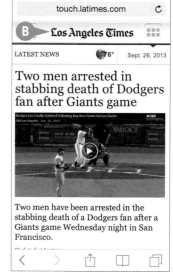

---

**TIP**

### How can I quickly access a website?

Creating a bookmark within Safari — as discussed in the next task, "Create Bookmarks" — is good for sites you access now and then. But if you access a site frequently, create an icon for it on your Home screen. Open the site in Safari. Tap **Share** (⬆), tap **Add to Home Screen** (Ⓐ), type the name on the Add to Home screen, and then tap **Add**. You can then go straight to the page by tapping its icon on the Home screen.

# Create Bookmarks

While browsing the web on your iPhone, you will likely find web pages you want to access again. To access such a web page easily, create a bookmark for it. If you have set your iPhone to sync bookmarks with your computer or an online account, the bookmark becomes available on your computer or online account as well when you sync.

If you create many bookmarks, it is usually helpful to store them in multiple folders. You can create folders easily on the iPhone and choose which folder to store each bookmark in.

## Create Bookmarks

### Create a Bookmark on the iPhone

**1** Press the Home button.

The Home screen appears.

**2** Tap **Safari**.

Safari opens and displays the last web page you were viewing.

**3** Navigate to the web page you want to bookmark.

**4** Tap **Share** (⬆).

The Share screen appears.

**5** Tap **Bookmark**.

The Add Bookmark screen appears.

**6** Edit the suggested name, or type a new name.

**7** Tap **Location**.

The Choose a Folder screen appears.

**8** Tap the folder in which to store the bookmark.

The Add Bookmark screen appears.

**9** Tap **Save**.

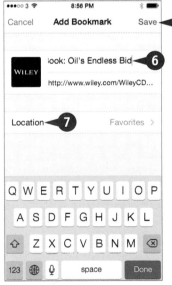

172

## Create a New Folder for Bookmarks

**1** In Safari, tap **Bookmarks** (□).

The Bookmarks screen appears.

**2** Tap **Edit**.

The editing controls appear.

**3** Tap **New Folder**.

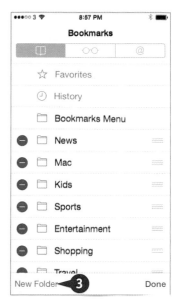

The Edit Folder screen appears.

**4** Tap **Location**.

The Choose a Folder screen appears.

**5** Tap the folder in which to store the bookmark.

The Edit Folder screen appears.

**6** Type the name for the folder.

**7** Tap **Bookmarks**.

The Bookmarks screen appears, still with editing controls displayed.

**8** Tap **Done**.

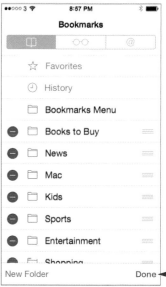

## TIP

**Can I change a bookmark I have created?**

Yes. Tap **Bookmarks** (□) to display the Bookmarks screen, and then navigate to the bookmark you want to change. Tap **Edit** to switch to editing mode. You can then tap a bookmark to open it on the Edit Bookmark screen, where you can change its name, address, or location. In editing mode, you can also delete a bookmark by tapping ● and then tapping **Delete**, or rearrange your bookmarks by tapping ≡ and dragging up or down the list.

# Keep a Reading List of Web Pages

**B**ookmarks are a handy way of marking pages you want to be able to visit repeatedly, but you may also want to be able to save some web pages for later reading without creating bookmarks for them. You can do this easily by using Safari's Reading List feature.

You can quickly add the current web page to Reading List by using the Share screen. Once you have added pages, you access Reading List through the Bookmarks feature. When viewing Reading List, you can display either all the pages it contains or only those you have not read.

## Keep a Reading List of Web Pages

### Add a Web Page to Reading List

**1** Press the Home button.

The Home screen appears.

**2** Tap **Safari**.

Safari opens and displays the last web page you were viewing.

**3** Navigate to the web page you want to bookmark.

**4** Tap **Share** (⬆).

The Share screen appears.

**5** Tap **Add to Reading List**.

Safari adds the web page to Reading List.

**Note:** You can also add a web page to Reading List by touching and holding a link to that page. In the dialog that opens, tap **Add to Reading List**.

## Open Reading List and Display a Page

**1** In Safari, tap **Bookmarks** (▢).

The Bookmarks screen appears.

**2** Tap **Reading List** ( ◯◯ ).

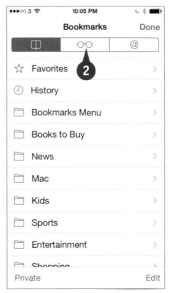

The Reading List screen appears.

**3** Tap **Show All**.

Reading List displays all the pages it contains, including those you have read.

**Ⓐ** You can tap **Show Unread** to display only unread pages.

**4** Tap the page you want to open.

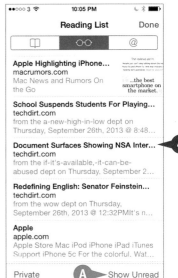

---

### TIP

**How do I remove an item from Reading List?**

To remove an item from Reading List, tap **Bookmarks** (▢) and then **Reading List** ( ◯◯ ). In the list of pages, tap the page you want to remove and swipe left, and then tap the **Delete** button that appears.

# Share Web Pages with Others

When browsing the web, you will likely come across pages you want to share with other people. Safari makes it easy to share web page addresses via e-mail, instant messaging, Twitter, Facebook, and other apps.

When others share web pages with you via Twitter and similar apps, Safari adds them to the Shared Links list. You can open this list, browse the pages, and quickly display any pages you want to view.

## Share Web Pages with Others

### Share a Web Page with Others

**1** Press the Home button.

The Home screen appears.

**2** Tap **Safari**.

Safari opens and displays the last web page you were viewing.

**3** Navigate to the web page you want to share.

**4** Tap **Share** (⬆).

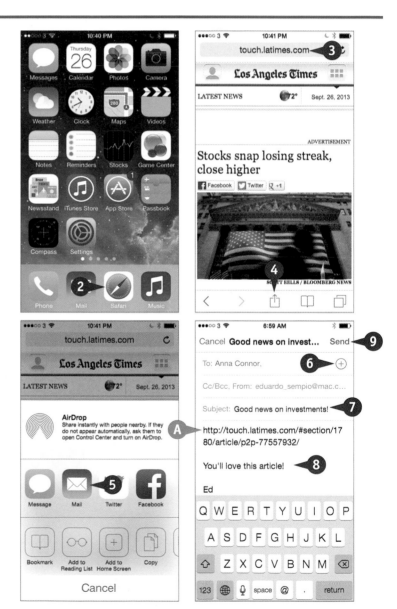

The Share screen appears.

**5** Tap **Mail**.

Your iPhone starts a new message in the Mail app.

**Ⓐ** The URL appears in the body of the message.

**6** Tap ⊕ and type an address for the message.

**7** Edit the suggested subject line as needed.

**8** Type any explanatory text needed.

**9** Tap **Send**.

## Open a Page Someone Has Shared with You

**1** In Safari, tap **Bookmarks** (□).

The Bookmarks screen appears.

**2** Tap **Shared Links** (@).

The Shared Links list appears.

**3** If necessary, tap and drag up to scroll down to locate the link you want.

**4** Tap the link.

Safari displays the linked page.

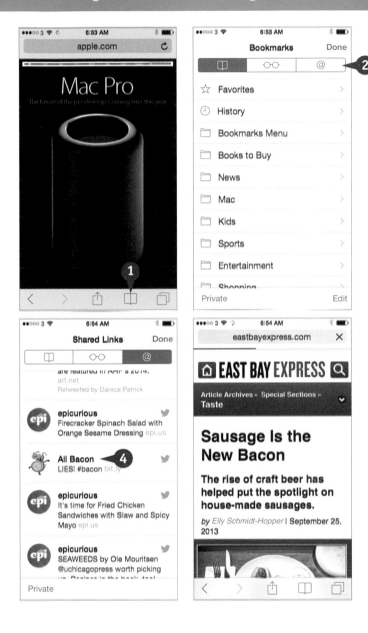

**What other ways can I use to share a web page?**

You can also share a web page address by including it in an instant message, by tweeting it to Twitter, or by posting it to Facebook. Another option is to use AirDrop to share the address with a local device. See Chapter 6 for instructions on using AirDrop.

# Navigate among Open Web Pages Using Tabs

If you browse the web a lot, you will probably need to open many web pages in Safari at the same time. Safari presents your open pages as a list of scrollable tabs, making it easy to navigate from one page to another.

You can change the order of the tabs to suit your needs, and you can quickly close a tab by either tapping its **Close** button or simply swiping it off the list.

## Navigate among Open Web Pages Using Tabs

### Open Safari and Display the List of Tabs

**1** Press the Home button.

The Home screen appears.

**2** Tap **Safari**.

Safari opens or becomes active.

**3** Tap **Pages** (▢).

The list of pages appears.

### Close Pages You Do Not Need to Keep Open

**1** Tap ✕ on the tab for a page you want to close.

The page closes, and the tab disappears from the list.

**2** Tap a tab and swipe it left off the screen.

The page closes, and the tab disappears from the list.

## Change the Order of the Pages

**1** Tap and hold the tab for a page you want to move.

The tab moves to the foreground.

**2** Drag the tab to where you want it to appear in the list, and then release it.

## Find a Page and Display It

**1** Scroll up and down to browse through the tabs.

**A** Your current iCloud tabs from your other devices logged into iCloud appear at the bottom of the screen. You can tap a page to open it.

**2** Tap the tab for the page you want to display.

The page opens.

---

## TIP

**How do I return from the list of tabs to the page I was viewing before?**

To return to the page you were viewing before, either tap the page's tab in the list of tabs, or tap **Done** in the lower right corner of the screen.

# Configure Your Default Search Engine

To find information with Safari, you often need to search using a search engine. Safari's default search engine is Google, but you can change to another search engine. Your choices are Google, Yahoo!, and Bing.

Google, Yahoo!, and Bing compete directly with one another and return similar results for many searches. But if you experiment with the three search engines, you will gradually discover which one suits you best. And if you find you prefer a search engine other than these three, you can search by using its website.

## Configure Your Default Search Engine

### Set the Default Search Engine for Safari

**1** Press the Home button.

The Home screen appears.

**2** Tap **Settings**.

The Settings screen appears.

**3** Scroll down the screen, and then tap **Safari**.

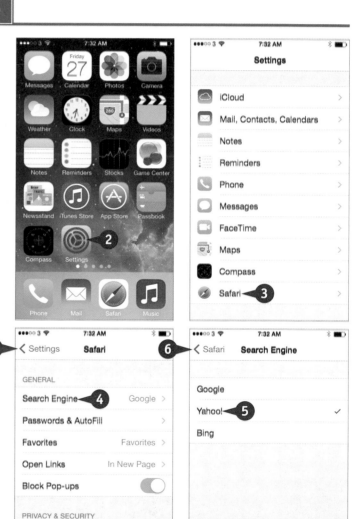

The Safari screen appears.

**4** Tap **Search Engine**.

The Search Engine screen appears.

**5** Tap the search engine you want — for example, **Yahoo!**.

A check mark appears next to the search engine you tapped.

**6** Tap **Safari**.

The Safari screen appears again, now showing the search engine you chose.

**7** Tap **Settings**.

The Settings screen appears.

## Search with a Search Engine Other than Google, Yahoo!, or Bing

1. Press the Home button.

   The Home screen appears.

2. Tap **Safari**.

   Safari opens.

3. Tap the Address box.

4. Enter the address of the search engine's website.

5. Tap **Search** or **Go**, depending on which button appears.

   The search engine appears.

6. Tap in the Search box.

7. Type your search terms.

8. Tap **Search** ( 🔍 ).

   The search results appear.

9. Tap a result to display its page.

**Which is the best search engine?**

This depends on what you are searching for and what is important to you. For most purposes, Google is the most comprehensive search engine, but you may be able to discover a more specialized search engine that focuses on your area of interest.

If you value your privacy, use a search engine that emphasizes privacy, and verify its claims as far as possible.

# Fill In Forms Quickly with AutoFill

If you fill in forms using your iPhone, you can save time and typos by enabling the AutoFill feature. AutoFill can automatically fill in standard form fields, such as name and address fields, using the information from a contact card you specify.

AutoFill can also automatically store other data you enter in fields, and can store usernames and passwords to enter them for you automatically. You can also add one or more credit cards to AutoFill so that you can easily pay for items online.

## Fill In Forms Quickly with AutoFill

**1** Press the Home button.

The Home screen appears.

**2** Tap **Settings**.

The Settings screen appears.

**3** Scroll down, and then tap **Safari**.

The Safari screen appears.

**4** Tap **Passwords & AutoFill**.

The Passwords & AutoFill screen appears.

**5** Set the **Use Contact Info** switch to On ( ) if you want to use AutoFill with contact info.

**6** Tap **My Info**.

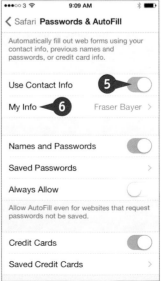

The Contacts screen appears.

**7** Tap the contact record that contains the information you want to use.

The AutoFill screen appears again.

**8** Set the **Names and Passwords** switch to On ( ◉ ) or Off ( ○ ), as needed.

**9** If you set the Names and Passwords switch to On ( ◉ ), tap **Saved Passwords**. On the Saved Passwords screen, review the sites that have saved passwords, and clear any you do not want to use. Tap **AutoFill** to return.

**10** Set the **Always Allow** switch to On ( ◉ ) if you want to use AutoFill for websites that request you not save passwords.

**11** Set the **Credit Cards** switch to On ( ◉ ) or Off ( ○ ), as needed.

**12** If you set the Credit Cards switch to On ( ◉ ), tap **Saved Credit Cards**.

The Credit Cards screen appears.

**13** Tap **Add Credit Card**.

The Add Credit Card screen appears.

**14** Enter your credit card details.

**15** Tap **Done**.

**16** Tap **AutoFill**.

The AutoFill screen appears.

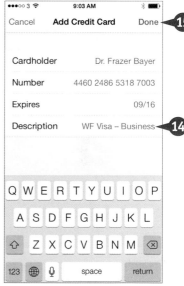

**TIP**

**Is it safe to store my passwords and credit card information in AutoFill?**

There is no hard-and-fast answer, but storing this sensitive information is reasonably safe because your iPhone encrypts it securely. The main threat to this data is from someone picking up your iPhone, so be sure to protect the device with a passcode or — better — a password (see Chapter 2). On the iPhone 5s, set up the Touch ID feature (see Chapter 1) to enable yourself to log in quickly without having to type the passcode or password.

# Tighten Up Safari's Security

Some websites try to infect computers with malevolent software, or *malware*, or lure visitors into providing sensitive personal or financial information. To protect yourself against such threats, you can turn on Safari's Fraudulent Website Warning feature, which warns you if you try to access a blacklisted site, and turn off the JavaScript programming language, which can be used to attack your iPhone.

You can also block pop-up windows, which some websites use to display unwanted information; choose which cookies to accept; and turn on the Do Not Track feature to reduce the footprint you leave on the Internet.

## Tighten Up Safari's Security

**1** Press the Home button.

The Home screen appears.

**2** Tap **Settings**.

The Settings screen appears.

**3** Scroll down, and then tap **Safari**.

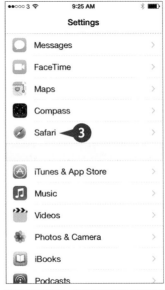

The Safari screen appears.

**4** Set the **Block Pop-ups** switch to On ( ◯● ) to block unwanted pop-up windows.

**5** Set the **Do Not Track** switch to On ( ◯● ) or Off ( ◯ ), as needed.

**6** Tap **Block Cookies**.

The Block Cookies screen appears.

**7** Tap **Always**, **From third parties and advertisers**, or **Never**, as needed. See the tip for advice.

**8** Tap **Safari**.

The Safari screen appears.

**9** Tap **Smart Search Field**.

The Smart Search Field screen appears.

**10** Set the **Search Suggestions** switch to On (⬤) if you want to receive search suggestions.

**11** Set the **Preload Top Hit** switch to On (⬤) if you want Safari to preload the first search result page so it will load quickly.

**12** Tap **Safari**.

The Safari screen appears.

**13** Set the **Fraudulent Website Warning** switch to On (⬤).

**14** Scroll down the screen.

**15** If you want to clear your browsing history, tap **Clear History**.

**16** If you want to clear your cookies and cached data, tap **Clear Cookies and Data**.

**17** Tap **Advanced**.

The Advanced screen appears.

**18** Set the **JavaScript** switch to On (⬤) or Off (◯), as needed.

**Note:** Turning off JavaScript may remove some or most functionality of harmless sites.

**19** Tap **Safari**.

---

**TIP**

**What are cookies, and what threat do they pose?**

A *cookie* is a small text file that a website places on a computer to identify that computer in the future. This is helpful for many sites, such as shopping sites in which you add items to a shopping cart, but when used by malevolent sites, cookies can pose a threat to your privacy. You can set Safari to block all cookies, but this prevents many legitimate websites from working properly. So blocking cookies from third parties and advertisers is normally the best compromise.

# Read Your E-Mail Messages

fter you have set up Mail by synchronizing accounts from your computer, as described in Chapter 1, or by setting up accounts manually on the iPhone, as described in Chapter 4, you are ready to send and receive e-mail messages using your iPhone.

This task shows you how to read your incoming e-mail messages. You learn to reply to messages and write messages from scratch later in this chapter.

## Read Your E-Mail Messages

**1** Press the Home button.

The Home screen appears.

**2** Tap **Mail**.

The Mailboxes screen appears.

**Note:** If Mail does not show the Mailboxes screen, tap the button in the upper left corner until the Mailboxes screen appears.

**3** Tap the inbox you want to see.

**A** To see all your incoming messages together, tap **All Inboxes**. Depending on how you use e-mail, you may find seeing all your messages together helpful.

The inbox opens.

**B** A blue dot to the left of a message indicates that you have not read the message yet.

**C** A gray star to the left of a message indicates the message is from a VIP. See the second tip for information about VIPs.

**4** Tap the message you want to open.

The message opens.

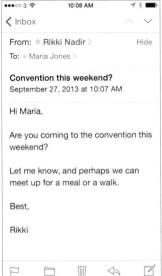

**5** Turn the iPhone sideways if you want to view the message in landscape orientation.

In landscape orientation, you can see the message at a larger size, so it is easier to read.

**6** Tap ∨.

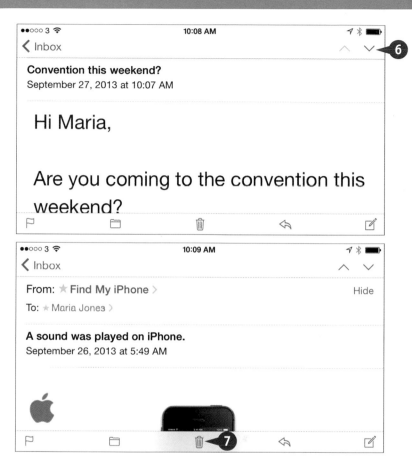

The next message appears.

**7** If you want to delete the message, tap 🗑.

**Note:** If you want to reply to the message, see the next task, "Reply To or Forward an E-Mail Message." If you want to file the message in a folder, see the task "Organize Your Messages in Mailbox Folders."

**Note:** The badge on the Mail icon on the Home screen shows how many unread messages Mail has found so far.

**How do I view the contents of another mailbox?**

From an open message, tap **Inbox** or **All Inboxes** to return to the inbox or the screen for all the inboxes. Tap **Mailboxes** to go back to the Mailboxes screen. You can then tap the mailbox you want to view.

**What is the VIP inbox on the Mailboxes screen?**

The VIP inbox is a tool for identifying important messages, no matter which e-mail account they come to. You mark particular contacts as being very important people to you, and Mail then adds messages from these VIPs to the VIP inbox. To add a VIP, tap the sender's name in an open message, then tap **Add to VIP** on the Sender screen.

# Reply To or Forward an E-Mail Message

After receiving an e-mail message, you often need to reply to it. You can choose between replying only to the sender of the message and replying to the sender and all the other recipients in the To field and the Cc field, if there are any. Recipients in the message's Bcc field, whose names you cannot see, do not receive your reply.

Other times, you may need to forward a message you have received to one or more other people. The Mail app makes both replying and forwarding messages as easy as possible.

## Reply To or Forward an E-Mail Message

### Open the Message You Will Reply To or Forward

**1** Press the Home button.

The Home screen appears.

**2** Tap **Mail**.

The Mailboxes screen appears.

**Note:** When you launch Mail, the app checks for new messages. This is why the number of new messages you see on the Mailboxes screen may differ from the number on the Mail badge on the Home screen.

**3** Tap the inbox you want to see.

The inbox opens.

**4** Tap the message you want to open.

The message opens.

**5** Tap **Action** (⤺).

The Action dialog opens.

**Note:** You can also reply to or forward a message by using Siri. For example, say "Reply to this message" or "Forward this message to Alice Smith," and then tell Siri what you want the message to say.

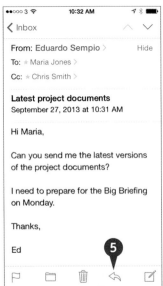

## Reply To the Message

**1** In the Action dialog, tap **Reply**.

**A** To reply to all recipients, tap **Reply All**. Reply to all recipients only when you are sure that they need to receive your reply. Often, it is better to reply only to the sender.

A screen containing the reply appears.

**2** Type your reply to the message.

**3** Tap **Send**.

Mail sends the message.

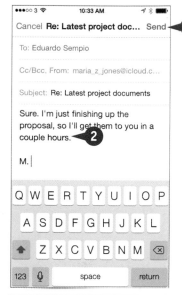

## Forward the Message

**1** In the Action dialog, tap **Forward**.

A screen containing the forwarded message appears.

**2** Type the recipient's address.

**B** Alternatively, you can tap ⊕ and choose the recipient in your Contacts list.

**3** Type a message if needed.

**4** Tap **Send**.

Mail sends the message.

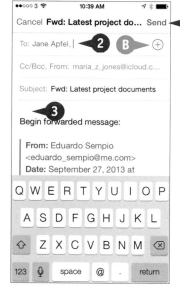

---

**Can I reply to or forward only part of a message?**
Yes. The quick way to do this is to select the part of the message you want to include before tapping **Action** (◁). Mail then includes only your selection. Alternatively, you can start the reply or forwarded message, and then delete the parts you do not want to include.

**How do I check for new messages?**
In a mailbox, tap and drag your finger down the screen, pulling down the messages. When a progress circle appears at the top, lift your finger. Mail checks for new messages.

# Organize Your Messages in Mailbox Folders

To keep your inbox or inboxes under control, you should organize your messages into mailbox folders.

You can quickly move a single message to a folder after reading it or after previewing it in the message list. Alternatively, you can select multiple messages in your inbox and move them all to a folder in a single action. You can also delete any message you no longer need.

## Organize Your Messages in Mailbox Folders

### Open Mail and Move a Single Message to a Folder

**1** Press the Home button.

The Home screen appears.

**2** Tap **Mail**.

The Mailboxes screen appears.

**3** Tap the mailbox you want to open.

The mailbox opens.

**4** Tap the message you want to read.

The message opens.

**5** Tap **Move** (🗀).

The Move This Message to a New Mailbox screen appears.

**6** Tap the mailbox to which you want to move the message.

Mail moves the message.

The next message in the mailbox appears, so that you can read it and file it if necessary.

**Note:** You can delete the open message by tapping 🗑.

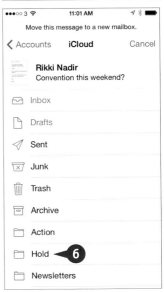

## Move Multiple Messages to a Folder

**1** In the mailbox, tap **Edit**.

An empty selection button ( ) appears to the left of each message, and the Trash button, Move button, and Mark button appear.

**2** Tap the selection button ( changes to ) next to each message you want to move.

**3** Tap **Move**.

The Mailboxes screen appears.

**4** Tap the mailbox to which you want to move the messages.

**Note:** To move the messages to a mailbox in another account, tap **Accounts** on the Move This Message to a New Mailbox screen. On the Accounts screen, tap the account, and then tap the mailbox.

Mail moves the messages.

## Move a Message from a Mailbox

**1** In the mailbox list, tap the message and swipe to the left.

The More button and Trash button appear.

**Note:** Tap **Trash** to delete the message.

**2** Tap **More**.

The More dialog opens.

**3** Tap **Move Message**.

The Mailboxes screen appears.

**4** Tap the mailbox to which you want to move the message.

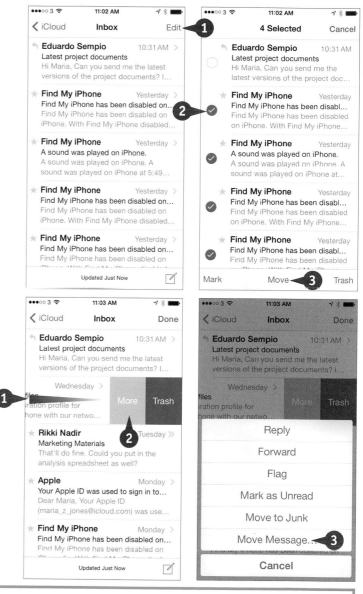

### TIP

**What do the Flag command and the Mark as Unread command do?**

Tap **Flag** (⚑) to set a flag on the message — for example, to indicate that you need to pay extra attention to it. The flag appears as an orange dot ( ● ).

Tap **Mark as Unread** to mark the message as not having been read, even though you have opened it. Sometimes it is helpful to mark a message as unread as a reminder that you need to read it properly later.

# Write and Send E-Mail Messages

Your iPhone is great for reading and replying to e-mail messages you receive, but you will likely also need to write new messages. When you do, you can use the data in the Contacts app to address your outgoing messages quickly and accurately. If the recipient's address is not one of your contacts, you can type the address manually.

You can attach one or more files to an e-mail message to send those files to the recipient. This works well for small files, but many mail servers reject files larger than several megabytes in size.

## Write and Send E-Mail Messages

**1** Press the Home button.

The Home screen appears.

**2** Tap **Mail**.

The Mailboxes screen appears.

**3** Tap **New Message** (✎).

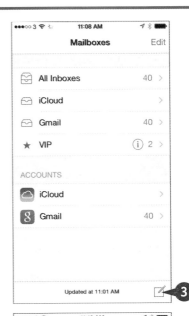

The New Message screen appears.

**4** Tap ⊕.

The Contacts list appears.

**Note:** If necessary, change the Contacts list displayed by tapping **Groups**, making your choice on the Groups screen, and then tapping **Done**.

**Ⓐ** If the person you are e-mailing is not a contact, type the address in the To area. You can also start typing here and then select a matching contact from the list that the Mail app displays.

**5** Tap the contact you want to send the message to.

**B** The contact's name appears in the To area.

**Note:** You can add other contacts to the To area by repeating steps **4** and **5**.

**6** If you need to add a Cc or Bcc recipient, tap **Cc/Bcc, From**.

The Cc, Bcc, and From fields expand.

**7** Tap the Cc area or Bcc area, and then follow steps **4** and **5** to add a recipient.

**C** To change the e-mail account you are sending the message from, tap **From**, and then tap the account to use.

**8** Tap **Subject**, and then type the message's subject.

**9** Tap below the Subject line, and then type the body of the message.

**10** Tap **Send**.

Mail sends the message.

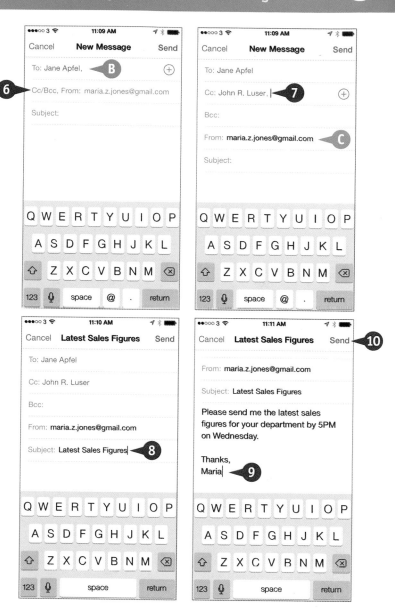

**How do I attach a file to a message?**
To attach a file to the message, start the message from the app that contains the file. For example, to send a photo, open the Photos app. Select the photo, tap **Share** (⬆), and then tap **Mail**. Mail starts a message with the photo attached. You then address the message and send it.

# View Files Attached to Incoming E-Mail Messages

E-mail is not just a great way to communicate; it is also a great way to transfer files quickly and easily. When you receive an e-mail message with a file attached to it, you can quickly view the file from the Mail app.

The Mail app automatically downloads small attachments. But if the attachment is a large file, the Mail app starts downloading it only when you open the message for reading. This behavior gives you the chance to delete the message and terminate the download if necessary.

## View Files Attached to Incoming E-Mail Messages

**1** Press the Home button.

The Home screen appears.

**2** Tap **Mail**.

The Mailboxes screen appears.

**3** Tap the inbox you want to open.

The inbox opens.

**A** A paperclip icon (📎) indicates that a message has one or more files attached.

**4** Tap the message you want to open.

The message opens.

**B** If Mail has not yet downloaded the file, tap the **Tap to Download** prompt to download it. A progress indicator appears.

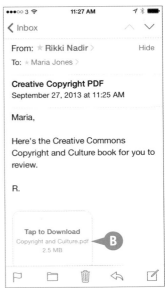

A button for the attachment appears.

**5** Tap the attachment's button.

The attached file opens in Mail's Viewer feature.

**Note:** The Viewer feature provides basic features for viewing widely used document types, such as PDF files, Microsoft Word documents, and Microsoft Excel workbooks. If the Viewer feature cannot open the file you try to open, your iPhone tries to suggest a suitable app.

**6** Tap **Share** (⬆).

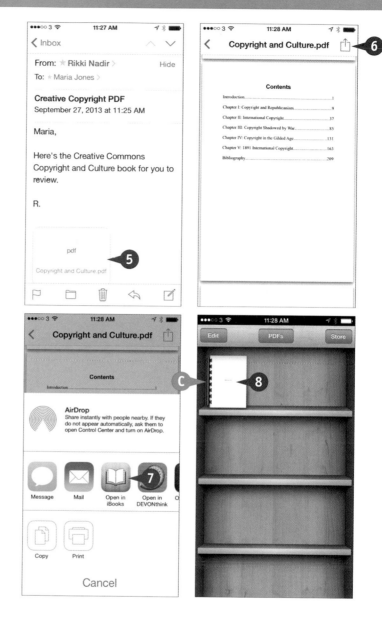

A screen for opening or using the attachment appears.

**7** Tap the app in which you want to open the document. For example, tap **Open in iBooks**.

**ⓒ** The file opens in the app you chose.

**8** Depending on the app, tap the file to open it.

**Note:** After you open an attached file in an app, your iPhone stores a copy of the file in that app's storage. You can then open the file again directly from that app.

---

**TIP**

**How can I delete an attached file from an e-mail message?**

You cannot directly delete an attached file from an e-mail message on the iPhone at this writing. You can delete only the message along with its attached file. If you use an e-mail app such as Apple Mail or web-based e-mail such as iCloud.com to manage the same e-mail account, you can remove the attached file using that app. When you update your mailbox on your iPhone, the iPhone deletes the attached file but leaves the message.

# Search for E-Mail Messages

To find a particular e-mail message, you can open the mailbox for the account that contains it and then browse for the message. But often you can locate a message more quickly by searching for it using a name or keyword that you know appears in the message.

You can search either in a single mailbox or in all your mailboxes together. Searching all mailboxes is useful when you are not sure what e-mail account contains the message.

## Search for E-Mail Messages

**1** Press the Home button.

The Home screen appears.

**2** Tap **Mail**.

The Mailboxes screen appears.

**3** Tap the mailbox you want to open. For example, tap **All Inboxes** to search all your inboxes for the message.

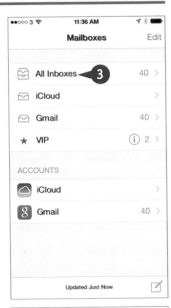

The mailbox opens.

**4** Tap and drag down to scroll up to the top of the screen.

**Note:** You can also tap the bar at the top of the screen to scroll to the top far enough to reveal the Search box.

The Search box appears.

**5** Tap in the Search box.

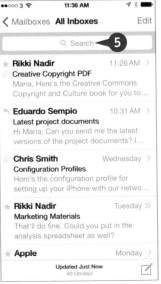

The keyboard appears.

**6** Type your search term.

A list of search results appears.

**7** If you need to change the scope of the search, drag down the screen, and then tap **All Mailboxes** or **Current Mailbox**, as needed.

**8** Tap the message you want to open.

The message opens.

---

**Is there another way to search for e-mail messages?**
Yes. You can use the iPhone's general search functionality to return e-mail matches along with other search results. Press the Home button to display the Home screen, and then drag down to display the Search box. Type your search term, locate the Mail search results, and then tap the message you want to see.

# CHAPTER 9

# Keeping Your Life Organized

You can use your iPhone to manage your contacts, keep your schedule, track commitments, and carry important documents.

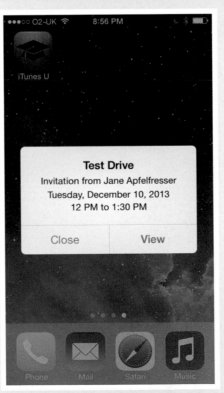

# Browse or Search for Contacts

Your iPhone's Contacts app enables you to store contact data that you sync from your computer or online accounts or that you enter directly on your iPhone. You can access the contacts either via the Contacts app itself or through the Contacts tab in the Phone app.

To see which contacts you have synced to your iPhone, or to find a particular contact, you can browse through the contacts. You can either browse through your full list of contacts or display particular groups, such as your business contacts. You can also locate contacts by searching for them.

## Browse or Search for Contacts

### Browse Your Contacts

**1** Press the Home button.

The Home screen appears.

**2** Tap **Extras**.

The Extras folder opens.

**3** Tap **Contacts**.

The Contacts screen appears.

**Note:** You can also access your contacts by pressing the Home button, tapping **Phone**, and then tapping **Contacts**.

**A** To navigate the screen of contacts quickly, tap the letter on the right that you want to jump to. To navigate more slowly, scroll up or down.

**4** Tap the contact whose information you want to view.

The contact's screen appears.

**Note:** From the contact's screen, you can quickly phone the contact by tapping the phone number you want to use.

**5** If necessary, tap and drag up to scroll down the screen to display more information.

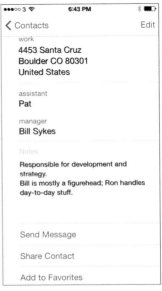

## Choose Which Groups of Contacts to Display

**1** From the Contacts screen, tap **Groups**.

The Groups screen appears.

**2** Tap **Show All Contacts**.

Contacts displays a check mark next to each group.

**Note:** When you tap **Show All Contacts**, the Hide All Contacts button appears in place of the Show All Contacts button. You can tap **Hide All Contacts** to remove all the check marks.

**3** Tap a group to apply a check mark to it or to remove the existing check mark.

**4** Tap **Done**.

The Contacts screen appears, showing the contacts in the groups you selected.

## Search for Contacts

**1** From the Contacts screen, tap **Search**.

The Search screen appears.

**2** Type the name you want to search for.

**3** From the list of matches, tap the contact you want to view.

The contact's information appears.

### How do I make my iPhone sort my contacts by last names instead of first names?

Press the Home button. Tap **Settings** and then **Mail, Contacts, Calendars**. In the Contacts area, tap **Sort Order**. Tap **Last, First**.

# Create a New Contact

Normally, you put contacts on your iPhone by syncing them from existing records on your computer or on an online service such as iCloud. But when necessary, you can create a new contact on your iPhone itself — for example, when you meet someone you want to remember.

You can then sync the contact record back to your computer or online service, adding the new contact to your existing contacts.

## Create a New Contact

**1** Press the Home button.

The Home screen appears.

**2** Tap **Phone**.

The Phone app opens.

**3** Tap **Contacts**.

The Contacts screen appears.

**Note:** You can also access the Contacts app by tapping the **Extras** folder on the Home screen, and then tapping the **Contacts** app.

**4** Tap **Add** (+).

The New Contact screen appears.

**5** Tap **First**.

The on-screen keyboard appears.

**6** Type the first name.

**7** Tap **Last**.

**8** Type the last name.

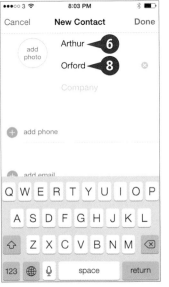

**9** Add other information as needed by tapping each field and then typing the information.

**10** To add a photo of the contact, tap **add photo**.

The Photo dialog opens.

**11** Tap **Take Photo**.

The Take Picture screen appears.

**12** Compose the photo, and then tap **Take Picture** (◯).

The Move and Scale screen appears.

**13** Position the part of the photo you want to use in the middle.

**Note:** Pinch in with two fingers to zoom the photo out. Pinch out with two fingers to zoom the photo in.

**14** Tap **Use Photo**.

The photo appears in the contact record.

**15** Tap **Done**.

**TIP**

**How do I assign my new contact an existing photo?**

**1** In the Photo dialog, tap **Choose Photo**.

**2** On the Photos screen, tap the photo album.

**3** Tap the photo.

**4** On the Move and Scale screen, position the photo, and then tap **Choose**.

# Share Contacts via E-Mail and Messages

Often in business or your personal life, you will need to share your contacts with other people. Your iPhone makes it easy to share a contact record via either e-mail or an instant message using the Multimedia Messaging Service, or MMS, as explained in this task. You can also share a contact record via AirDrop; see Chapter 6 for information on using AirDrop.

The iPhone shares the contact record as a virtual business card in the widely used vCard format. Most phones and personal-organizer software can easily import vCard files.

## Share Contacts via E-Mail and Messages

### Open the Contact You Want to Share

**1** Press the Home button.

The Home screen appears.

**2** Tap **Extras**.

The Extras folder opens.

**3** Tap **Contacts**.

The Contacts screen appears.

**Note:** You can also access the Contacts app from within the Phone app. From the Home screen, tap **Phone**, and then tap the **Contacts** tab at the bottom.

**4** Tap the contact you want to share.

The Info screen for the contact appears.

**5** Tap **Share Contact**.

The Share Contact Using dialog opens.

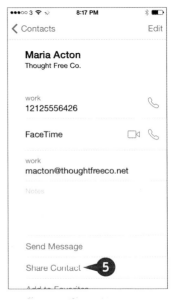

## Share a Contact via E-Mail

**1** In the Share Contact Using dialog, tap **Mail**.

**A** A new message appears in the Mail app, with the contact record attached as a vCard file.

**B** The contact's name appears in the Subject line.

**2** Address the message by typing the address or by tapping ⊕ and choosing a contact as the recipient.

**3** Type a message.

**4** Tap **Send**, and Mail sends the message with the contact record attached.

## Share a Contact via Message

**1** In the Share Contact Using dialog, tap **Message**.

**C** The New MMS screen appears, with the contact record attached to the message.

**2** Address the message by typing the name or number or by tapping ⊕ and choosing a contact as the recipient.

**3** Type a message.

**4** Tap **Send**, and the iPhone sends the message with the contact record attached.

## TIP

**How do I add a vCard I receive in an e-mail message to my contacts?**

In the Mail app, tap the button for the vCard file. A screen appears showing the vCard's contents. Scroll down to the bottom, and then tap **Create New Contact**. If the vCard contains extra information about an existing contact, tap **Add to Existing Contact**, and then tap the contact.

# Browse Existing Events in Your Calendars

Your iPhone's Calendar app gives you a great way of managing your schedule and making sure you never miss an appointment.

After setting up your calendars to sync using iTunes, iCloud, or another calendar service, as described in Chapter 1, you can take your calendars with you everywhere and consult them whenever you need to. You can view either all your calendars or only ones you choose.

## Browse Existing Events in Your Calendars

### Browse Existing Events in Your Calendars

**1** Press the Home button.

The Home screen appears.

**2** Tap **Calendar**.

The Calendar screen appears.

**A** The black circle indicates the day shown. When today is selected, the circle is red.

**B** Your events appear on a scrollable timeline.

**C** An event's background color indicates the calendar it belongs to.

**D** You can tap **Today** to display the current day.

**3** Tap the day you want to see.

The events for the day appear.

**4** Tap the month.

The calendar for the month appears.

**E** You can tap the year to display the calendar for the full year, in which you can navigate quickly to other months.

**5** Scroll up or down as needed, and then tap the date you want.

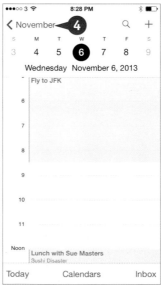

The date's appointments appear.

**6** Tap an event to see its details.

The Event Details screen appears.

**7** To edit the event, tap **Edit**.

The Edit screen appears, and you can make changes to the event. When you finish, tap **Done**.

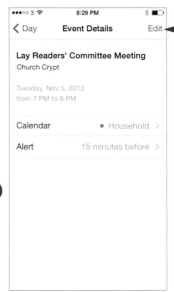

## Choose Which Calendars to Display

**1** At the bottom of the screen, tap **Calendars**.

**2** On the Calendars screen, tap to place a check mark next to a calendar you want to display, or tap to remove the check mark from a calendar you want to hide.

**F** Tap **Show All Calendars** to place a check mark next to each calendar. Tap **Hide All Calendars** to remove all check marks.

**G** The Birthdays calendar automatically displays birthdays of contacts whose contact data includes the birthday.

**H** You can set the **Show Declined Events** switch to On ( ) if you want to include invitations you have declined.

**3** Tap **Done**.

The calendars you chose appear.

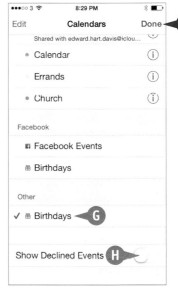

## TIP

**How can I quickly find an event?**
In the Calendar app, tap **Search** (🔍). Calendar displays a list of your events. Type your search term. When Calendar displays a list of matches, tap the event you want to view.

# Create New Events in Your Calendars

Normally, you will probably create most new events in your calendars on your computer, and then sync them to your iPhone. But when you need to create a new event using the iPhone, you can easily do so.

You can create either a straightforward, one-shot appointment or an appointment that repeats on a schedule. You can also choose the calendar in which to store the appointment.

## Create New Events in Your Calendars

1. Press the Home button.

   The Home screen appears.

2. Tap **Calendar**.

   The Calendar screen appears.

3. Tap the day on which you want to create the new event.

**Note:** You can also tap the current month and use the month-by-month calendar to navigate to the date. Alternatively, leave the current date selected, and then change the date when creating the event.

4. Tap **Add** (+).

   The Add Event screen appears.

5. Tap **Title** and type the title of the event.

6. Tap **Location** and type the location of the event.

7. Tap **Starts**.

The time and date controls appear.

**8** Tap the date and time controls to set the start time.

**9** Tap **Ends**.

**10** Tap the date and time controls to set the end time.

**A** If this is an all-day appointment, set the **All-day** switch to On (⬤).

**B** If you need to change the time zone, tap **Time Zone**, type the city name, and then tap the time zone.

**11** Tap **Alert**.

**12** On the Event Alert screen, tap the timing for the alert.

**13** Tap **Add Event**.

**14** On the Add Event screen, tap **Calendar**.

**15** On the Calendar screen, tap the calendar for the event.

**16** Tap **Add Event**.

**17** On the Add Event screen, tap **Done**.

The event appears on your calendar.

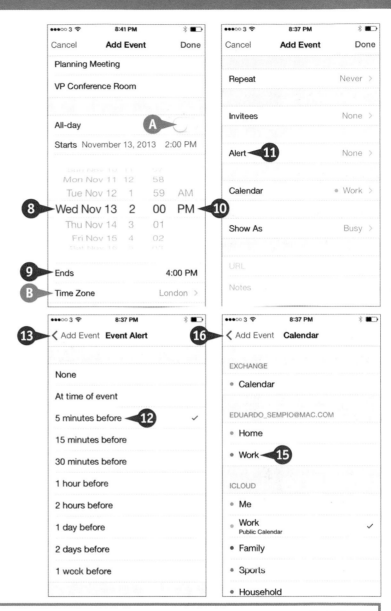

## TIP

**How do I set up an event that repeats every week?**
On the Add Event screen, tap **Repeat**. On the Repeat screen, tap **Every Week** (**A**), placing a check mark next to it.

# Work with Calendar Invitations

As well as events you create yourself, you may receive invitations to events that others create. When you receive an event invitation attached to an e-mail message, you can choose whether to accept the invitation or decline it. If you accept the invitation, you can add the event automatically to your calendar.

## Work with Calendar Invitations

### Deal with an Invitation from an Alert

**1** When an invitation alert appears, tap **View**.

**2** On the Event Details screen, tap **Calendar**, if you decide to accept the invitation.

**3** On the Calendar screen, tap the Calendar to which you want to assign the event.

**Ⓐ** A check mark appears next to the calendar.

**4** Tap the event's name.

**5** On the Event Details screen, tap **Alert**, if you want to set an alert to remind yourself about the event.

**6** On the Event Alert screen, tap the button for the alert interval. For example, tap **15 minutes before**.

**Ⓑ** A check mark appears on the button.

**7** Tap the event's name.

**8** On the Event Details screen, tap **Show As** if you need to change whether the time appears in your calendar as Busy or Free.

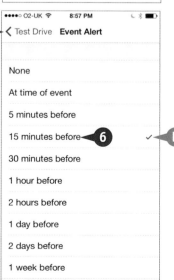

The Show As screen appears.

**9** Tap **Busy** or **Free**, as appropriate.

**C** A check mark appears on the button you tapped.

**10** Tap the event's name.

The Event Details screen appears.

**11** Tap **Accept** to accept the invitation.

Calendar adds the invitation to your calendar.

**Note:** After you set an alert for an event, the Second Alert button appears. You can tap this button to set a second alert for the event.

## Deal with an Invitation from the Inbox Screen

**D** In your calendar, the Inbox button shows an alert giving the number of invitations.

**1** Tap **Inbox**.

The Inbox screen appears.

**2** Tap **Accept**, **Decline**, or **Maybe**, as needed.

**Note:** To see the full detail of the invitation, tap its button on the Inbox screen. The Event Details screen then appears, and you can accept the invitation as described earlier in this task.

**3** Tap **Done**.

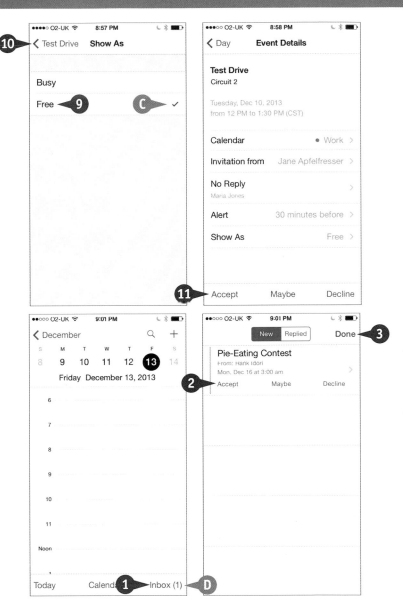

## TIP

**Why does an event appear at a different time than that shown in the invitation I accepted?**
When you open the invitation, you see the event's time in the time zone in which it was created. If your iPhone is currently using a different time zone, the appointment appears in your calendar using that time zone's time, so the time appears to have changed.

# Keep Track of Your Commitments with Reminders

Your iPhone's Reminders app gives you an easy way to note your commitments and keep track of them. The Reminders app comes with a built-in list called Reminders, but you can create as many other lists as you need — for example, Errands, Shopping, or Household.

You can create a reminder with no due time or location, but it is often more useful to tie each reminder to a due time, arriving at or leaving a location, or both. When you create such reminders, your iPhone can remind you of them at the appropriate time or place.

## Keep Track of Your Commitments with Reminders

### Open the Reminders App and Create Your Reminder Lists

**1** Press the Home button.

The Home screen appears.

**2** Tap **Reminders**.

The Reminders app opens. At first, the Lists screen appears.

**A** The Tasks list appears on the Lists screen if you sync your iPhone with an Exchange account for which you have enabled Reminders.

**3** Tap **New List**.

The New List screen appears.

**Note:** If you have only one Notes account, Reminders does not prompt you to choose the account to use.

**4** Tap the account in which you want to store the list.

The keyboard appears.

**5** Type the name for the list.

**6** Tap the color to use for the list.

**Note:** Use different colors for your reminders lists so you can see at a glance to which list a task belongs.

**7** Tap **Done**.

The list appears.

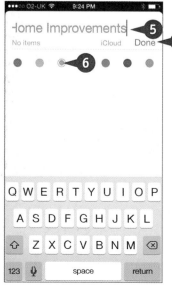

## Create a New Reminder

**1** To create a new reminder in this list, tap the first line.

**B** To return to the Lists screen so you can switch to another list, tap the tabbed pages at the bottom of the screen.

The keyboard appears.

**2** Type the text for the reminder.

**3** Tap ⓘ.

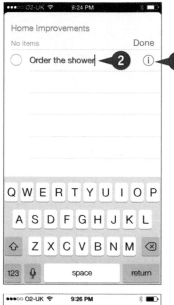

The Details screen appears.

**4** To create a time-based reminder, set the **Remind me on a day** switch to On ( ◯ ).

The Alarm and Repeat controls appear.

**5** Tap **Alarm**.

The date and time controls appear.

**6** Set the date and time for the reminder.

**7** If you need to repeat the reminder, tap **Repeat**, choose the repeat interval on the Repeat screen, and then tap **Details** to return to the Details screen.

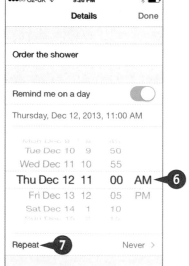

## TIP

**How do I sync my iPhone's reminders with my Mac's reminders?**

You can sync your iPhone's reminders with your Mac's reminders via your iCloud account.

On your iPhone, press the Home button to display the Home screen, and then tap **Settings** to display the Settings screen. Tap **iCloud** to display the iCloud screen, and then set the **Reminders** switch to On ( ◯ ).

On your Mac, click  and **System Preferences** to open System Preferences. Click **iCloud** to display the iCloud pane, and then select the **Calendars & Reminders** check box ( ☐ changes to ☑ ).

continued ▶

You can assign different priorities to your reminders to give yourself a quick visual reference of their urgency. You can also add notes to a reminder to keep relevant information at hand.

When you have completed a reminder, you can mark it as completed. You can view your list of scheduled reminders for quick reference, and you can choose whether to include your completed reminders in the list. If you no longer need a reminder, you can delete it from the list.

## Keep Track of Your Commitments with Reminders (continued)

**8** To create a location-based reminder, set the **Remind me at a location** switch to On (⬤).

**Note:** If Reminders prompts you to allow it to use your current location, tap **OK.**

**9** Tap **Location**.

The Location screen appears.

**10** Type the location in the Search box.

**Ⓐ** You can tap **Current Location** to use your current location.

**11** Tap the location in the list of results.

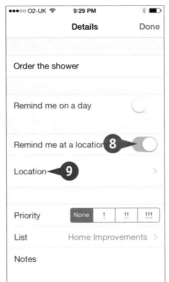

A map of the location appears.

**12** Tap **When I arrive** or **When I leave**.

**13** Tap **Details**.

The Details screen appears.

**14** To assign a priority to the reminder, tap **None**, **!**, **!!**, or **!!!**.

**Ⓑ** To assign the reminder to a different list than the current list, tap **List**. On the Change List screen, tap the list you want to use.

**15** To add a note to the reminder, tap **Notes** and type the text.

**16** Tap **Done**.

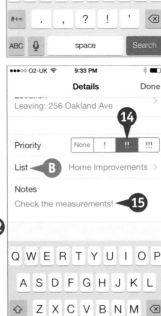

The new reminder appears on your list of reminders.

**17** Tap the next line to start creating a new reminder.

**C** When you finish a task, tap ○ (○ changes to ◉) to mark the reminder as complete.

**Note:** To delete a reminder, tap **Edit** on the screen that contains it. Tap ● to its left, and then tap **Delete**.

**18** Tap the tabbed pages at the bottom of the screen to switch to another reminder list.

## View a List of Your Scheduled Reminders

**1** From the Lists screen, tap **Scheduled** (▦).

The Scheduled list appears.

**D** You can tap **Show Completed** to include the reminders you have marked as complete. Tap **Hide Completed** when you no longer need to see these.

**2** Tap the reminder you want to see.

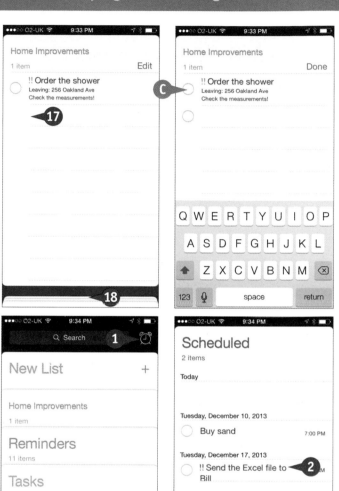

**How do I change the default list that Reminders puts my reminders in?**
Press the Home button to display the Home screen, and then tap **Settings** to display the Settings screen. Tap **Reminders** to display the Reminders screen, tap **Default List** to display the Default List screen, and then tap the list you want to make the default. On the Reminders screen, you can also choose how many reminders to sync — **Reminders 2 Weeks Back**, **Reminders 1 Month Back**, **Reminders 3 Months Back**, **Reminders 6 Months Back**, or **All Reminders**.

# Keep Essential Documents at Hand with Passbook

Passbook is an app for storing electronic versions of essential documents such as boarding passes, cinema tickets, and hotel reservations.

To get your documents into Passbook, you use apps such as Mail and Safari. For example, when an airline sends you your travel details attached to an e-mail message, you can add the boarding pass to Passbook from Mail. You can also add documents using custom apps for shopping, booking hotels, and booking flights.

## Keep Essential Documents at Hand with Passbook

### Add a Document to Passbook

1 In Mail, tap the message with the document attached.

The message opens.

2 Tap the document's button.

The document appears.

3 Tap **Add**.

**Note:** If there are multiple documents, tap **Add All**.

Mail adds the document to Passbook.

The message appears again.

**Note:** In Safari, open the web page containing the document, and then tap **Add** to add it to Passbook.

### Open Passbook and Find the Documents You Need

1 Press the Home button.

The Home screen appears.

2 Tap **Passbook**.

Passbook opens.

The documents you have added appear.

**Note:** Until you add one or more documents to Passbook, the app displays an information screen highlighting its uses.

3 Tap the document you want to view.

**Ⓐ** The document appears above the other documents. You can then hold its barcode in front of a scanner to use the document.

**④** To see another document, tap the current top document and drag down.

**⑤** At the bottom of the screen, release the document.

Passbook reshuffles the documents so you can see them all.

## Choose Settings for a Document or Delete It

**①** Tap ⓘ.

The document rotates so you can see its back.

**②** Set the **Automatic Updates** switch to On (⬜) if you want to receive updates to this document.

**③** Set the **Show On Lock Screen** switch to On (⬜) if you want notifications about the document to appear on the lock screen.

**Ⓑ** If you have no further need for the document, tap **Delete** to delete it.

**④** When you finish reviewing the document, tap **Done**.

The document rotates to display its front.

---

**TIP**

**What other actions can I take with documents in Passbook?**
You can share a document with other people via e-mail, instant messaging, or AirDrop. To access these features, tap **Share** (⬆), and then tap **AirDrop**, **Mail**, or **Message** on the sharing sheet that appears.

# CHAPTER 10

# Playing Music and Videos

As well as being a phone and a powerful hand-held computer, your iPhone is also a full-scale music and video player. To play music, you use the Music app; to play videos, you use the Videos app. In this chapter, you learn to use the Music app to play back music and radio and create playlists. You also learn how to enjoy podcasts and iTunes U lectures, play videos, and shop on the iTunes Store.

# Play Back Music Using the Music App

After loading music on your iPhone, as described in the task "Choose Which Items to Sync from Your Computer" in Chapter 1, you can play it back using the Music app.

You can play music in several ways. You can play music by song or by album, as described in this task. You can play songs in exactly the order you want by creating a custom playlist, as described in the task "Create a Playlist with the Music App." You can also play by artist, genre, or composer.

## Play Back Music Using the Music App

**1** Press the Home button.

**2** On the Home screen, tap **Music**.

**3** On the Music screen, tap the button by which you want to sort. This example uses **Songs**.

The list of songs appears.

**Ⓐ** To see the music listed by another category, such as Genres, tap **More**, and then tap the category by which you want to sort.

**Ⓑ** Tap a letter on the right side to jump to the first item starting with that letter.

**4** Tap the song you want to play.

The song's details appear, and the song plays.

**5** Tap and drag the playhead to change the position in the song.

**6** Tap and drag the volume control.

**7** Tap the album artwork.

If the song contains the text of its lyrics, the Song Lyrics panel appears.

**8** Tap the Song Lyrics panel to display the album artwork again.

**9** Tap **Shuffle** if you want to shuffle the order of songs. Shuffle All replaces Shuffle. Tap **Shuffle All** to turn off shuffling.

**10** Tap **Repeat**.

The Repeat dialog appears.

**11** Tap **Repeat Song** to repeat just this song. Tap **Repeat All** to repeat all songs in the current list. Tap **Repeat Off** to turn off repeating.

**12** Tap **Song List** (⊟).

The list of songs in the current album appears.

**13** Tap the song you want to play, or tap **Done** to continue playing the current song.

**14** To navigate to another album visually, turn your iPhone to landscape orientation.

A screen of album covers appears.

**15** Tap the album you want to play.

The list of songs on the album appears.

**16** Tap the song you want to play.

The song starts playing.

**Note:** Only some songs include the text of their lyrics. You may need to add the text to other songs using iTunes or another app on your computer.

## TIP

**Is there a way to control the Music app's playback when I have switched to another app?**
Yes. You can quickly control the Music app from Control Center. Press the Home button to display the Home screen, and then swipe up from the bottom of the screen to display Control Center. You can then use the playhead to move through the song, control playback using the playback buttons, and tap and drag the volume slider to adjust the volume. When you finish using Control Center, drag down from the top to close it.

# Play Back Videos Using the Videos App

To play videos — such as movies, TV shows, or music videos — you use the iPhone's Videos app. You can play back a video either on the iPhone's screen, which is handy when you are traveling, or on a TV to which you connect the iPhone, or to a TV connected to an Apple TV box. Using a TV is great when you need to share a movie or other video with family, friends, or colleagues.

## Play Back Videos Using the Videos App

**1** Press the Home button.

The Home screen appears.

**Note:** You can also play videos included on web pages. To do so, press the Home button, tap **Safari**, navigate to the page, and then tap the video.

**2** Tap **Videos**.

The Videos screen appears.

**3** Tap the video you want to play.

The information screen for the video appears, showing the video's preview frame and name.

**4** Scroll down to see further details about the video.

**Note:** If you are about to play a landscape video, turn your iPhone sideways to view the video in landscape orientation.

**5** Tap **Play** (▶).

The playback controls appear at first, but then disappear within a few seconds if you do not use them.

The video starts playing.

6 When you need to control playback, tap the screen.

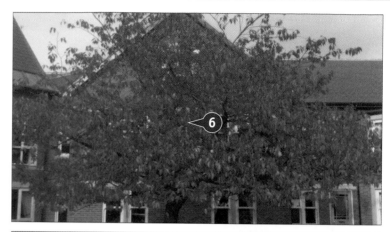

The playback controls appear, and you can pause the video, move forward, or take other actions.

7 Tap **Done** when you want to stop playing the video.

TIP

**How do I play back videos on my television from my iPhone?**

If you have an Apple TV or AirPlay-compatible device, use AirPlay, as explained in the next task, "Play Music and Videos Using AirPlay."

Otherwise, use the Apple Lightning Digital AV Adapter and an HDMI cable to connect your iPhone to a TV. The content of your iPhone's screen then appears on the TV's screen.

# Play Music and Videos Using AirPlay

Playing music and videos on your iPhone can be great, but sharing them with others is often even better. Using the AirPlay feature, you can play music from your iPhone on remote speakers connected to an AirPlay-compatible device such as an AirPort Express or Apple TV.

Similarly, you can play video from your iPhone on a TV or monitor connected to an Apple TV. Even better, you can use the iOS feature called AirPlay Mirroring to display an iPhone app on a TV or monitor. For example, you can display a web page in Safari on your TV screen.

## Play Music and Videos Using AirPlay

### Play Music on External Speakers Using AirPlay

1. In the Music app, tap the song you want to play.

   The song's screen appears, and the song starts playing.

2. Tap and swipe up from the bottom of the screen.

   Control Center opens.

3. Tap **AirPlay**.

   The AirPlay dialog opens.

4. Tap the speakers or Apple TV you want to use.

5. Tap **Done**.

   The AirPlay dialog closes.

   The AirPlay button shows the device you selected.

   The music starts playing through the AirPlay device.

6. Tap in the Music app above Control Center.

   Control Center closes, and the Music app appears full screen.

## Play a Video from Your iPhone to Your TV's Screen

1 In the Videos app, start the video playing.

2 Tap **AirPlay** (■).

3 Tap the AirPlay device to use.

The video content appears on the TV or monitor connected to the AirPlay device. The Videos app displays a message that the content is playing on an AirPlay device.

## Display an iPhone App on Your TV's Screen

1 With the app open, navigate to the content to display, the Maps app for example.

2 Tap and swipe up from the bottom of the screen to open Control Center.

3 Tap **AirPlay** (■).

4 Tap the AirPlay device to use.

5 Set the **Mirroring** switch to On (■).

6 Tap **Done**.

The TV or monitor mirrors the iPhone's screen.

7 Tap in the app to close Control Center.

## TIPS

**Why does the AirPlay button not appear in Control Center?**
The AirPlay button appears only when your iPhone is connected to a wireless network to which AirPlay devices are attached. If you use multiple wireless networks, make sure your iPhone is connected to the right network.

**Can AirPlay play music through multiple sets of speakers at the same time?**
AirPlay can play music through two or more sets of speakers at the same time, enabling you to play music throughout your home. But at this writing, AirPlay on the iPhone can play only to a single device at a time. To play to multiple devices, you need to use AirPlay on a Mac or PC.

# Create a Playlist with the Music App

**I**nstead of playing individual songs or playing a CD's songs from start to finish, you can create a playlist that contains only the songs you want in your preferred order. Playlists are a great way to enjoy music on your iPhone.

You can either create a standard playlist by putting the songs in order yourself, or use the Genius Playlist feature to have the Music app create the playlist for you.

## Create a Playlist with the Music App

**1** Press the Home button.

The Home screen appears.

**2** Tap **Music**.

The Music screen appears.

**3** Tap **Playlists**.

The Playlists screen appears.

**A** The Genius symbol (⚛) indicates a Genius playlist.

**4** Tap **New Playlist**.

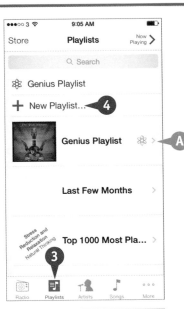

The New Playlist dialog opens.

**5** Type the name for the playlist.

**6** Tap **Save**.

The Songs screen appears.

**7** Tap + for each song you want to add, or simply tap the song's button.

**B** The text on the song button fades to gray to show you have added the song to the playlist.

**C** To browse by artists for songs to add, tap **Artists**. To browse by playlists, tap **Playlists**. To browse by albums, tap **Albums**.

**8** Tap **Done**.

The playlist screen appears.

**9** Tap **Edit**.

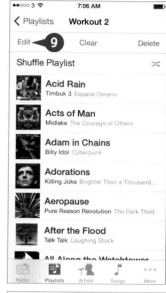

The screen for editing the playlist appears.

**10** Tap ≡ and drag a song up or down to move it.

**D** To remove a song, tap ⊖.

**11** Tap **Done** at the top of the playlist editing screen.

**12** Tap a song to start the playlist playing.

**E** Tap **Shuffle Playlist** if you want to play the playlist's songs in random order.

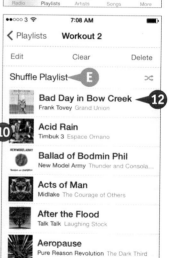

---

**TIP**

**How do I create a Genius playlist on my iPhone?**

Press the Home button. Tap **Music**, tap **Playlists**, and then tap **Genius Playlist**. Tap the song (**A**) to base the playlist on. The Music app creates the playlist and sets it playing.

# Customize the Music App's Interface

The Music app comes set up so that you can easily browse by playlists, artists, songs, or albums. If you want to browse by other categories, such as by composers or by genres, you can customize the Music app's interface to put these items at the tip of your finger.

## Customize the Music App's Interface

**1** Press the Home button.

The Home screen appears.

**2** Tap **Music**.

The Music screen appears.

**3** Tap **More**.

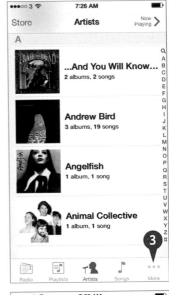

The More screen appears.

**4** Tap **Edit**.

The Configure screen appears.

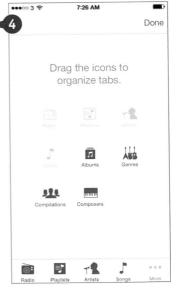

**5** Tap a button and drag it to replace a button on the button bar. For example, tap **Genres** and drag it on top of **Albums**.

The button you dropped replaces the button you dropped it on.

**6** Change other buttons as needed.

**Note:** You can change the position of the buttons on the button bar by tapping a button and dragging it left or right to where you want it.

**7** Tap **Done**.

**A** You can then use your customized version of the Music screen.

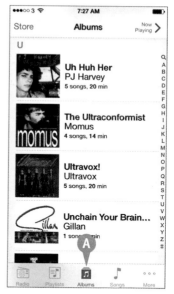

---

## TIP

**How do I reset the Music screen to its default settings?**

The straightforward way to reset the Music app's screen to its default settings is to display the Configure screen as described in this task, and drag the icons into their default order: Playlists, Artists, Songs, Albums, and More.

You can also return the Music app's screen to its default configuration from the Reset screen in Settings, but this is a wide-ranging change that you normally do not want to make.

# Listen to iTunes Radio

Your iPhone's Music app includes iTunes Radio, a feature for listening to streaming radio across the Internet and setting up personalized stations that play the types of music you prefer. While listening to a song, you can choose to hear more songs like it, ask not to hear this song again, or create a custom station based on the artist or the song. When you find a song you must have, you can buy it from the iTunes Store.

At this writing, iTunes Radio is available only in the United States because of the complexities of licensing music. Some features are available only if you have an iTunes Match subscription.

## Listen to iTunes Radio

### Open the Music App and Launch iTunes Radio

**1** Press the Home button.

The Home screen appears.

**2** Tap **Music**.

The Music app opens.

**3** Tap **Radio**.

The Radio screen appears.

**4** Tap a station you want to hear.

The station's screen appears.

The station starts playing.

**A** Tap **❚❚** to pause playback.

**B** Tap **▶▶** if you want to skip to the next song.

**5** To control whether you hear music like the current song, tap ★.

The control dialog opens.

**6** Tap the appropriate button:

**C** Tap **Play More Like This** to indicate you like this type of music.

**D** Tap **Never Play This Song** to register your dislike.

**E** Tap **Add to iTunes Wish List** to add the song to your Wish List in iTunes.

The dialog closes.

**F** If you tapped **Play More Like This**, the star icon turns red (★ changes to ★).

If you tapped **Never Play This Song**, Radio starts playing the next song.

**7** Tap ⓘ.

The information screen appears.

**8** Tap the appropriate button:

**G** Tap the price button to display this song in the iTunes Store.

**H** Tap **New Station from Artist** if you want to create a new station based on the artist.

**I** Tap **New Station from Song** to create a new station based on the song.

## Add a Station to Your List

**1** On the Radio home screen, tap **Edit** to the left of My Stations.

The Edit Stations screen appears.

**2** Tap **New Station**.

The New Station screen appears.

**3** Tap the type of music you want. For example, tap **Classic Rock**.

**J** Alternatively, tap the Search box and type an artist name, song name, or genre on which to base the station.

**4** On the screen that appears, tap the station you want to add.

 **TIP**

**How do I remove a station I no longer want to listen to?**
In the Music app, tap the **Radio** button, and then tap **Edit** to the left of My Stations. On the Edit Stations screen, tap the station you want to remove. At the bottom of the station's screen, tap **Delete Station**, then tap **Delete** in the confirmation dialog.

# Watch Podcasts and iTunes U Lessons

**B**esides listening to music and watching videos, you can use your iPhone to watch or listen to *podcasts*, which are video or audio programs released via the Internet.

You can find podcasts covering many different topics by using Apple's Podcasts app. Similarly, you can use the iTunes U app to access podcasts containing free educational content. iTunes U also acts as a portal to other types of content including paid material.

## Watch Podcasts and iTunes U Lessons

**1** Press the Home button.

The Home screen appears.

**2** Tap **Podcasts**.

**Note:** If the Podcasts app does not appear on the Home screen, go to the App Store and install it. See Chapter 7 for instructions on installing apps.

The Podcasts app opens.

**Note:** At first, when you have added no podcasts, you see an informational message.

**3** Tap **Store**.

The Podcasts app displays the Podcasts area in the iTunes Store.

**4** Tap **Categories**.

The Categories screen appears.

**5** Tap the category you want to see.

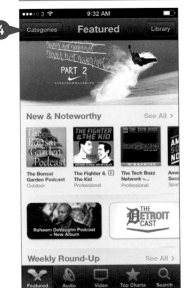

The screen for the category appears.

**6** Tap **Featured**, **Audio**, **Video**, or **Top Charts**, as needed.

**Note:** You can also search for podcasts by tapping **Search** and then typing search terms in the Search box.

**7** Tap the podcast you want to view.

**8** Tap **Subscribe** if you want to subscribe to the podcast.

**9** Tap ⬇ to download an episode of the podcast.

**10** Tap the button in the upper left corner to display the previous screen.

**11** Tap **Library**.

**12** Tap the podcast whose episodes you want to see.

**13** Tap the episode you want to play.

The episode starts playing.

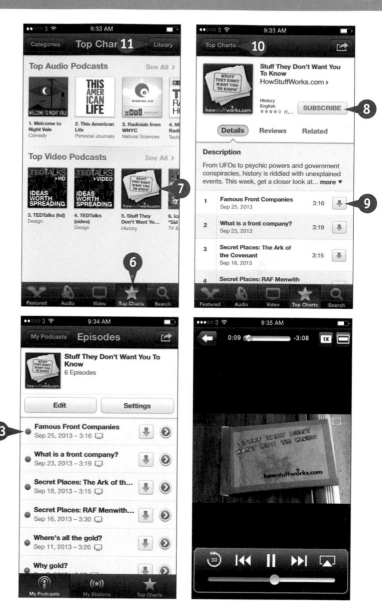

**How do I use iTunes U?**

iTunes U works in a similar way to the Podcasts app. Press the Home button, and then tap **iTunes U** to launch the app. Tap **Catalog** to display the Catalog screen, and then browse to find lectures you want to view. Tap **Library** to display the Library screen, and then tap the item you want to play.

# Shop for Music and Video at the iTunes Store

To find music and videos for your iPhone, you can shop at Apple's iTunes Store by using the iTunes app.

When you buy music or videos from the iTunes Store using the iTunes app, the iPhone downloads the files, so you can play them immediately. When you sync your iPhone with your computer, iTunes copies the music or videos you have bought to your computer. If you use your iPhone without a computer, you can sync the files to iCloud so that you can use them on your other devices — for example, on an iPad.

## Shop for Music and Video at the iTunes Store

**1** Press the Home button.

The Home screen appears.

**2** Tap **iTunes Store**.

The iTunes screen appears.

**3** Tap **Music** or **Videos** on the button bar to display the type of content you want. This example uses **Music**.

The screen you chose appears.

**4** Tap **Genres**.

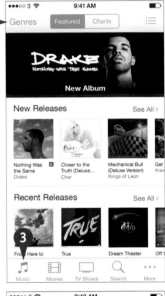

The Genres screen appears.

**5** Tap the genre you want — for example, **Alternative**.

The genre's screen appears.

**6** Tap the album or song you want to display.

The album's screen appears.

**7** Tap a song title to play a preview.

**A** Tap **Stop** (⊙) to stop the preview playing.

**8** To buy a song, tap the price button.

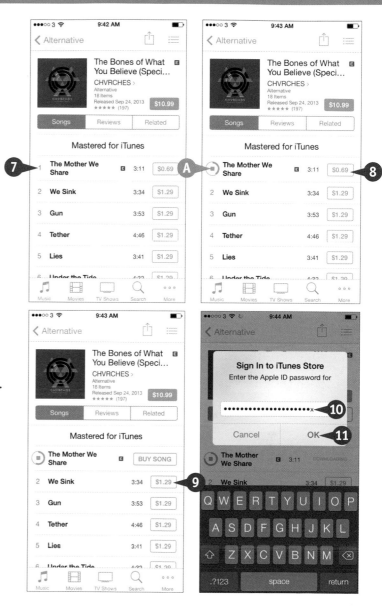

The Buy Song button replaces the price button.

**9** Tap **Buy Song**.

The Sign In to iTunes Store dialog opens.

**10** Type your password.

**11** Tap **OK**.

iTunes downloads the song, and you can play it using the Music app.

---

**TIP**

**How can I find the music I want at the iTunes Store?**
You can easily search for music within the iTunes app. Tap **Search** on the button bar at the bottom of the screen, and then type a search term. iTunes shows matching results as you type. Tap the result you want to view.

# CHAPTER 11

# Working with Photos and Books

In this chapter, you learn to use the Photos app to view and share photos. You also learn to use iBooks to read e-books and PDF files.

# Browse Photos Using Years, Collections, and Moments

You can use the Photos app to browse the photos you have taken with your iPhone's camera, photos you have synced using iTunes or via iCloud's Shared Streams feature, and images you receive in e-mail messages or download from web pages.

You can browse your photos by date and locations using the smart groupings that Photos creates. You open a Year grouping to reach the Collections it contains, tap a collection to access the Moments within it, and then tap a Moment to browse its photos. Alternatively, you can browse by albums, as explained in the next task, "Browse Photos Using Streams."

## Browse Photos Using Years, Collections, and Moments

**1** Press the Home button.

The Home screen appears.

**2** Tap **Photos**.

The Photos app opens.

**3** Tap **Photos**.

The Photos screen appears, showing the Years list.

**4** Tap the year you want to open.

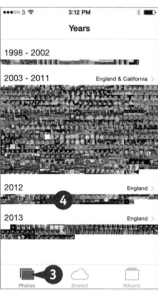

The Collections screen for the year appears.

**5** Tap the collection you want to open.

**Note:** Scroll up or down as needed to see other collections.

The Moments screen for the collection appears.

**6** Tap the photo you want to view.

The photo opens.

Ⓐ You can tap **Edit** to edit the photo, as explained in Chapter 13.

Ⓑ You can tap **Share** (⬆) to share the photo, as explained later in this chapter.

Ⓒ You can tap **Trash** (🗑) to delete the photo.

**Note:** If the Trash icon does not appear, this photo is one you cannot delete — for example, because it belongs to a shared photo stream rather than to your photo library.

**7** Tap and swipe left or right to display other photos in the moment.

Another photo appears.

**8** Tap **Moments**.

The Moments screen appears.

**Note:** You can scroll up or down to display other moments, and then tap a photo to open it.

**9** Tap **Collections**.

The Collections screen appears.

**Note:** You can scroll up or down to display other collections, and then tap a collection to open it.

**10** Tap **Years**.

The Years screen appears, and you can navigate to another year.

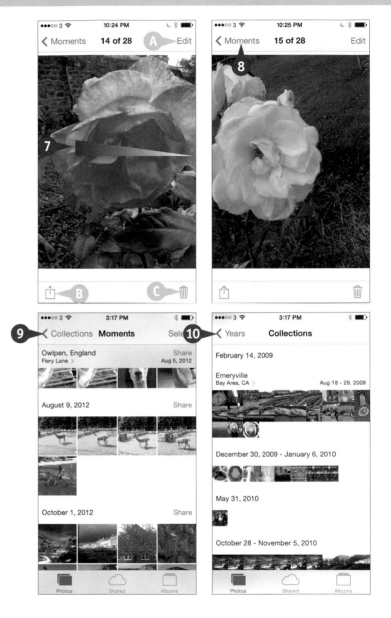

---

## TIP

**How can I move a photo to a different year?**

To move a photo to a different year, you need to change the date set in the photo's metadata. You cannot do this with the Photos app, but you can change the date with a third-party app such as Pixelgarde, which is free from the App Store at this writing. Alternatively, if you sync the photos from your computer, you can change the date in the photo on your computer. For example, in iPhoto on OS X, click **Photos** and **Adjust Date and Time**.

# Browse Photos Using Streams

Your iPhone's Photos app includes a feature called Shared Streams that enables you to share photos easily with others via iCloud and enjoy the photos they are sharing. In this task, you learn how to add other people's shared streams to the Photos app on your iPhone by accepting invitations. You also learn how to browse through the photos they are sharing.

Later in this chapter, you learn to share your own photos via Shared Streams.

## Browse Photos Using Streams

### Accept an Invitation to a Shared Stream

1. When you receive an invitation to a photo stream, open the e-mail message in Mail.

2. Tap **Subscribe to this Photo Stream**.

   The Photos app becomes active, and the Shared Streams screen appears.

   The new stream appears on the Shared Streams screen.

**Note:** The Activity item at the top of the Shared Streams screen shows new activity on your shared streams. When you add a shared stream, the Activity thumbnail shows the new stream's thumbnail.

3. Tap the new stream.

   The new stream's screen appears.

4. Tap a photo.

   The photo opens.

Ⓐ You can tap **Add a comment** to add a comment on the photo.

Ⓑ You can tap **Share** (⏏) to share the photo with others.

Ⓒ You can swipe left or right to display other photos.

5. Tap the stream's name.

   The Shared Streams screen appears.

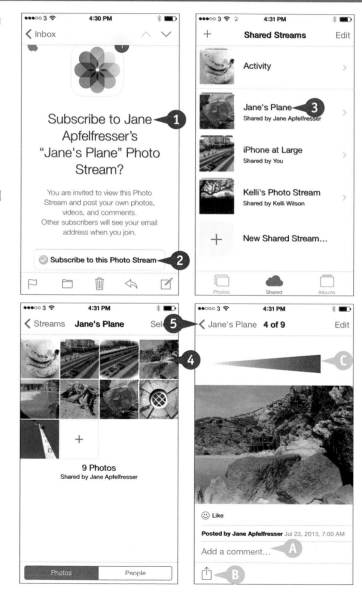

## Browse the Latest Activity on Shared Streams

1 In the Photos app, tap **Shared**.

The Shared Streams screen appears.

2 Tap **Activity**.

The Activity screen appears.

3 Tap a photo.

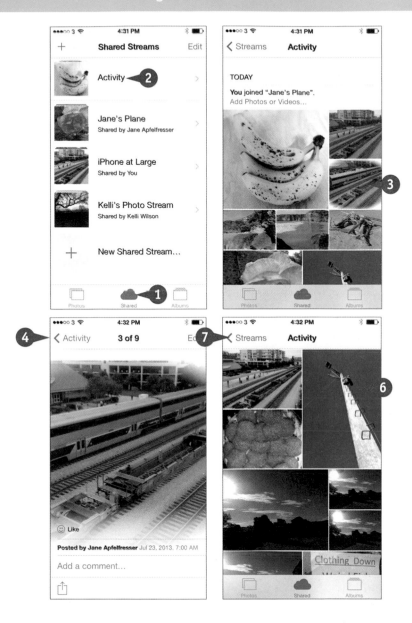

The photo opens.

4 Tap **Activity**.

The Activity screen appears.

5 Scroll down the screen to view further new items.

6 Tap a photo you want to view.

7 When you finish browsing the latest activity, tap **Streams**.

The Shared Streams screen appears.

---

**TIP**

**How do I remove a shared stream?**

In the Photos app, tap **Shared** to display the Shared Streams screen. Tap **Edit** to turn on Editing mode, and then tap ⊖ to the left of the stream you want to remove. Tap the **Unsubscribe** button that then appears.

# Browse Photos Using Albums

As well as browsing by collections and browsing shared photo streams, you can browse your photos by albums. Your iPhone's Camera app automatically maintains several albums, storing each conventional photo you take in an album called Camera Roll, each panorama photo in an album called Panoramas, and each video in an album called Videos. You can also create other albums manually from your photos or sync existing albums from your computer.

If you sync your iPhone with iPhoto on the Mac, you can sync an album called Faces that contains known faces that iPhoto has recognized in your photos.

## Browse Photos Using Albums

### Open the Photos App and Browse an Album

**1** Press the Home button.

The Home screen appears.

**2** Tap **Photos**.

The Photos app opens.

**3** Tap **Albums**.

The Albums screen appears.

**4** Tap **Camera Roll**.

The Camera Roll album appears.

**Note:** Camera Roll is the album in which the Camera app places the photos you take; photos you save from web pages, e-mail messages, and instant messages; and photos you edit from other people's streams.

**5** Tap the photo you want to view.

The photo opens.

**Note:** Swipe left to display the next photo or right to display the previous photo.

**6** Tap the album's name — in this case, **Camera Roll**.

The album appears.

**7** Tap **Albums**.

The Albums screen appears.

## Create an Album

**1** In the Photos app, tap **Albums**.

The Albums screen appears.

**2** Tap **New** (+).

The New Album dialog opens.

**3** Type the name to give the album.

**4** Tap **Save**.

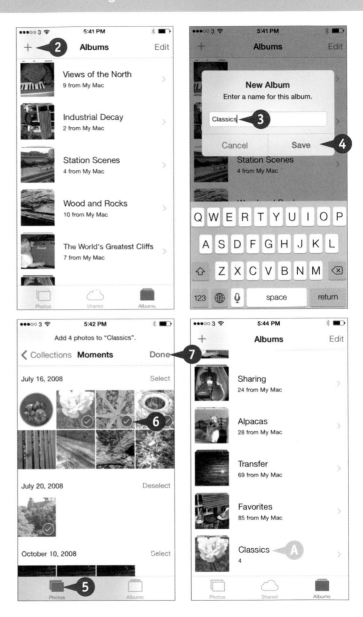

The Add Photos screen appears.

**5** Tap the source of the photos. For example, tap **Photos**, tap the year, tap the collection, and then tap the moment.

**6** Tap each photo to add to the collection, placing ⊘ on each.

**7** Tap **Done**.

Ⓐ The album appears on the Albums screen.

---

### TIP

**How can I move through a long list of photos more quickly?**

You can move through the photos more quickly by using momentum scrolling. Tap and flick up with your finger to set the photos scrolling. As the momentum drops, you can tap and flick up again to scroll further. Tap and drag your finger in the opposite direction to stop the scrolling.

# Share Photos Using My Photo Stream

If you have an iCloud account, you can use the My Photo Stream feature to share your photos among your iOS devices and your computer.

After you turn on My Photo Stream on your iPhone, other iOS devices, and your Macs or PCs, Photo Stream automatically syncs your 1,000 most recent photos among the devices and your computers.

## Share Photos Using My Photo Stream

### Turn On My Photo Stream on Your iPhone

**1** Press the Home button.

The Home screen appears.

**2** Tap **Settings**.

The Settings screen appears.

**3** Scroll down and then tap **iCloud**.

The iCloud screen appears.

**4** Tap **Photos**.

The Photos screen appears.

**5** Set the **My Photo Stream** switch to On ( ).

**6** If you want to share photo streams with others, set the **Photo Sharing** switch to On ( ). See the next task, "Share Photo Streams with Other People," for more.

**7** Tap the name of the iCloud account.

The iCloud screen appears.

**8** Tap **Settings**.

The Settings screen appears.

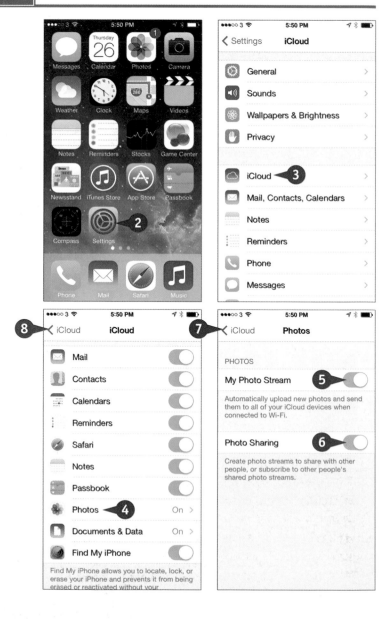

## Use Photo Stream on Your Mac

**1** Click  and **System Preferences**.

The System Preferences window opens.

**2** Click **iCloud**.

The iCloud pane appears.

**3** Click **Photos** (☐ changes to ☑).

**4** Click **Options**.

The iCloud Photos dialog opens.

**5** Click **My Photo Stream** (☐ changes to ☑).

**6** If you want to share photo streams with others, click **Photo Sharing** (☐ changes to ☑).

**7** Click **OK**.

**8** Click **System Preferences** and **Quit System Preferences**.

**9** Click **iPhoto** () on the Dock.

**10** In iPhoto, click **iCloud**.

The iCloud screen appears, showing your streams and your family and friends' streams.

---

**TIP**

**How do I use Photo Stream in Windows?**
Click **Start** and **Control Panel**. Click **View By** and **Large Icons**, and then click **iCloud**. Click **Photo Stream** (☐ changes to ☑) and **Close**. Now click **Start** and **Computer**, navigate to the Photo Stream folder, and open it.

# Share Photo Streams with Other People

our iPhone enables you to share your photo streams with other people easily. After turning on the Photo Sharing feature on the iCloud screen in the Settings app, you can create shared photo streams, invite people to subscribe to them, and add photos as needed. See the previous task, "Share Photos Using My Photo Stream," to turn on the Photo Sharing feature.

You can also control whether subscribers can post photos and videos to your shared photo stream, decide whether to make the stream publicly available on the iCloud.com website, and choose whether to receive notifications when subscribers comment on your photos or post their own.

## Share Photo Streams with Other People

**1** Press the Home button.

The Home screen appears.

**2** Tap **Photos**.

The Photos app opens.

**3** Tap **Shared**.

The Shared Streams screen appears.

**4** Tap **New Shared Stream**.

**Note:** You can also tap **New** (+) to start creating a new shared stream.

The New Stream dialog opens.

**5** Type the name for the stream.

**6** Tap **Next**.

Another New Stream dialog opens.

**7** Tap ⊕ to display the Contacts screen, and then tap the contact to add.

**8** Repeat step **7** to add other contacts as needed. You can also type contact names.

**9** Tap **Create**.

The Shared Streams screen appears.

**10** Tap the new stream.

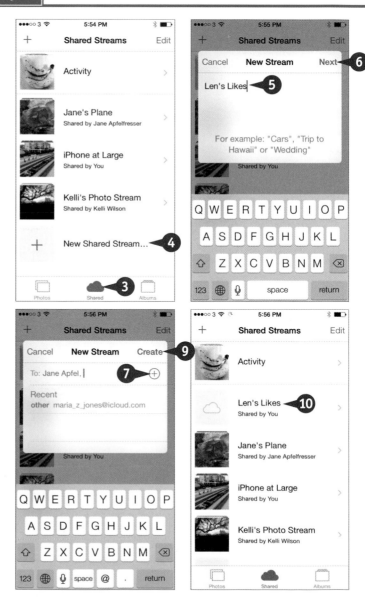

The stream's screen appears.

**11** Tap **New** (+).

The Moments screen appears, with the selection controls displayed.

**12** Tap each photo you want to add.

**13** Tap **Done**.

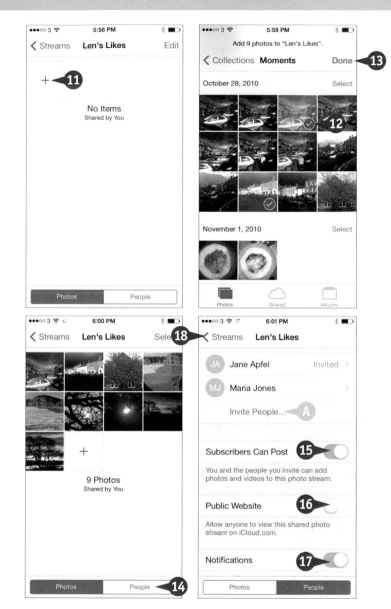

The stream's screen appears.

**14** Tap **People**.

The People screen appears.

**Ⓐ** To invite others to the stream, tap **Invite People**.

**15** Set the **Subscribers Can Post** switch to On (⬤) or Off (◯), as needed.

**16** Set the **Public Website** switch to On (⬤) or Off (◯) to control whether to make the stream publicly accessible on the iCloud.com website.

**17** Set the **Notifications** switch to On (⬤) or Off (◯), as needed.

**18** Tap **Streams**.

The Streams screen appears.

---

**TIP**

**If I make a photo stream public, how do people find the website?**

When you set the **Public Website** switch on the People screen for a photo stream to On (⬤), a Share Link button appears. Tap **Share Link** to display the Share screen, and then tap the means of sharing you want to use — for example, Message, Mail, Twitter, or Facebook.

# Share Photos via E-Mail and Instant Messaging

From your iPhone's Photos app, you can quickly share a photo either by sending it as an attachment to an e-mail message or by inserting it in an instant message.

When you send a photo via e-mail, your iPhone prompts you to choose whether to send the photo at its actual size or at a smaller size.

## Share Photos via E-Mail and Instant Messaging

### Select the Photo and Display the Share Screen

**1** Press the Home button.

The Home screen appears.

**2** Tap **Photos**.

The Photos app opens.

**3** Navigate to the photo you want to share. For example, tap **Years**, tap the appropriate collection, and then tap the moment that contains the photo.

**4** Tap the photo to open it.

**5** Tap **Share** (⬆).

The Share screen appears.

## Share the Photo via Instant Messaging

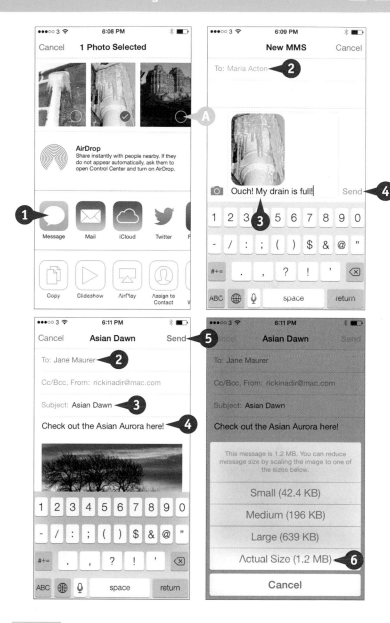

If you want to send another photo at the same time, tap it (○ changes to ✓).

**1** On the Share screen, tap **Message**.

Your iPhone creates a new Multimedia Messaging Service, or MMS, message in the Messages app with the photo attached to the message.

**2** Tap in the To field and address the message.

**3** Tap in the body area, and then type any text needed.

**4** Tap **Send**.

The Messages app sends the message.

## Share the Photo via E-Mail

**1** On the Share screen, tap **Mail**.

Your iPhone creates a new e-mail message in the Mail app with the photo attached to the message.

**2** Tap in the To field and address the e-mail message.

**3** Tap in the Subject line and type the subject for the e-mail message.

**4** Tap in the body area, and then type any text needed.

**5** Tap **Send**.

**6** If the Photos Size dialog opens, tap the button for the size of photo you want to send.

Mail sends the message.

---

### TIP

**What is the best size for sending photos via e-mail?**
This depends on what the recipient will do with the photo. If the recipient needs to edit or print the photo, choose **Actual Size**. If the recipient will merely view the photo on-screen, choose **Large** or **Medium**. The **Small** size works for contact card images, but its picture quality is too low for most other uses.

# Play Slide Shows of Photos

Your iPhone can not only display your photos but also play them as a slide show. The slide show feature is limited to using existing groups of photos — you cannot create a slide show group on the iPhone — but you can shuffle the photos into a different order. You can also choose to repeat the slide show or run the photos in random order. Then, when you start the slide show, you can choose which transition to use and add music. To make the most of your slide shows, you can choose the slide timing in the Photos screen in Settings.

## Play Slide Shows of Photos

**1** Press the Home button.

The Home screen appears.

**Note:** To play your photos on a bigger screen, either use AirPlay to a TV connected to an Apple TV or use the Apple Lightning Digital AV Adapter and an HDMI cable to connect your iPhone to a TV or monitor with an HDMI input.

**2** Tap **Photos**.

The Photos screen appears.

**3** Navigate to the photo with which you want to start the slide show. For example, tap **Photos**, tap the appropriate year, tap the appropriate collection, and then tap the moment that contains the photo.

The moment or other photo collection opens.

**4** Tap the photo you want to use at the beginning of the slide show.

The photo opens.

**5** Tap **Share** (⬆).

The Share screen appears.

**6** Tap **Slideshow**.

The Slideshow Options screen appears.

**7** If you have a choice of output devices, such as an Apple TV instead of your iPhone, tap the one you want to use.

**8** Tap **Transitions**.

The Transitions screen appears.

**9** Tap the transition you want.

**10** Tap **Back**.

The Slideshow Options screen appears.

**11** If you want to play music during the slide show, set the **Play Music** switch to On ( ).

The Music button appears.

**12** Tap **Music**.

The Music screen appears.

**13** Tap the song, album, or playlist you want to play.

The Slideshow Options screen appears.

**14** Tap **Start Slideshow**.

The slideshow starts.

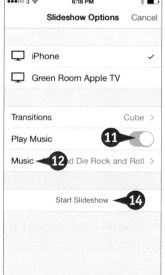

**TIP**

**How do I choose other settings for a slide show?**
You can set timing, repeat, and shuffling in the Settings app. Press the Home button to display the Home screen, and then tap **Settings**. On the Settings screen, tap **Photos & Camera**. In the Slideshow area, tap **Play Each Slide For**, and then tap the length of time — for example, **10 Seconds**. On the Photos & Camera screen, set the **Repeat** switch and the **Shuffle** switch to On ( ) or Off ( ), as needed.

# Read Digital Books with iBooks

To enjoy electronic books, or *e-books*, on your iPhone, download the free iBooks app from the App Store. Using iBooks, you can read e-books that you load on the iPhone from your computer, download free or paid-for e-books from online stores, or read PDF files you transfer from your computer.

If you have already loaded some e-books, you can read them as described in this task. If iBooks contains no books, see the next task, "Browse and Buy Digital Books with iBooks," for instructions on finding and downloading e-books.

## Read Digital Books with iBooks

**1** Press the Home button.

The Home screen appears.

**2** Tap **iBooks**.

iBooks opens, and the Books screen appears.

**Ⓐ** If the Books button does not appear in the upper middle area of the iBooks screen, tap the button that appears there. On the Collections screen that appears, tap **Books** to display the Books screen.

**3** If you want to view the books as a list, tap **List** (▤) at the top of the screen.

**Ⓑ** You can search to locate the book you want.

The list of books appears.

**4** Tap the book you want to open.

The book opens.

**Note:** When you open a book, iBooks displays your current page. When you open a book for the first time, iBooks displays the book's cover, first page, or default page.

**5** Tap anywhere on the screen to hide the reading controls.

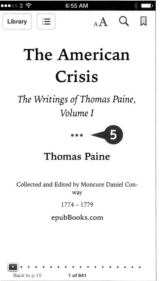

The reading controls disappear.

**Note:** To display the reading controls again, tap anywhere on the screen.

**6** Tap the right side of the page to display the next page.

**Note:** To display the previous page, tap the left side of the page. Alternatively, tap the left side of the page and drag to the right.

**7** To look at the next page without fully revealing it, tap the right side and drag to the left. You can then either drag further to turn the page or release the page and let it fall closed.

**8** To jump to another part of the book, tap **Table of Contents** (≡).

**Note:** Alternatively, you can drag the indicator at the bottom of the screen.

**9** When the table of contents appears, tap the part of the book you want to display.

**10** To search in the book, tap **Search** (🔍).

**11** On the Search screen, type the search term.

**12** Tap the match you want to display.

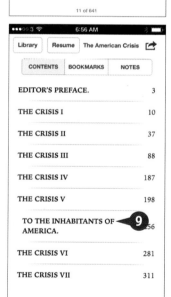

---

**TIP**

**How do I change the font iBooks uses?**
Tap the screen to display the controls, and then tap **Font Settings** (ₐA). In the Font Settings dialog, tap **Small** (Ⓐ) or **Large** (Ⓑ) to change the font size. Tap **Fonts** (Ⓒ) to display the font list, and then tap the font you want to use. Finally, tap outside the Font Settings dialog to close it.

# Browse and Buy Digital Books with iBooks

The iBooks app connects directly to Apple's online bookstore, which you can browse to find e-books. Some e-books are free; others you have to pay for, but many have samples that you can download to help you decide whether to buy the book.

After you download an e-book, it appears on your iBooks bookshelf. You can then open it and read it as described in the previous task, "Read Digital Books with iBooks."

## Browse and Buy Digital Books with iBooks

**1** Press the Home button.

The Home screen appears.

**2** Tap **iBooks**.

iBooks opens, and the Books screen appears.

**3** Tap **Store**.

The iBooks Store appears, showing a screen such as Top Charts.

**A** You can tap another button, such as **Top Authors**, or tap **Search** to search for books.

**4** Tap **Categories**.

The Categories screen appears.

**5** Tap the category you want to view. For example, tap **History**.

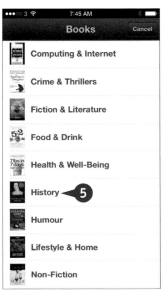

The screen appears for the category you chose.

**6** Tap the book whose information you want to view.

The book's screen appears.

**7** To learn more about the book, read the Details section.

**B** You can tap **Reviews** to see reviews of the book.

**C** You can tap **Related** to see books that may be related to this one.

**8** Tap **Sample** to get a sample of the book; tap **Free** to get the book if it is free; or tap the price button to buy the book.

The sample or book appears on your iBooks bookshelf.

**9** Tap the sample or book.

The book opens.

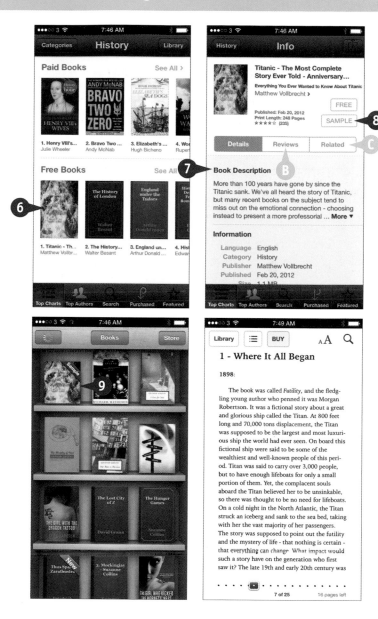

---

**TIP**

**Where can I find free e-books to read in iBooks?**
The iBooks Store has a good selection of free e-books. Look at the Free Books listing on the Top Charts screen or the Top Authors screen, or tap **Featured** and then tap **Free Books** in the Browse area.

Other sources of free e-books include ManyBooks.net (www.manybooks.net), Project Gutenberg (www.gutenberg.org), and the Baen Free Library (www.baen.com/library).

# Add PDF Files to iBooks and Read Them

These days, many books, reports, and other documents are available as Portable Document Format files, or PDF files. You can load PDF files on your iPhone and read them using iBooks. This is a great way to take your required reading with you so that you can catch up on it anywhere.

## Add PDF Files to iBooks and Read Them

### Add PDFs to iBooks Using iTunes

**1** Connect your iPhone to your computer via the USB cable or Wi-Fi.

**2** Click your iPhone's button.

The iPhone's control screens appear.

**3** Click **Books**.

The Books screen appears.

**4** Make sure the **Sync Books** check box is selected (☑).

**5** Click the **File** menu.

The File menu opens.

**6** Click **Add to Library**.

The Add To Library dialog opens.

**7** Click the PDF file or select the PDF files you want to add.

**8** Click **Open**.

iTunes adds the PDF file or files to the Books list.

**9** Click **Apply** or **Sync**, whichever button appears.

iTunes syncs the PDF files to the iPhone.

**10** Disconnect the iPhone from your computer.

## Read a PDF File Using iBooks

**1** Press the Home button.

The Home screen appears.

**2** Tap **iBooks**.

The Books screen appears.

**3** Tap **Books**.

The Collections screen appears.

**4** Tap **PDFs**.

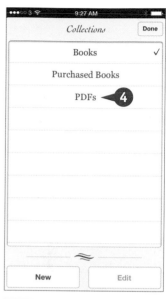

The PDFs screen appears.

**5** Tap the PDF file you want to open.

The PDF file appears. You can then read the PDF file by scrolling up and down and zooming in and out as needed.

**Note:** If you open a PDF file while browsing the web in Safari, you can open the file in iBooks. To do so, tap the screen, and then tap **Open in iBooks** on the command bar that pops up.

**How do I change the font size on the PDF file?**
You cannot change the font size on the PDF file. This is because PDF is a graphical format — essentially a picture — instead of a text format. To make the PDF file more readable on the iPhone, rotate the iPhone to a landscape orientation, so that the screen is wider than it is tall. Then pinch outward to zoom the text to a larger size.

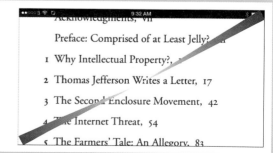

# CHAPTER 12

# Using the Built-In Apps

Your iPhone comes with apps that enable you to make the most of its features right out of the box. You can get your bearings with Compass, find your way and explore with Maps, track prices with Stocks, keep the time with Clock, or check the forecast with Weather.

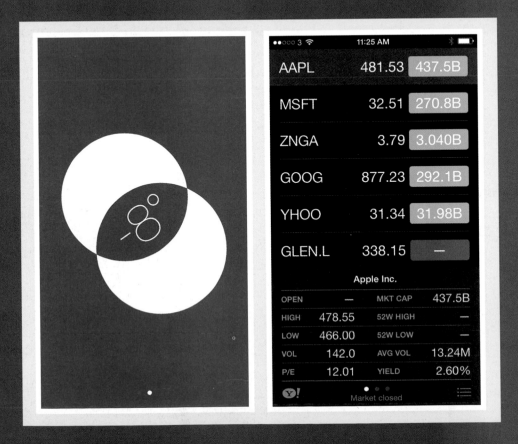

# Get Your Bearings with Compass

When you need to get your bearings, use the Compass app that comes installed on your iPhone. With Compass, you can establish your relationship to the points of the compass, learn your precise GPS location, and measure an angle between two points.

Compass includes a Level feature that you can use to level an object or surface precisely or to measure its current slant.

## Get Your Bearings with Compass

### Open Compass and Get Your Bearings

1. Press the Home button.

   The Home screen appears.

2. Tap **Compass**.

   The Compass screen appears.

**Note:** If Compass displays a message prompting you to complete the circle to calibrate it, turn your iPhone this way and that until the circle is filled in. The compass then appears.

3. Point your iPhone in the direction whose bearing you want to take.

Ⓐ The readout shows the bearing.

Ⓑ You can tap the GPS location to switch to the Maps app and display the map for that location.

### Measure an Angle

1. On the Compass screen, tap anywhere on the compass to fix the current bearing.

Ⓒ The bearing appears at the top of the compass.

2. Turn the iPhone toward the target point.

Ⓓ The red arc measures the difference between the two bearings.

## Use the Level Feature

**1** From the Compass screen, tap and drag left.

**E** You can also tap the gray dot to switch to the Level screen.

The Level screen appears.

**F** The figure shows the angle of the object or surface.

**2** Tilt your iPhone toward a level position to move the circles on top of each other.

**3** If the black-and-white color scheme is hard to see, tap one of the circles.

The background color changes to red.

**G** When you align the circles, the screen goes green.

---

## TIP

**Does the Compass app use True North or Magnetic North?**
The Compass app can show either True North or Magnetic North. To switch, press the Home button, and then tap **Settings**. In the Settings app, tap **Compass**, and then set the **Use True North** switch (**A**) to On (⬤) or Off (   ), as needed.

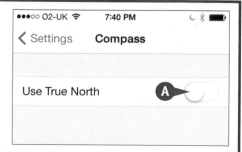

# Find Your Location with Maps

Your iPhone's Maps app can pinpoint your location by using the Global Positioning System, known as GPS, or wireless networks. You can view your location on a road map, a satellite picture, or a hybrid that shows street and place names on the satellite picture. You can easily switch among map types to find the most useful one for your current needs. To help you get your bearings, the Tracking feature in the Maps app can show you which direction you are facing.

## Find Your Location with Maps

**1** Press the Home button.

The Home screen appears.

**2** Tap **Maps**.

The Maps screen appears.

**A** A blue dot shows your current location. The expanding circle around the blue dot shows that Maps is determining your location.

**Note:** It may take a minute for Maps to work out your location accurately. While Maps determines the location, the blue dot moves, even though the iPhone remains stationary.

**3** Tap and pinch in with two fingers.

**Note:** You can tap and pinch out with two fingers to zoom in.

The map zooms out, showing a larger area.

**4** Tap ⓘ.

The Maps dialog opens.

**5** Tap **Satellite**.

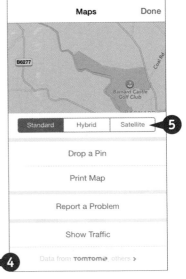

The Satellite view appears.

**6** Tap ⓘ.

The Maps dialog opens.

**7** Tap **Hybrid**.

The satellite map appears with street and place names overlaid on it.

**8** Tap **Location** (⟋ changes to ➤), turning on the Location service.

**9** Tap **Location** (➤ changes to ⋏).

**Ⓑ** The Compass icon appears (⬤). The red arrow indicates north.

**Ⓒ** The map turns to show the direction the iPhone is facing, so that you can orient yourself.

## TIP

**How can I tell the scale of the map?**

Place two fingers on the screen as if about to pinch outward or inward. Maps displays a scale in the upper left part of the screen (**Ⓐ**).

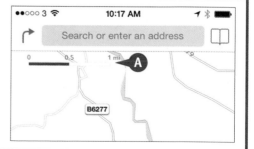

# Find Directions with Maps

Your iPhone's Maps app can give you directions to where you want to go. Maps can also show you current traffic congestion in some locales to help you identify the most viable route for a journey.

Maps displays driving directions by default, but you can also display public transit directions and walking directions.

## Find Directions with Maps

**1** Press the Home button.

The Home screen appears.

**2** Tap **Maps**.

The Maps screen appears.

**3** Tap ↱.

The Directions screen appears.

**4** Tap **Start**.

The Current Location text changes to a blue button.

**5** Tap ⊗ to delete the Current Location button.

**Note:** If you want the directions to start from your current location, leave Current Location in the Start field. Skip to step **7**.

**6** Type the start location for the directions.

**Note:** If the starting location or ending location is an address in the Contacts app, start typing the name, and then tap the match in the list.

**7** Type the end location.

**A** Tap **Switch Places** (⇅) if you need to switch the start location and end location.

**8** Tap **Route**.

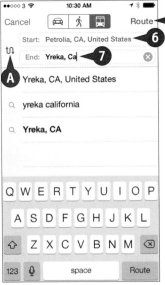

**B** A screen showing the driving directions appears. The green pin marks the start, and the red pin marks the end.

**C** If multiple routes are available, tap a time button to view a different route. The time button changes to blue to indicate it is active.

**9** Tap **Start**.

The first screen of directions appears.

**10** Tap and scroll as needed to follow the directions.

**11** If you want to see the full list of directions, tap **Overview**.

The overview screen appears.

**12** Tap **Directions** (≔).

The Directions screen appears, showing a complete list of the directions.

**D** You can tap a direction to display it on the map.

**13** Tap **Done** to return to the map.

**14** Tap **Resume** to resume step-by-step navigation.

---

**TIP**

**How do I get directions for public transit or walking?**

Tap 🚌 to display the details of available public transport. Tap 🚶 to display the distance and time for walking the route.

It is a good idea to double-check public transit directions against the latest published schedules because the information is sometimes out of date.

Be aware that walking directions may be inaccurate. Before walking the route, check that it does not send you across pedestrian-free bridges or through rail tunnels.

# Explore with 3D Flyover

Maps is not only great for finding out where you are and for getting directions to places, but it can also show you 3D flyovers of the places on the map.

After switching on the 3D feature, you can zoom in and out, pan around, and move backward and forward.

## Explore with 3D Flyover

**1** Press the Home button.

The Home screen appears.

**2** Tap **Maps**.

The Maps screen appears.

**3** Display the area of interest in the middle of the screen. For example, tap and drag the map, or search for the location you want.

**4** Tap 🏢 in an urban area or 3D outside urban areas.

The screen switches to Flyover view or 3D view.

**5** Pinch out with two fingers to zoom in.

**Note:** You can pinch in with two fingers to zoom out.

**Note:** Tap and drag to scroll the map as needed.

**6** Place two fingers on the screen and twist clockwise or counterclockwise to rotate the view.

The rotated view appears.

**A** The Compass arrow (●) appears. You can tap it to restore the direction to north.

**7** Pan and zoom as needed to explore the area.

**8** Tap and drag down with two fingers.

The viewing angle steepens until you reach a straight-down position.

**9** Tap and drag up with two fingers.

The viewing angle becomes shallower.

**10** Tap 🏢 or 3D.

The standard view reappears.

---

**TIP**

**What does 3D do with the Standard map?**

When you tap 3D to switch on Flyover with the Standard map displayed, Maps tilts the map at an angle, as you might do with a paper map. For most purposes, 3D and Flyover are most useful with the Satellite map and the Hybrid map.

# Use Maps' Bookmarks and Contacts

When you need to be able to return to a location easily in the Maps app, you can place a bookmark at the location.

Similarly, you can add a location to your contacts, so that you can access it either from the Contacts app or from the Maps app. You can either create a new contact or add the location to an existing contact. You can also return quickly to locations you have visited recently but not created a bookmark or contact for.

## Use Maps' Bookmarks and Contacts

**1** Press the Home button.

The Home screen appears.

**2** Tap **Maps**.

The Maps screen appears.

**3** Find the place you want to bookmark. For example, tap and drag the map, or search for the location you want.

**4** Tap and hold the place you want to bookmark.

The Maps app drops a pin on the place.

**Note:** To get rid of a pin you have dropped, tap the pin to display its pop-up label, and then tap the label. On the Location screen that appears, tap **Remove Pin**.

**5** Tap >.

The Location screen appears.

**6** At the bottom of the screen, tap **Add Bookmark**.

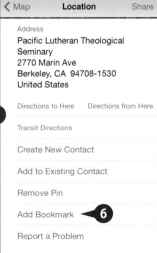

The Add Bookmark screen appears.

**7** Type the name for the bookmark. Alternatively, you can accept the default name, if there is one.

**8** Tap **Save**.

**A** You can quickly get directions to or from this location by tapping **Directions to Here** or **Directions from Here**.

**9** To create a new contact record for this location, tap **Create New Contact**. Go to step **11**.

**10** To add this location to an existing contact record, tap **Add to Existing Contact**. Go to step **12**.

**11** On the New Contact screen, type the details for the contact, and then tap **Done**.

**12** On the Contacts screen that appears, tap the contact to which you want to add the location.

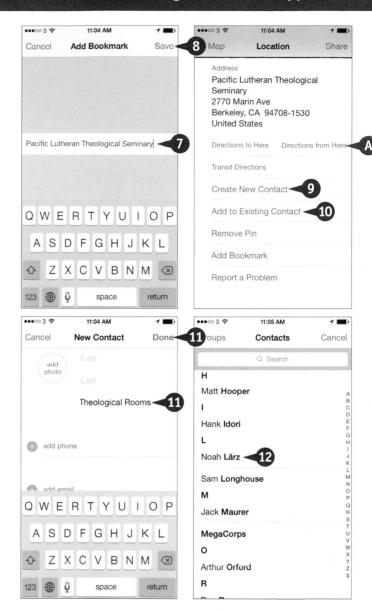

**How do I go to a location I have bookmarked or created a contact for?**

In the Maps app, tap **Bookmarks** (▢). On the Bookmarks screen, tap **Bookmarks** or **Contacts**, and then tap the location.

You can also go back to a recent location by tapping **Recents**, and then tapping the location.

# Share a Location via E-Mail and Instant Messaging

Often, you will find it useful to share a location with other people. The Maps app enables you to share a location in moments via either e-mail or instant messaging.

You can share your current location, a location you have bookmarked or created a contact for, or a location on which you drop a pin.

## Share a Location via E-Mail and Instant Messaging

### Find the Location and Open the Share Dialog

**1** Press the Home button.

The Home screen appears.

**2** Tap **Maps**.

The Maps screen appears.

**3** Find the location you want to bookmark.

**4** If the location does not already have a bookmark or contact, tap and hold it to drop a pin on it.

**5** Tap >.

The Location screen appears.

**Note:** If you have just dropped a pin, you may want to name it instead of leaving the default name, Dropped Pin. Tap **Add Bookmark** on the Location screen, type the name, and then tap **Save**.

**6** Tap **Share**.

The Share dialog opens.

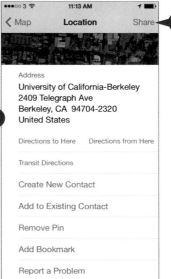

## Share the Location via E-Mail

**1** In the Share dialog, tap **Mail**.

Your iPhone creates a new e-mail message in the Mail app with the location's link inserted in the message.

**2** Tap in the To field, and address the e-mail message.

**3** Tap in the Subject line, and type the subject for the e-mail message.

**4** Tap in the body area, and type any text needed.

**5** Tap **Send**.

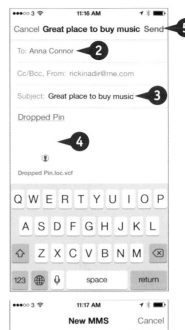

## Share the Location via Instant Messaging

**1** In the Share dialog, tap **Message**.

Your iPhone creates a new message in the Messages app with the location attached to the message.

**2** Tap in the To field, and address the message.

**3** Tap in the body area, and type any text needed.

**4** Tap **Send**.

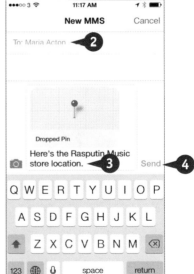

## TIP

**How else can I share a location?**

You can also share a location on Twitter or Facebook, or AirDrop. To share via Twitter, tap **Twitter**, type a suitable message on the Tweet screen, and then tap **Send**. To share via Facebook, tap **Facebook**, type any explanation needed, and then tap **Post**. To share via AirDrop, use the technique explained in Chapter 6.

If you have created a contact for the location, you can share the contact from the Contacts app. Tap the contact's entry to display the Info screen, and then tap **Share Contact**. In the Share Contact Using dialog, tap **Mail** or **Message**, complete the message, and send it.

# Track Stock Prices with the Stocks App

I f you own or follow stocks, you can use the iPhone's Stocks app to track stock prices so that you can take immediate action as needed.

The Stocks app displays a default selection of stock information at first, including the Dow Jones Industrial Average, the NASDAQ Composite, the Standard & Poor's 500, and Apple, Google, and Yahoo! stocks. You can customize the Stocks app to display only those stocks that interest you.

## Track Stock Prices with the Stocks App

### Open the Stocks App

**1** Press the Home button.

The Home screen appears.

**2** Tap **Stocks**.

The Stocks screen appears, showing a default selection of stocks.

### Choose the Stocks You Want to Track

**1** Tap **Info** (▤).

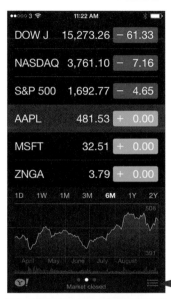

The Stocks configuration screen appears.

**2** Tap **Add** (➕).

The Search screen appears.

**3** Type the company's name or stock ID.

**4** Either tap **Search** or simply wait for the Stocks app to search.

A list of matching company names and stock symbols appears.

**5** Tap the item you want to add.

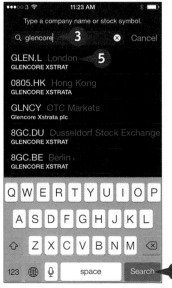

The stock listing appears.

**6** To remove a stock listing, tap ⊖, and then tap **Delete**.

The stock listing disappears.

**7** To change the order, tap ▤ and drag up or down.

**8** Tap **percentage**, **price**, or **market cap** to control which statistic the Stocks app displays first.

**9** Tap **Done**.

## View Information for a Stock

**1** On the Stocks screen, tap the stock for which you want to see information at the bottom of the screen.

**2** Tap the first dot to see the summary information, the second dot to see the stock chart, or the third dot to see stock-related headlines.

**Note:** You can also scroll the lower part of the screen to switch among the summary information, the stock chart, and the headlines.

**3** Tap to switch among percentage changes, price changes, and market capitalization.

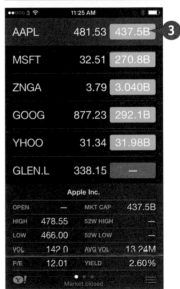

## TIPS

**What does the Y! button do?**

Tap **Yahoo!** (🔘) to display the Yahoo! Finance page for the selected stock listing in Safari.

**How can I read the stock chart more easily?**

Turn the iPhone to landscape orientation to see the stock chart on its own and at a larger size.

# Set Up the Clock App with Multiple Locations

When you travel, or when you work with people in different time zones, you may need to track the time in different time zones. You can set up the World Clock feature in your iPhone's Clock app with the different locations you need so that you can instantly see the local time in each location you need to track.

You can add locations to World Clock from a long list, remove any locations you do not need, and drag the locations into your preferred order.

## Set Up the Clock App with Multiple Locations

**1** Press the Home button.

The Home screen appears.

**2** Tap **Clock**.

The Clock app appears.

**Note:** When you open the Clock app, it displays the last screen you used in the app.

**3** Tap **World Clock**.

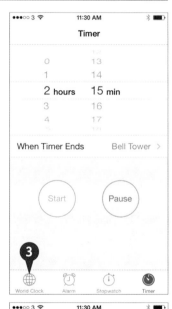

The World Clock screen appears.

**4** Tap +.

The Choose a City screen appears.

**5** Tap the city you want to add to World Clock.

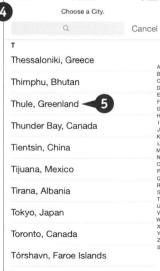

The World Clock screen shows
the clock you added.

**6** Tap **Edit**.

The World Clock screen opens
for editing.

**7** Tap ≡ next to a clock,
and drag it up or down the
list as needed.

**Note:** To delete a clock, tap ⊖
next to it, and then tap **Delete**.

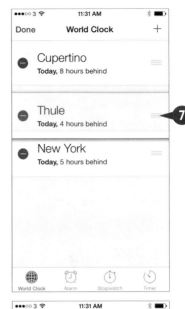

**8** Tap **Done**.

The clocks appear in your
chosen order.

You can now easily see what
time it is in each of the
locations you are tracking.

**Note:** Tap a clock's button to
toggle the clock's display
between analog and digital.

---

## TIPS

**Why do some clocks have black faces and others white faces?**

A black clock face indicates that it is currently
between 6 p.m. and 6 a.m. in that time zone. A
white clock face indicates that it is between 6 a.m.
and 6 p.m.

**How do I set the time on my iPhone's main clock?**

Normally, your iPhone sets the time automatically,
but you can set the time manually if you want.
From the Home screen, tap **Settings**, and then tap
**General**. Tap **Date & Time**, and then use the
controls on the Date & Time screen.

# Set Alarms

As well as showing the time in multiple locations, the Clock app includes full Alarm features. You can set as many alarms as you need, give each alarm a distinctive tone, and create different schedules for the alarms. For example, you can set an alarm to wake you each weekday but not on the weekend.

You can assign names to your alarms to help you identify them easily, turn them on and off as needed, and delete any alarms you no longer require.

## Set Alarms

1 Press the Home button.

The Home screen appears.

2 Tap **Clock**.

The Clock screen appears.

3 Tap **Alarm**.

The Alarm screen appears.

4 Tap +.

The Add Alarm screen appears.

5 Scroll the time controls to set the alarm time.

6 If you want to be able to use snooze on the alarm, set the **Snooze** switch to On ( ).

7 To create a repeating alarm, tap **Repeat**.

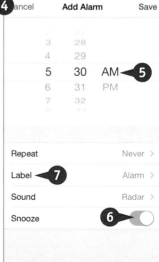

The Repeat screen appears.

**8** Tap to place a check mark next to each day you want the alarm to sound.

**9** Tap **Back**.

The Add Alarm screen appears again.

**10** Tap **Label**.

The Label screen appears.

**11** Type the name for the alarm.

**12** Tap **Back**.

The Add Alarm screen appears again.

**13** Tap **Sound**.

The Sound screen appears.

**14** Tap a sound to preview it.

A check mark appears next to the sound.

**15** When you have chosen the alarm sound, tap **Back**.

The Add Alarm screen appears again.

**16** Tap **Save**.

The Alarm screen appears.

**17** Set the alarm's switch to On ( ) or Off ( ), as needed.

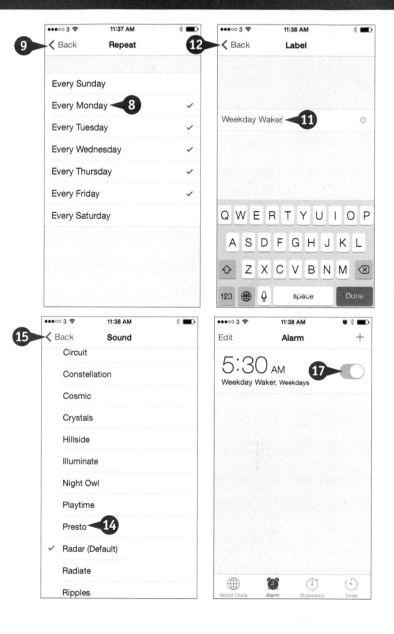

---

## TIP

**Is there an easy way to tell whether an alarm is set?**
Yes. The alarm icon ( ) appears in the status bar when an alarm is set. Only one icon appears even if you set multiple alarms.

# Use the Stopwatch and Timer Features

Your iPhone's Clock app includes a Stopwatch feature and a Timer feature. The Stopwatch feature provides a handy way of timing events such as races, including the ability to log the time for each lap in a track race.

The Timer feature enables you to count down from a set time and sound an alarm when the time elapses. You can pause the timer as necessary. You can also use Siri to set timers, which is useful when your hands are otherwise occupied.

## Use the Stopwatch and Timer Features

### Use the Stopwatch Feature

1. Press the Home button.

   The Home screen appears.

2. Tap **Clock**.

   The Clock screen appears.

3. Tap **Stopwatch**.

   The Stopwatch screen appears.

4. Tap **Start**.

The stopwatch starts running.

5. Tap **Lap** to mark a lap time.

   Ⓐ The lap time appears in the list.

   Ⓑ The main readout shows the total time elapsed.

   Ⓒ The upper readout shows the time since the last lap mark.

6. Tap **Stop**.

7. Tap **Reset** when you need to reset the stopwatch.

## Use the Timer Feature

**1** Press the Home button.

The Home screen appears.

**2** Tap **Clock**.

The Clock screen appears.

**3** Tap **Timer**.

The Timer screen appears.

**4** Scroll the time controls to set the number of hours and minutes.

**5** Tap **When Timer Ends**.

The When Timer Ends screen appears.

**6** Tap a sound to preview it.

A check mark appears next to the sound.

**7** When you have chosen the sound, tap **Set**.

The Timer screen reappears.

**8** Tap **Start**.

The timer starts running.

**D** Tap **Pause** if you need to pause the timer. You can then tap **Resume**, which replaces Pause, to resume it.

**E** Tap **Cancel** if you need to cancel the timer. Clock resets the timer to the time you set in step **4**.

## TIPS

**How can I make my iPhone play music for a while as I go to sleep?**

To play music and shut it off automatically after a set time, set Timer to the interval you want. Tap **Sounds**, scroll down to the bottom of the When Timer Ends screen, and tap **Stop Playing**. Then tap **Set**.

**How do I tell Siri to set a timer?**

Say "Set a timer for" and the period of time. For example, say "Set a timer for 20 minutes." To see the timer, say "Show me my timer" or a similar phrase. To stop the timer running and reset it, say "Cancel the timer."

# Look Up Forecasts in Weather

Along with much other useful information, your iPhone can put the weather forecasts in the palm of your hand. By using the Weather app, you can quickly learn the current conditions and forecast for as many cities as you need. The Weather app comes set to show the weather in Cupertino, the city where Apple's headquarters are located, but you can choose whatever cities you want. You can also make Weather show the weather for your current location. You can then move quickly from location to location as needed.

## Look Up Forecasts in Weather

**1** Press the Home button.

The Home screen appears.

**2** Tap **Weather**.

The Weather app opens and displays the weather for either your current location or for Cupertino.

**Note:** To get local weather, you must allow Weather to use Location Services. On the Home screen, tap **Settings**, tap **Privacy**, and then tap **Location Services**. On the Location Services screen, tap the **Weather** switch and set it to On ( ).

**3** Tap the temperature.

**A** Further details appear, including the humidity, chance of rain, and wind speed and direction.

**B** Tap the hourly weather timeline and drag left to display later hours.

**4** Tap .

The list of weather locations appears.

**5** Tap .

The Search screen appears.

**6** Start typing the city or location.

**7** Tap **Search**.

**8** Tap the appropriate result in the list.

The city appears on the list of weather locations.

**Note:** You can now add other cities as needed.

**9** Tap and hold a location until it moves, and then drag it to where you want it in the list.

**10** Tap the location you want to display.

**Note:** To delete a city, swipe it to the left, and then tap **Delete**.

The location's weather appears.

**11** Swipe left or right.

**C** You can also tap a dot to the left or right of the current dot to display a different screen.

The next screen in that direction appears.

**How do I change from Centigrade to Fahrenheit?**
Tap **Info** (▭) to display the Weather screen, and then tap **°F** or **°C**, as needed.

**What does the Y! button in the Weather app do?**
Tap the **Yahoo!** (▣!) button to display the Yahoo! Weather page for the current city in Safari.

# CHAPTER 13

# Taking Photos and Videos

With your iPhone's Camera app, you can take high-quality still photos, apply filters to give different looks, and edit the photos to improve them. You can also capture video and trim your clips down to length. You can easily share both the photos and the videos you take.

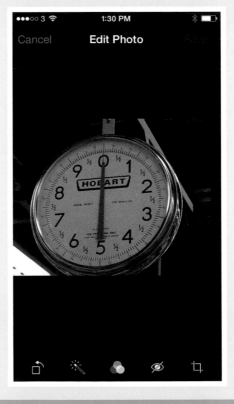

# Take Photos with the Camera App

Your iPhone includes a high-resolution camera in its back for taking both still photos and videos, plus a lower-resolution camera in the front for taking photos and videos of yourself and for making video calls.

To take photos using the camera, you use the Camera app. This app includes a digital zoom feature for zooming in and out, and a flash that you can set to On, Off, or Auto.

## Take Photos with the Camera App

### Open the Camera App

**1** Press the Home button.

The Home screen appears.

**Note:** From the lock screen, you can open the Camera app by tapping the Camera icon in the lower right corner and dragging up.

**2** Tap **Camera**.

The Camera app opens and displays whatever is in front of the lens.

### Compose the Photo and Zoom If Necessary

**1** Aim the iPhone so that your subject appears in the middle of the photo area. To focus on an item not in the center of the frame, tap that item to move the focus rectangle to it.

**Note:** If you need to take tightly composed photos, get a tripod mount for the iPhone. You can find various models on eBay and photography sites.

**2** If you need to zoom in or out, place two fingers together on the screen and pinch outward.

The zoom slider appears.

**3** Tap ➕ to zoom in or ➖ to zoom out. Tap as many times as needed.

**A** You can also zoom by tapping and dragging the zoom slider (⊖).

## Choose Whether and How to Use the Flash

**1** Tap the **Flash** button.

The Flash settings appear.

**2** Tap **On** to use the flash, **Auto** to use the flash if there is not enough light without it, or **Off** to turn the flash off.

## Take the Photo and View It

**1** Tap **Take Photo** (⬤).

**Note:** To prevent the iPhone moving when you take the picture, tap and hold **Take Photo** (⬤), and then lift your finger when you are ready to take the photo.

The Camera app takes the photo and displays a thumbnail.

**2** Tap the thumbnail.

The photo appears.

**Ⓑ** From the photo screen, you can navigate as discussed in Chapter 11. For example, swipe your finger to the left to display the next photo, or swipe to the right to display the previous photo. Tap 🗑 to delete the photo.

**3** Tap **Done** when you want to go back to the Camera app.

---

### TIP

**How do I switch to the front-facing camera?**

Tap **Switch Cameras** (📷) to switch from the rear-facing camera to the front-facing camera. The image that the front-facing camera is seeing appears on-screen, and you can take pictures as described in this task. Tap **Switch Cameras** (📷) again when you want to switch back to the rear-facing camera.

# Take HDR, Square, and Panorama Photos

The Camera app includes a feature called *high dynamic range*, or HDR. HDR takes three photos in immediate succession with slightly different exposure settings, and then combines them into a single photo that has a better color balance and intensity than a single photo.

To take an HDR photo with your iPhone, you turn on the HDR feature in the Camera app, and then take the photo as normal. The Camera app also includes a feature for capturing square photos and a panorama mode for capturing landscapes.

## Take HDR, Square, and Panorama Photos

### Open the Camera App

**1** Press the Home button.

The Home screen appears.

**2** Tap **Camera**.

The Camera app opens.

### Turn On the HDR Feature and Take a Photo

**1** Tap **HDR Off**.

Ⓐ The HDR readout changes to HDR On.

**Note:** You cannot use the HDR feature together with flash. So when you turn HDR on, your iPhone automatically turns the flash off; when you turn the flash on, your iPhone turns HDR off.

**2** Tap **Take Photo** (◎).

**B** The Camera app takes the photo, displaying an animation in the Take Photo button as it does so.

**3** Tap the thumbnail.

The HDR version of the photo appears.

**C** The HDR logo indicates this is the HDR version.

**Note:** Swipe your finger left to display the first version of the photo.

**4** When you want to return to the Camera app, tap the screen to display the controls, and then tap **Done**.

**Note:** HDR combines three differently exposed photos into a single picture. It also saves the normal version of the photo — a version with a single exposure. If you do not want to save the normal version, set the Keep Normal Photo switch to Off ( ) on the Photos & Camera screen in the Settings app.

### Take a Square Photo

**1** If you need to take a square photo, tap **Square**.

**Note:** Square photos are useful for adding to contact records and similar needs.

Camera reduces the frame to a square.

**2** Tap **Take Photo** (⬜).

Camera takes a photo.

## TIP

**How do I take panorama photos?**
Tap **Pano**. Hold the iPhone in portrait orientation, aim at the left end of the panorama, and then tap **Take Photo** (⬜). Follow the on-screen prompts to move the iPhone to the right, keeping the white arrow on the horizontal line. If Camera prompts you to slow down, do so.

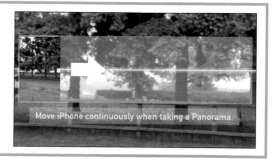

Move iPhone continuously when taking a Panorama.

# Apply Filters to Your Photos

You can use the Filter feature in the Camera app to change the look of a photo by applying a filter such as Mono, Tonal, Chrome, Transfer, or Instant.

You can apply a filter either before taking the photo or after taking it. If you apply the filter before taking the photo, you can remove the filter afterward; the filter is an effect applied to the photo, not an integral part of the photo.

## Apply Filters to Your Photos

**1** Press the Home button.

The Home screen appears.

**2** Tap **Camera**.

The Camera app opens.

**3** Tap **Filters** (◨).

The Filters screen appears.

**4** Tap the filter you want to apply.

**A** Camera applies the filter to the screen.

**5** Tap **Take Photo** (◯).

**6** Tap the photo's thumbnail.

The photo appears.

**7** Tap **Edit**.

The Edit Photo screen appears, showing the editing tools.

**8** Tap **Filters** (■).

The Choose Filter screen appears.

**9** Tap the filter you want to apply. Scroll left or right to display other filters.

**Note:** Tap **None** if you want to remove filtering.

**10** Tap **Apply**.

The Edit Photo screen appears, showing the photo with the filter applied.

**11** Tap **Save**.

iOS saves the change to the photo.

## TIP

**Is it better to apply a filter before taking a photo or after taking it?**
This is up to you. Sometimes it is helpful to have the filter effect in place when composing a photo so that you can arrange the composition and lighting to complement the filtering. Other times, especially when you do not have time to experiment with filters, it is more practical to take the photos and then try applying filters afterward.

# Edit Your Photos

To improve your photos, you can use the five powerful but easy-to-use editing tools your iPhone includes. You can rotate a photo to a different orientation, enhance its colors, apply a filter to change its colorization, remove red eye from eyes, and crop off the parts of the photo you do not need.

You can access the editing tools either through the Camera Roll album in the Photos app or through the Photos app. To start editing a photo, you open the photo by tapping it, and then tap **Edit**.

## Edit Your Photos

### Rotate a Photo

**1** With the photo open, tap **Edit**.

The Edit Photo screen appears.

**2** Tap **Rotate** (⤵).

The photo rotates 90° counterclockwise.

**Note:** Tap **Rotate** (⤵) again if you need to rotate the photo further.

**3** Tap **Save**.

iOS saves the changes.

### Enhance the Colors in a Photo

**1** With the photo open, tap **Edit**.

The Edit Photo screen appears.

**2** Tap **Auto-Enhance** (✦).

iOS enhances the colors.

**Note:** Tap **Auto-Enhance** (✦) again if you want to remove the color change.

**A** The Auto-Enhance On readout appears.

**3** Tap **Save**.

## Remove Red Eye from a Photo

**1** With the photo open, tap **Edit**.

The Edit Photo screen appears.

**Note:** You may need to zoom in on the photo in order to touch the red-eye patches accurately.

**2** Tap **Red-Eye Reduction** (⊘).

**B** iOS prompts you to tap each eye.

**3** Tap each red eye.

iOS removes the red eye.

**4** Tap **Apply**.

## Crop a Photo

**1** With the photo open, tap **Edit**.

The Edit Photo screen appears.

**2** Tap **Crop** (⬚).

The Crop Photo screen appears.

**3** Tap and drag the crop handles to the size you want.

**4** If necessary, tap inside the cropping area and drag the photo to change the part shown.

**5** Tap **Crop**.

iOS crops the photo.

### TIP

**What does the Aspect button on the Crop Photo screen do?**

Tap **Aspect** when you need to crop to a specific aspect ratio, such as a square or the 16:9 widescreen aspect ratio. In the Aspect dialog, tap the constraint you want to use. iOS adjusts the current cropping to match the aspect ratio. You may then need to move the portion of the photo shown to get the composition you want. If you adjust the cropping, tap **Aspect** again and reapply the aspect ratio.

| |
|---|
| 4 × 6 |
| 5 × 7 |
| 8 × 10 |
| 16 × 9 |

# Capture Video

As well as capturing still photos, your iPhone's camera can capture high-quality, full-motion video in either portrait orientation or landscape orientation. The iPhone 5s can also capture slow-motion video, which is great for increasing your cinematic repertoire. The iPhone 5c does not have this capability.

To capture video, you use the Camera app. You launch the Camera app as usual, and then switch it to Video mode. After taking the video, you can view it on the iPhone's screen.

## Capture Video

1 Press the Home button.

The Home screen appears.

2 Tap **Camera**.

The Camera screen appears, showing the image the lens is seeing.

3 Move the slider to **Video**. On an iPhone 5s, you can move the slider to **Slo-Mo** to capture slow-motion footage.

The video image and video controls appear.

**Note:** If the still camera is zoomed out all the way when you switch to the video camera, the picture appears to zoom in. This is because the video camera uses a focal length longer than the wide-angle setting of the still camera.

4 Aim the camera at your subject.

Ⓐ If you need to use the flash for the video, tap the flash button, and then tap **Auto** or **On**. When you are shooting video, the flash is effective only at short range.

**Note:** To focus on a particular area of the screen, tap that area.

5 Tap **Record** (⊙).

Ⓑ The camera starts recording, and the time readout shows the time that has elapsed.

**6** To zoom in, place two fingers on the screen and pinch outward. You can then tap ⊞ to zoom in, tap ⊟ to zoom out, or drag the zoom slider (⊜).

**C** To take a still photo while shooting video, tap **Take Photo** (◻).

**7** To finish recording, tap **Stop** (◉).

The Camera app stops recording and displays a thumbnail of the video's first frame.

**8** Tap the thumbnail.

The video appears.

**9** Tap **Play** (▶).

The video starts playing.

**10** Tap anywhere on the screen to display the video controls. These disappear automatically after a few seconds of not being used.

**Note:** If you want to trim the video, follow the procedure described in the next task, "Edit Video with the Trim Feature," before tapping **Done**.

**11** When you finish viewing the video, tap **Done**.

The Camera app appears again.

## TIP

**What does the bar of miniature pictures at the top of the video playback screen do?**
The navigation bar gives you a quick way of moving forward and backward through the movie. Tap the vertical playhead bar, and then drag to the right or to the left until the movie reaches the part you want. You can use the navigation bar either when the movie is playing or when it is paused.

# Edit Video with the Trim Feature

When you capture video, you normally shoot more footage than you want to keep. You then edit the video down to keep only the footage you need.

The Camera app includes a straightforward Trim feature that you can use to trim the beginning and end of a video clip to where you want them. For greater precision in editing, or to make a movie out of multiple clips, you can use the iMovie app, which is available from the App Store.

## Edit Video with the Trim Feature

**1** Press the Home button.

The Home screen appears.

**2** Tap **Camera**.

The Camera screen appears, showing the image the lens is seeing.

**3** Move the slider to **Video**.

**4** Tap the thumbnail.

The photos and videos in the Camera Roll appear.

**Note:** If the latest photo appears, tap **Camera Roll** to display the Camera Roll photos and videos.

**5** Tap the thumbnail for the video you want to trim.

The video opens.

**6** Drag the white playhead to move through the video. Alternatively, tap **Play** (▶) to play the video.

**7** Tap the left trim handle and drag it to the right.

The trim handles and the bottom of the navigation bar turn yellow to indicate that they are active.

**8** Stop dragging when the frame appears where you want to trim the clip.

9 Tap the right handle and drag it to the left until the frame to which you want to trim the end appears.

10 Tap **Trim**.

The Trim dialog appears.

11 Tap **Trim Original** if you want to trim the original clip. Tap **Save as New Clip** to create a new clip from the trimmed content, leaving the original clip unchanged.

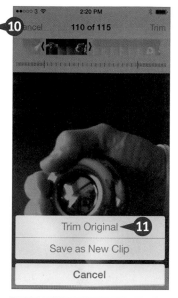

A The Trimming Video progress indicator appears while the Camera app trims the video.

**Note:** Tap **Play** (▶) if you want to play back the trimmed video.

12 Tap **Done**.

## TIP

**Is there an easier way of trimming my videos?**

If you need to trim your videos on your iPhone, try turning the iPhone to landscape orientation. This makes the navigation bar longer and the trimming handles easier to use.

If you have a Mac, you can trim your videos more precisely, and make many other changes, by importing the clips into iMovie on the Mac, and then working with them there.

# Share Your Photos and Videos

After taking photos and videos with your iPhone's camera, or after loading photos and videos on the iPhone using iTunes, you can share them with other people.

Chapter 11 explains how to share photos via e-mail and instant messaging, and Chapter 6 explains how to share items via the AirDrop feature. This task explains how to tweet photos to your Twitter account, assign photos to contacts, use photos as wallpaper, or print photos.

## Share Your Photos and Videos

### Select the Photo or Video to Share

1. Press the Home button.

2. On the Home screen, tap **Photos**.

3. On the Photos screen, tap the item that contains the photo or video you want to share. For example, tap an album.

4. Tap the photo or video you want to share.

5. Tap **Share** (📤) to open the Share screen.

### Share a Photo on Twitter

1. On the Share screen, tap **Twitter**.

2. Type the text of the tweet.

3. Tap **Location** if you want to add your location to the tweet.

4. Tap **Post**.

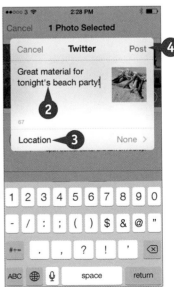

## Assign a Photo to a Contact

1. On the Share screen, tap **Assign to Contact**.

   The list of contacts appears.

2. Tap the contact to which you want to assign the photo.

   The Move and Scale screen appears.

3. If necessary, move the photo so that the face appears centrally.

4. If necessary, pinch in to shrink the photo or pinch out to enlarge it.

5. Tap **Choose**.

## Set a Photo as Wallpaper

1. On the Share screen, tap **Use as Wallpaper**.

   The Move and Scale screen appears.

2. Move the photo to display the part you want.

3. If necessary, pinch in to shrink the photo or pinch out to enlarge it.

4. Tap **Set**.

   The Set Wallpaper dialog appears.

5. Tap **Set Lock Screen**, **Set Home Screen**, or **Set Both**, as needed.

---

**TIP**

**How do I print a photo?**

Display the photo you want to print, and then tap **Share** (⬆) to display the Share screen. Tap **Print** to display the Printer Options screen. If the Printer readout does not show the correct printer, tap **Select Printer**, and then tap the printer. Tap **Print** to print the photo.

# CHAPTER 14

# Advanced Features and Troubleshooting

**You can connect your iPhone to VPNs and Exchange Server, troubleshoot problems, and locate it when it goes missing.**

# Install Configuration Profiles on Your iPhone

You can configure your iPhone directly by choosing settings in the Settings app, but you can also configure the iPhone by installing one or more configuration profiles provided by an administrator. The most common way of providing a configuration profile is via e-mail.

Usually, you need to install configuration profiles only when your iPhone is managed by an administrator instead of by yourself. For example, a configuration profile can contain the settings needed for your iPhone to connect to a corporate network or a campus network.

## Install Configuration Profiles on Your iPhone

**1** Press the Home button.

The Home screen appears.

**2** Tap **Mail**.

The Mailboxes screen appears.

**3** Tap the mailbox that contains the message with the configuration profile.

**A** You can tap **All Inboxes** to display all your inboxes.

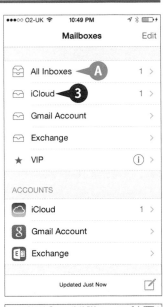

The Inbox opens.

**4** Tap the message that contains the configuration profile.

The message opens.

**5** Tap the button for the configuration profile.

**6** On the Install Profile screen, look for the Verified readout.

**Note:** Never install a configuration profile that does not have the Verified readout. The configuration profile may not be from the source claimed and may damage your iPhone, compromise your data, or both.

**7** Review the configuration profile.

**8** Tap **More Details** for more information.

**Note:** You can tap an item on the Details screen to see further details.

**9** Tap the profile's name.

**10** On the Install Profile screen, tap **Install** to open the Install Profile dialog.

**11** Tap **Install Now**.

Your iPhone installs the configuration profile.

**Note:** If the configuration profile requires you to enter information, the appropriate screens appear. For example, if the configuration profile requires you to set a passcode, the Set Passcode screen appears.

**12** On the Profile Installed screen, tap **Done**.

---

## TIP

**Is there a way of installing a configuration profile other than using e-mail?**

Yes. An administrator can place a configuration profile on a web page. You download the configuration profile using Safari, and then install it using installation screens similar to those shown in this task. By sending a text message to your iPhone, an administrator can easily direct you to a web page that contains a configuration profile specific to your iPhone rather than a general profile for iPhones.

# Connect to a Network via VPN

If you use your iPhone for work, you may need to connect it to your work network. By using the settings, username, and password that the network's administrator provides, you can connect via virtual private networking, or VPN, across the Internet. You can also use VPN to connect to your home network if you set up a VPN server on it.

VPN uses encryption to create a secure connection across the Internet. By using VPN, you can connect securely from anywhere you have an Internet connection.

## Connect to a Network via VPN

### Set Up the VPN Connection on the iPhone

1 Press the Home button.

The Home screen appears.

2 Tap **Settings**.

The Settings screen appears.

**Note:** After you have set up a VPN, the VPN switch appears in the top area of the Settings screen. You can connect to the VPN by tapping the switch and moving it to On ( ○ changes to ⬤ ).

3 Tap **General**.

The General screen appears.

4 At the bottom of the screen, tap **VPN**.

The VPN screen appears.

5 Tap **Add VPN Configuration**.

**Note:** If your iPhone already has a VPN you want to use, tap it, and then go to step 1 of the next set of steps, "Connect to the VPN."

The Add Configuration screen appears.

**6** Tap the tab for the VPN type: **L2TP**, **PPTP**, or **IPSec**.

**7** Fill in the details of the VPN.

**Note:** Set the **Send All Traffic** switch to On (⬤) if you want your iPhone to send all Internet traffic across the VPN after you connect.

**8** Tap **Save**.

The VPN configuration appears on the VPN screen.

## Connect to the VPN

**1** On the VPN screen, tap the **VPN** switch and move it to On (◯ changes to ⬤).

The iPhone connects to the VPN.

**A** The VPN indicator appears in the status bar.

**2** Work across the network connection as if you were connected directly to the network.

**3** To see how long your iPhone has been connected, or to learn its IP address, tap **Status**.

**4** On the Status screen, tap **VPN**.

**5** When you are ready to disconnect from the VPN, tap the **VPN** switch on the VPN screen and move it to Off (⬤ changes to ◯ ).

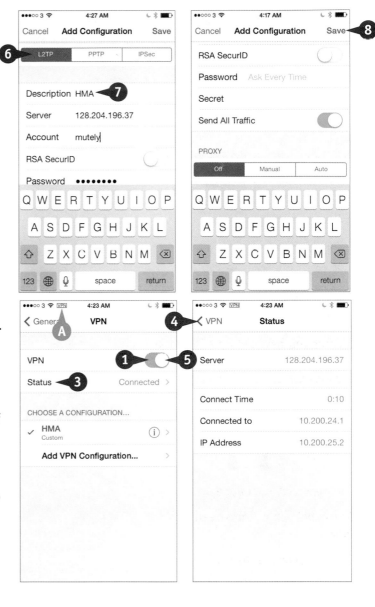

---

**TIP**

**Is there an easier way to set up a VPN connection?**

Yes. An administrator can provide the VPN details in a configuration profile, as discussed earlier in this chapter. When you install the configuration profile, your iPhone adds the VPN automatically. You can then connect to the VPN.

# Connect Your iPhone to Exchange Server

I f your company or organization uses Microsoft Exchange Server, you can set up your iPhone to connect to Exchange for e-mail, contacts, calendaring, reminders, and notes.

Before setting up your Exchange account, ask an administrator for the details you need. These are your e-mail address, your password, the server name, and the domain name. You may be able to set up the account using only the e-mail address and password, but often you need the server name and domain as well.

## Connect Your iPhone to Exchange Server

**1** Press the Home button.

The Home screen appears.

**2** Tap **Settings**.

The Settings screen appears.

**Note:** If you have not yet set up an e-mail account on the iPhone, you can also open the Add Account screen by tapping **Mail** on the iPhone's Home screen.

**3** Tap and drag up to scroll down, and then tap **Mail, Contacts, Calendars**.

The Mail, Contacts, Calendars screen appears.

**4** Tap **Add Account**.

The Add Account screen appears.

**5** Tap **Microsoft Exchange**.

**6** On the first Exchange screen, type your e-mail address.

**7** Type your password.

**8** Type a descriptive name for the account in the Description field.

**9** Tap **Next**.

If setting up the account needs more information, another screen appears.

**10** Type the server's address.

**11** Type the domain if needed.

**12** Type your username.

**13** Tap **Next**.

**14** On the next screen, set the **Mail** switch to On (⬤) or Off (◯), as needed.

**15** Set the **Contacts** switch to On (⬤) or Off (◯).

**16** Set the **Calendars** switch to On (⬤) or Off (◯).

**17** Set the **Reminders** switch to On (⬤) or Off (◯).

**18** Set the **Notes** switch to On (⬤) or Off (◯).

**19** Tap **Save**.

**A** The new account appears on the Mail, Contacts, Calendars screen.

## TIPS

**Is there an alternative way to set up an Exchange account?**

Yes. An administrator can provide the Exchange details in a configuration profile, as discussed earlier in this chapter. If you have another e-mail account on your iPhone, the administrator can send you the profile. Otherwise, you may need to download the profile from a web page.

**How do I know whether to enter a domain name when setting up my Exchange account?**

You need to ask an administrator because some Exchange implementations require you to enter a domain, whereas others do not.

# Update Your iPhone's Software

Apple periodically releases new versions of the iPhone's software to fix problems, improve performance, and add new features. To keep your iPhone running quickly and smoothly, and to add the latest features that Apple provides, you should update the iPhone's software when a new version becomes available.

iTunes and your iPhone notify you automatically when a new version of the iPhone's software is available. You can also check manually for new versions of the software.

## Update Your iPhone's Software

**1** Connect your iPhone to your computer via the USB cable.

The iPhone appears on the navigation bar in iTunes.

A dialog appears, telling you that a new software version is available.

**2** Click **Update**.

iTunes downloads the new software, extracts it, and begins to install it.

The Summary screen shows the progress of the installation.

**3** If iTunes does not display the iPhone's management screens, click the iPhone button on the navigation bar to make the management screens appear.

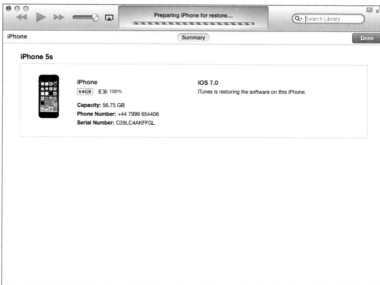

When the installation is complete, iTunes displays a dialog telling you that the iPhone will restart in 15 seconds.

**4** Click **OK**, or wait for the countdown to complete.

The iPhone restarts, and its button then appears on the navigaion bar in iTunes.

**5** If iTunes does not display the management screens for your iPhone, click the iPhone buton on the navigation bar.

The iPhone's management screens appear.

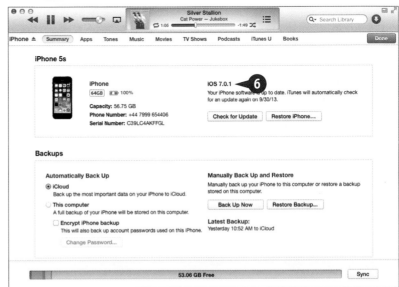

**6** Verify the version number in the Software Version readout in the iPhone area.

**7** Disconnect your iPhone from the USB cable. You can now start using the iPhone as usual.

---

## TIPS

**How do I make iTunes check for a new version of my iPhone's software?**

Connect your iPhone to your computer via the USB cable so that the iPhone appears on the navigation bar in iTunes. When the Summary screen appears, click **Check for Update** in the upper area.

**Can I update my iPhone's software without using a computer?**

Yes. You can update your iPhone "over the air" by using a wireless network. Press the Home button, tap **Settings**, tap **General**, and then tap **Software Update** to check for new software. You can also update over the air using the cellular network, but because iPhone software updates may involve transferring hundreds of megabytes of data, it is faster and less expensive to use a wireless network.

# Extend Your iPhone's Runtime on the Battery

To keep your iPhone running all day long, you need to charge the battery fully by plugging the iPhone into a USB socket, the iPhone Power Adapter, or another power source. You can extend your iPhone's runtime by reducing the demands on the battery. You can dim your iPhone's screen so that it consumes less power. You can set your iPhone to go to sleep quickly. You can turn off Wi-Fi and Bluetooth when you do not need them, and you can turn off the power-hungry GPS feature when you do not need to track your iPhone with the Find My iPhone feature.

## Extend Your iPhone's Runtime on the Battery

### Dim the iPhone's Screen

**1** Press the Home button.

**2** On the Home screen, tap **Settings**.

**3** On the Settings screen, tap **Wallpapers & Brightness**.

**4** On the Wallpaper & Brightness screen, tap the **Brightness** slider and drag it to the left to dim the screen.

**A** Move the **Auto-Brightness** switch to On (⬤) if you want the iPhone to adjust the brightness automatically.

**Note:** To save power, set a short time for Auto-Lock. Press the Home button, tap **Settings**, tap **General**, and then tap **Auto-Lock**. Tap a short interval — for example, **1 Minute**.

**5** Tap **Settings**.

### Turn Off Wi-Fi and Bluetooth

**1** On the Settings screen, tap **Wi-Fi**.

**2** On the Wi-Fi screen, tap the **Wi-Fi** switch and move it to Off (◯).

**3** Tap **Settings**.

**4** On the Settings screen, tap **Bluetooth**.

The Bluetooth screen appears.

**5** Tap the **Bluetooth** switch and move it to Off ( ◯ ).

**6** Tap **Settings**.

The Settings screen appears.

## Turn Off the GPS Feature

**1** On the Settings screen, tap **Privacy**.

The Privacy screen appears.

**2** Tap **Location Services**.

The Location Services screen appears.

**3** Tap the **Location Services** switch and move it to Off ( ◯ ).

**Note:** If your iPhone warns you that turning off Location Services will turn off Find My iPhone, tap **Turn Off**.

**4** Tap **Privacy**.

The Privacy screen appears.

**5** Tap **Settings**.

The Settings screen appears.

### Is there a quicker way of controlling power consumption?

You can control Wi-Fi, Bluetooth, and screen brightness from Control Center. Swipe up from the bottom of the screen to open Control Center, and then tap **Wi-Fi** (Ⓐ) or **Bluetooth** (Ⓑ) or drag the Brightness slider (Ⓒ).

# Back Up and Restore Using Your Computer

When you sync your iPhone with your computer, iTunes automatically backs up the iPhone's data and settings. If your iPhone suffers a software or hardware failure, you can restore the data and settings to your iPhone. You can also sync your data and settings to a new iPhone, an iPad, or an iPod touch.

iTunes backs up the iPhone's unique data, such as the settings and notes you have created on the iPhone, but does not back up music files, video files, or photos that you have synced to the iPhone from your computer.

## Back Up and Restore Using Your Computer

**1** Connect your iPhone to your computer via the USB cable or via Wi-Fi.

The iPhone appears on the navigation bar in iTunes.

**2** Click the iPhone button on the navigation bar.

The iPhone's management screens appear.

**3** Click **Summary**.

**4** Click **Back Up Now**.

iTunes backs up your iPhone.

**5** Click **Restore iPhone**.

**Note:** If Find My iPhone is turned on for your iPhone, iTunes prompts you to turn it off. Press the Home button, tap **Settings**, tap **iCloud**, and then set the **Find My iPhone** switch to Off ( ◯ ).

**Note:** Instead of restoring the iPhone's software, you can restore only the iPhone's data by clicking **Restore Backup**.

iTunes confirms that you want to restore the iPhone to its factory settings.

**6** Click **Restore**.

iTunes backs up the iPhone's data, restores the software on the iPhone, and returns the iPhone to its factory settings.

**Note:** Do not disconnect the iPhone during the restore process. Doing so can leave the iPhone in an unusable state.

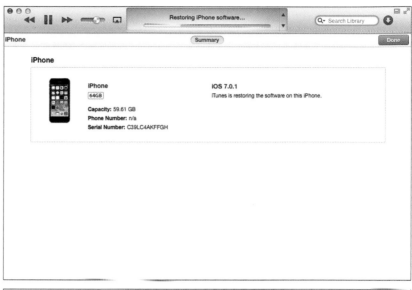

iTunes displays the Welcome to Your New iPhone screen.

**7** Click **Restore from this backup** ( ○ changes to ◉ ).

**8** Click ✦ and choose your iPhone by name.

**9** Click **Continue**.

iTunes restores the data and settings to your iPhone.

Your iPhone restarts, appears on the navigation bar in iTunes, and then syncs.

**10** Disconnect the iPhone.

## TIP

**How can I protect confidential information in my iPhone's backups?**

On the Summary screen in iTunes, click **Encrypt iPhone backup** ( ☐ changes to ☑ ). In the Set Password dialog, type the password (Ⓐ), and then click **Set Password** (Ⓑ). iTunes then encrypts your backups using strong encryption.

# Back Up and Restore Using iCloud

Instead of backing up your iPhone to your computer, you can back it up to iCloud. If your iPhone suffers a software or hardware failure, you can restore its data and settings from backup.

At this writing, a standard free iCloud account gives you 5GB of data storage, but you can buy more space as needed. You can choose which items to back up to iCloud. The iTunes Store lets you download again all the apps, media files, and games you have bought, so you do not need to back up these files.

## Back Up and Restore Using iCloud

**1** Press the Home button.

The Home screen appears.

**2** Tap **Settings**.

The Settings screen appears.

**3** Tap and drag up to scroll down, and then tap **iCloud**.

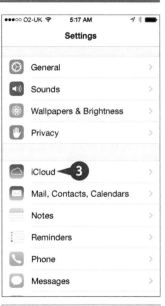

The iCloud screen appears, showing the name of the iCloud account you have set up.

**4** Choose the data you want to synchronize with iCloud by moving the Mail, Contacts, Calendars, Reminders, Safari, Notes, and Passbook switches to On ( ) or Off ( ) as needed.

**Note:** The 5GB of storage in a standard free iCloud account is enough space to store your iPhone's settings and your most important data and files. If you need to store more data, buy more space.

**5** If you need to buy more storage, tap your account name.

The Account screen appears, showing your storage amount in the Storage Plan area.

**6** Tap the **Storage Plan** button.

**7** Tap the storage plan you want, tap **Buy**, and follow the payment process.

**8** On the Account screen, tap **Photos**.

**9** On the Photos Stream screen, set the **My Photo Stream** switch and the **Photo Sharing** switch to On (⬤) or Off (◯), as needed.

**10** Tap **iCloud**.

**11** On the Account screen, tap **Documents & Data**.

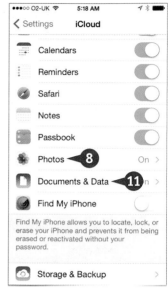

**12** Set the **Documents & Data** switch to On (⬤) or Off (◯), as needed.

**13** In the apps list, set each app's switch to On (⬤) or Off (◯), as needed.

**14** Tap **iCloud**.

**15** Set the **Find My iPhone** switch to On (⬤) or Off (◯), as needed.

**16** Tap **Storage & Backup**.

**17** Set the **iCloud Backup** switch to On (⬤).

**18** If you want to back up your iPhone now, tap **Back Up Now**.

## TIP

**How do I restore my iPhone from its iCloud backup?**

First, reset the iPhone to factory settings. Press the Home button, tap **Settings**, tap **General**, tap **Reset**, and tap **Erase All Content and Settings**. Tap **Erase iPhone** in the confirmation dialog. When the iPhone restarts and displays its setup screens, choose your language and country. On the Set Up iPhone screen, tap **Restore from iCloud Backup**, and then tap **Next**. On the Apple ID screen, enter your Apple ID, and then tap **Next**. On the Choose Backup screen, tap the backup you want to use — normally, the most recent backup — and then tap **Restore**.

# Reset Your Networks, Dictionary, and Home Screen

After experimenting with changes to your iPhone's settings, you may want to restore the iPhone to the default settings to undo the changes you have made. For example, you may want to restore your Home screen to its default settings to undo customizations.

From the Reset screen, you can quickly reset your network settings, your keyboard dictionary, your Home screen layout, or your location and privacy settings. You can also reset all settings, as discussed in the next task, "Restore Your iPhone to Factory Settings."

## Reset Your Networks, Dictionary, and Home Screen

**1** Press the Home button.

The Home screen appears.

**2** Tap **Settings**.

The Settings screen appears.

**3** Tap and drag up to scroll part of the way down the screen.

**4** Tap **General**.

The General screen appears.

**5** Tap and drag up to scroll down all the way to the bottom.

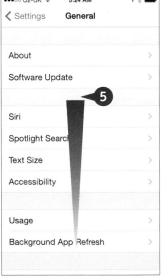

The lower part of the General screen appears.

**6** Tap **Reset**.

The Reset screen appears.

**7** Tap **Reset Network Settings**, **Reset Keyboard Dictionary**, or **Reset Home Screen Layout**, as needed.

**Note:** Resetting the network settings deletes all network information you have entered, such as passwords for wireless networks. Resetting the keyboard dictionary deletes the custom words you have added to it. Resetting the Home screen layout puts the Home screen icons back in their default places.

**Note:** If your iPhone prompts you to enter your passcode, type it to continue with the reset operation.

A confirmation dialog opens, showing a brief explanation of what the command will reset.

**8** Tap the **Reset** button in the dialog.

The iPhone resets the item you chose.

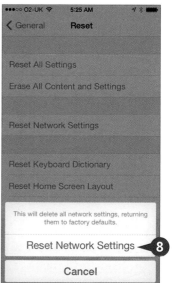

## TIP

**What does the Reset Location & Privacy button on the Reset screen do?**

When an app first requests location information, your iPhone asks your permission. For example, when you first take a photo using the Camera app, the Camera app requests your location so that it can store it in the photo. After you tap **OK** (Ⓐ) for such a request, your iPhone does not ask you again for the same app. Resetting your location and privacy settings makes each app request permission again.

# Restore Your iPhone to Factory Settings

If your iPhone starts malfunctioning and you cannot get iTunes to recognize it, you may need to restore the iPhone to factory settings. This is an operation you perform on the iPhone itself when severe problems occur with its settings, to get the iPhone into a state where it can communicate with iTunes again.

If iTunes can recognize the iPhone, use iTunes to restore the iPhone instead of resetting the iPhone as described here.

## Restore Your iPhone to Factory Settings

**1** Press the Home button.

The Home screen appears.

**2** Tap **Settings**.

The Settings screen appears.

**Note:** If your iPhone is not responding to the Home button or your taps, press and hold the Sleep/Wake button and the Home button for about 15 seconds to reset the iPhone.

**3** Tap and drag up to scroll part of the way down the screen.

**4** Tap **General**.

The General screen appears.

**5** Tap and drag up to scroll down all the way to the bottom.

316

The lower part of the General screen appears.

**6** Tap **Reset**.

The Reset screen appears.

**7** Tap **Reset All Settings**.

**Note:** If you have applied a restrictions passcode to the iPhone, you must enter the passcode after tapping Reset All Settings.

**Note:** If you are restoring your iPhone to factory settings in preparation for passing it on to someone else, tap **Erase All Content and Settings** to remove the iPhone's content. If Find My iPhone is on, you will need to sign out of iCloud.

**Note:** If your iPhone prompts you to enter your passcode, type it to continue with the reset operation.

A confirmation dialog appears.

**8** Tap **Reset All Settings**.

A second confirmation dialog appears.

**9** Tap **Reset All Settings**.

The iPhone resets all its settings.

## TIP

**Does resetting all the iPhone's settings delete my data and my music files?**

No, it does not. When you reset all the iPhone's settings, the settings go back to their defaults, but your data remains in place. But you need to set the iPhone's settings again, either by restoring them using iTunes or by setting them manually, in order to get your iPhone working the way you prefer.

# Troubleshoot Wi-Fi Connections

To get the most out of your iPhone without exceeding your data plan, use Wi-Fi networks whenever they are available instead of using your cellular connection.

Normally, the iPhone establishes and maintains Wi-Fi connections without problems. But you may sometimes need to request your iPhone's network address again, a process called renewing the lease on the IP address. You may also need to tell your iPhone to forget a network, and then rejoin the network manually, providing the password again.

## Troubleshoot Wi-Fi Connections

### Renew the Lease on Your iPhone's IP Address

**1** Press the Home button.

The Home screen appears.

**Note:** You can sometimes resolve a Wi-Fi problem by turning Wi-Fi off and back on. Swipe up from the bottom of the screen to open Control Center, tap **Wi-Fi** (📶 changes to 📶), and then tap **Wi-Fi** again (📶 changes to 📶).

**2** Tap **Settings**.

The Settings screen appears.

**3** Tap **Wi-Fi**.

The Wi-Fi screen appears.

**4** Tap ⓘ to the right of the network for which you want to renew the lease.

The network's screen appears.

**5** Tap **Renew Lease**.

The Renew Lease dialog opens.

**6** Tap **Renew Lease**.

**7** Tap **Wi-Fi Networks**.

The Wi-Fi screen appears.

318

## Forget a Network and Then Rejoin It

**1** On the Wi-Fi screen, tap ⓘ to the right of the network.

The network's screen appears.

**2** Tap **Forget this Network**.

The Forget this Network dialog opens.

**3** Tap **Forget**.

The iPhone removes the network's details.

**4** Tap **Wi-Fi**.

The Wi-Fi screen appears.

**5** Tap the network's name.

The password screen appears.

**6** Type the password for the network.

**7** Tap **Join**.

The iPhone joins the network.

---

**TIP**

### What else can I do to reestablish my Wi-Fi network connections?

If you are unable to fix your Wi-Fi network connections by renewing the IP address lease or by forgetting and rejoining the network, as described in this task, try restarting your iPhone. If that does not work, reset your network settings, as described earlier in this chapter, and then set up each connection again manually.

# Troubleshoot iTunes Sync Problems

To keep your iPhone charged and loaded with your current data and media files from your computer, connect it regularly to your computer and sync it using iTunes.

Connection and syncing are usually straightforward, but you may sometimes find that iTunes does not recognize your iPhone when you connect it. When this happens, you will have to troubleshoot the physical connection and iTunes' settings. If iTunes is not set to sync automatically with your iPhone, you must start the sync manually.

## Troubleshoot iTunes Sync Problems

### Check the USB Connection between Your Computer and Your iPhone

**1** Check that the Lightning connector end of the cable is firmly plugged into the Lightning port on the iPhone. If your iPhone has a case, you may need to remove it in order to make a good connection.

**Note:** Make sure the USB port you use is a full-power port instead of a low-power port. Use a USB port directly on your computer instead of a USB port on an unpowered hub or a peripheral device such as a keyboard.

**2** Check that the USB end of the cable is firmly plugged into a USB port on your computer.

### Restart the iPhone

**1** Press and hold the Power/Sleep button on the iPhone for several seconds.

**2** On the shutdown screen, tap and drag the slider to the right.

The iPhone turns off.

**3** Press and hold the Power/Sleep button for two seconds.

The Apple logo appears on the screen, and the iPhone restarts.

**4** Connect the iPhone to your computer via the USB cable.

## Restart iTunes

1 Close iTunes. In Windows, click **File** and **Exit**. On a Mac, click **iTunes** and **Quit iTunes**.

**Note:** If neither restarting your iPhone nor restarting iTunes enables the two to communicate, try restarting your PC or Mac.

2 Restart iTunes. In Windows, click **iTunes** on the Start menu or Start screen. On a Mac, click **iTunes** on the Dock.

3 Connect the iPhone to your computer via the USB cable.

## Verify Automatic Syncing or Start a Sync Manually

1 If iTunes does not launch or become active when you connect your iPhone, launch or activate iTunes manually.

2 Click the iPhone button on the navigation bar.

3 On the iPhone's management screen, click **Summary**.

4 Click **Automatically sync when this iPhone is connected** (☐ changes to ☑).

5 Click **Apply**.

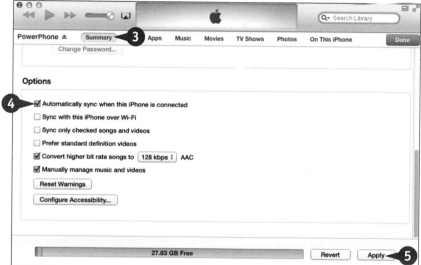

## TIP

**Why does nothing happen when I connect my iPhone to my computer?**
If your iPhone's battery is exhausted, nothing happens for several minutes after you connect your iPhone to your computer. This is because the iPhone is charging its battery via the USB cable. After a few minutes, when the iPhone's battery has enough charge to power the screen, the screen comes on, and syncing begins as usual.

# Locate Your iPhone with Find My iPhone

If you have an iCloud account, you can use the Find My iPhone feature to locate your iPhone when you have lost it or it has been stolen. You can also display a message on the iPhone — for example, to tell the person who has found the iPhone how to contact you — or remotely wipe the data on the iPhone.

To use Find My iPhone, you must first set up your iCloud account on your iPhone, and then enable the Find My iPhone feature.

## Locate Your iPhone with Find My iPhone

### Turn On the Find My iPhone Feature

1 Set up your iCloud account on your iPhone as discussed in "Set Up Your iPhone as New Using iCloud" in Chapter 1.

2 Press the Home button.

The Home screen appears.

3 Tap **Settings**.

The Settings screen appears.

4 Tap **iCloud**.

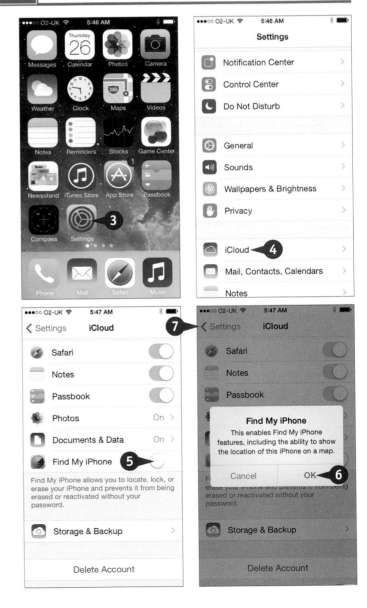

The iCloud screen appears.

5 Tap the **Find My iPhone** switch, and move it to On ( ◯ ).

The Find My iPhone dialog appears.

6 Tap **OK**.

7 Tap **Settings**.

The Settings screen appears.

## Locate Your iPhone Using Find My iPhone

**1** Open a web browser, such as Internet Explorer or Safari.

**2** Click the Address box.

**3** Type **www.icloud.com**, and press **Enter** in Windows or **Return** on a Mac.

The Sign In to iCloud web page appears.

**4** Type your username.

**5** Type your password.

**6** Click ⊕.

The iCloud site appears, displaying the page you last used.

**7** Click **iCloud** (☁).

The iCloud apps page appears.

**8** Click **Find My iPhone**.

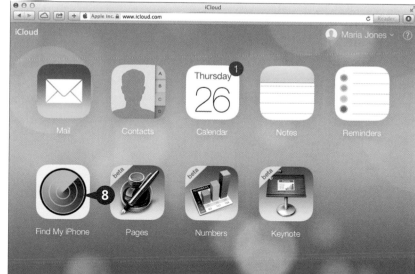

**Is it worth displaying a message on my iPhone, or should I simply wipe it?**

Almost always, it is definitely worth displaying a message on your iPhone. If you have lost your iPhone, and someone has found it, that person may be trying to return it to you. The chances are good that the finder is honest, even if he has not discovered that you have locked the iPhone with a passcode. That said, if you are certain someone has stolen your iPhone, you may prefer simply to wipe it, using the technique explained next.

continued ▶

Find My iPhone is a powerful feature that you can use both when you have mislaid your iPhone and when someone has deliberately taken it from you.

If Find My iPhone reveals that someone has taken your iPhone, you can wipe its contents to prevent whoever has taken it from hacking into your data. Be clear that wiping your iPhone prevents you from locating the iPhone again — ever — except by chance. Wipe your iPhone only when you have lost it, you have no hope of recovering it, and you must destroy the data on it.

## Locate Your iPhone with Find My iPhone (continued)

The iCloud Find My iPhone page appears.

**9** Click **All Devices**.

**A** The My Devices dialog appears.

**10** Click your iPhone.

The Info dialog appears, showing the iPhone's location.

**11** If you want to play a sound on the iPhone, click **Play Sound**. This feature is primarily helpful for locating your iPhone if you have mislaid it somewhere nearby.

**B** A message indicates that the iPhone has played the sound.

### Lock the iPhone with a Passcode

**1** Click **Lost Mode** in the Info dialog.

The Lost Mode dialog appears.

**2** Click the numbers for a new passcode to apply to the iPhone.

The Lost Mode dialog displays its Re-enter Passcode screen.

**3** Click the passcode numbers again.

**4** Type a contact phone number.

**5** Click **Next**.

**6** Type a message to whoever finds your iPhone.

**7** Click **Done**.

iCloud sends the lock request to the iPhone, and then displays a dialog telling you it sent the request.

## Remotely Erase the iPhone

**1** Click **Erase iPhone** in the Info dialog.

The Enter Your Apple ID Password dialog appears.

**2** Click **Erase**.

The Erase iPhone dialog appears.

**3** Type your password.

**4** Click **Done**.

iCloud sends the erase request to the iPhone, which erases its data.

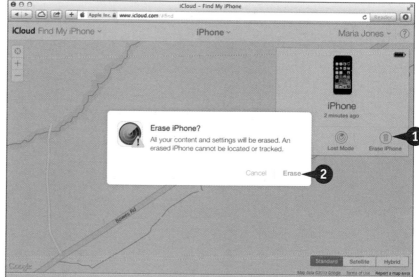

## TIP

**Can I remotely wipe the data on my iPhone if I do not have an iCloud account?**
You can set a passcode for the iPhone as discussed in Chapter 2, and then move the **Erase Data** switch on the Passcode Lock screen to On ( ⬤ ). This setting makes the iPhone automatically erase its data after ten successive failed attempts to enter the passcode. After five failed attempts, the iPhone enforces a delay before the next attempt; further failures increase the delay.

# Index

## Numerics
3D flyover, 266–267

## A
accessibility features. *See also* Siri
    other features, 78–79
    use in the car, 80–81
    VoiceOver, identifying items on-screen using, 76–77
accessories, 64–65
activation, 10–11
Adding Friends switch, 61
AirDrop, sharing items, 128–129, 204, 217
Airplane mode, 36, 120
AirPlay device, 37, 127, 224–225
AirPrint-enabled printers, 65
alarms, 69, 213, 276–277
albums, 242–243
alerts, 45, 93, 210–211
Always Bcc Myself switch, 87
angles, measuring, 260
App Store, 156–157
Apple ID, 42
Apple Mail, 195
apps. *See also* alarms; Clock app; Compass app; Maps app; Stocks app; Stopwatch feature; Timer feature; Weather app
    acquiring, 33, 61
    adding files to iTunes, 161
    App Store display, 157
    bolding, italicizing, underlining, replacing text, 164–165
    choosing ones that give notifications, 44–45
    customizing Home screen, 150–151
    cutting, copying, and pasting text, 162–163
    entries in Settings app, 41
    finding in App Store, 156–157
    installing ones provided by administrator, 160–161
    launching, 32–33
    making purchase from, 61
    opening attachments in e-mail, 194–195
    organizing with folders, 152–153
    putting default apps on Home screen, 151
    restricting Background App Refresh feature, 123
    setting restrictions on purchases, 61
    settings, 41
    stopping unresponsive apps, 155
    switching quickly between, 154–155
    syncing from your computer, 24
    updating and removing, 158–159
    updating using iTunes, 159
    using Location Services, 51
Ask Before Deleting feature, 87
Aspect button, 291
AssistiveTouch feature, 78
audiobooks, 26
Auto-Enhance button, 290
AutoFill, 182–183
Auto-Lock feature, 54, 55, 308

## B
background, refreshing, 122–123
backup, 17, 21, 310–311, 312–313
Badge App Icon switch, 45
banners, 45
battery, extending runtime, 308–309
Bing, 180
Block Pop-ups switch, 184
Bluetooth devices
    connecting to iPhone, 126–127
    turning on/off, 36, 308, 309
    using headset, 104
bold text, 164–165
bookmarks
    accessing websites, 170–171
    creating, changing, creating folders, 172–173
    naming, 270
    opening
        Reading List, 175
        Shared Links list, 177
    syncing from your computer, 23
    using in Maps, 268–269
books
    browsing and buying e-books, 254–255
    changing font size, 253

# There's a Visual book
# for every learning level...

## Simplified®

**The place to start if you're new to computers. Full color.**

- Computers
- Creating Web Pages
- Digital Photography
- Excel
- Internet
- Laptops
- Mac OS
- Office
- PCs
- Windows
- Word

## Teach Yourself VISUALLY™

**Get beginning to intermediate-level training in a variety of topics. Full color.**

- Access
- Adobe Muse
- Computers
- Digital Photography
- Digital Video
- Dreamweaver
- Excel
- Flash
- HTML5
- iLife
- iPad
- iPhone
- iPod
- Macs
- Mac OS
- Office
- Outlook
- Photoshop
- Photoshop Elements
- Photoshop Lightroom
- PowerPoint
- Salesforce.com
- Search Engine Optimization
- Social Media
- Web Design
- Windows
- Wireless Networking
- Word
- WordPress

## Top 100 Simplified® Tips & Tricks

**Tips and techniques to take your skills beyond the basics. Full color.**

- Digital Photography
- eBay
- Excel
- Google
- Office
- Photoshop
- Photoshop Elements
- PowerPoint
- Windows